ADVANCE PRAISE FOR CITIZEN HARIRI

'An insightful study of the neoliberal "reconstruction" period, seen through the political biography of its central character. Combining a political economy perspective with a sound grasp of multidimensional political realities, Baumann brilliantly shows how Hariri adapted to Lebanon's intricacies.'

Gilbert Achcar, Professor of Development Studies & International Relations, School of Oriental and African Studies, London

'Although colourful businessman-turned-politician Rafiq al-Hariri credited his success to the return of laissez-faire economics, Citizen Hariri reveals the surprisingly illiberal foundations of Lebanon's urban megaprojects and financial engineering. A treasure trove of essential insights into class, capitalism, and business-state relations in the contemporary Middle East.'

Daniel Neep, Assistant Professor, Center for Contemporary Arab Studies, School of Foreign Service, Georgetown University Qatar

'Political biography at its best. Hannes Baumann successfully uses the trajectory of Rafiq Hariri as a prism through which to understand Lebanon's political dynamics. The result is a convincing and multilayered analysis that helps us to grasp both Hariri's career and his enduring and complex legacy.'

Charles Tripp, Professor of Politics, School of Oriental and African Studies, London

'Baumann provides a brilliant study of the neoliberal reconstruction in postwar Lebanon by an oligarchy of warlords, bankers and contractors, who subordinated the state to private interests and enriched themselves on rent extraction, increasing unemployment, poverty and social inequalities.'

Fawwaz Traboulsi, author of *A History of Modern Lebanon*

'A masterly account of the introduction of neoliberalism in Lebanon. Combining sociological and economic analysis, Citizen Hariri provides a fresh look at clientelism, governance, class formation, and the state in Lebanon. It will be a key work for years to come.'

Sune Haugbølle, Associate Professor at Roskilde University, and author of *War and Memory in Lebanon*

CITIZEN HARIRI

HANNES BAUMANN

Citizen Hariri

Lebanon's Neoliberal Reconstruction

HURST & COMPANY, LONDON

First published in the United Kingdom in 2016 by
C. Hurst & Co. (Publishers) Ltd.,
41 Great Russell Street, London, WC1B 3PL
© Hannes Baumann, 2016
All rights reserved.
Printed in India

The right of Hannes Baumann to be identified as the author
of this publication is asserted by him in accordance with the
Copyright, Designs and Patents Act, 1988.

A Cataloguing-in-Publication data record for this book
is available from the British Library.

ISBN: 9781849046992

This book is printed using paper from registered sustainable
and managed sources.

www.hurstpublishers.com

In memory of Hildegard Baumann and Anna Uhly

CONTENTS

ACKNOWLEDGEMENTS

I would like to thank various individuals and institutions which have helped me put together this book. Special thanks go to my Ph.D. supervisor Charles Tripp for his calm and always encouraging guidance. I would also like to thank my examiners Gilbert Achcar and Elizabeth Picard for their invaluable comments. I am indebted to my second supervisor Laleh Khalili as well as Jamil Mouawad, Daniel Neep, Reinoud Leenders and Yair Wallach, who read parts of my original Ph.D. thesis or the manuscript and provided invaluable comments. Special thanks go to Alasdair Craig and Jon de Peyer at Hurst for shepherding the manuscript to completion.

Sections of chapters 2 and 5 previously appeared as a chapter in a volume edited by Sabrina Mervin and Franck Mermier and published by Karthala in 2012, titled *Leaders et partisans au Liban*. I would like to thank Karthala for their permission to reproduce these sections here.

In Beirut, I benefited from the insights of (and countless lunches and dinners with) Karim Eid-Sabbagh and Doris Summer. Without them this book would have been a very different beast, and a much tamer one at that. My understanding of Lebanese politics was also enriched in the many conversations with various friends, academics, activists, journalists, pundits, and well-informed Lebanese who took the time to share their views with me. Thanks also go to the Centre for Arab and Middle Eastern Studies (CAMES) at the American University in Beirut (AUB) who hosted me while I was there, especially to Aliya Saidi. Many thanks also go to the archivists in the AUB archives for the time and patience in digging up references to Rafiq Hariri. I would also like to thank my interviewees for taking the time to speak to me.

ACKNOWLEDGEMENTS

I would like to express my heartfelt thanks to various institutions which provided financial support for the original research and the completion of the book manuscript. The Leverhulme Trust supported my field research in Lebanon with a Study Abroad Studentship in 2007–2008. The Council for British Research on the Levant (CBRL) kindly supported my travels with a travel grant. I would like to thank Sarah Boucher and Media Eghbal for their patience and understanding when they were my line managers at Euromonitor International in 2005–2007. They were very understanding of my time commitments towards the Ph.D. My research at Euromonitor was completely separate from my academic work and I derived no commercial benefit from my Ph.D. research. I completed part of the manuscript as Jamal Daniel Levant Post-doctoral Fellow in 2013–2014, based at the Centre for Contemporary Arab Studies (CCAS) at Georgetown University. My thanks go to Mr Jamal Daniel personally for endowing the fellowship and to CCAS for hosting me. I am especially grateful to Osama Abi-Mershed for originally inviting me to Georgetown as a visiting assistant professor. Another part of the manuscript was written as a Leverhulme Early Career Fellow at the Institute of Middle Eastern Studies (IMES) at King's College London. I would like to thank Rory Miller and Michael Kerr for supporting my application and hosting me at IMES. I would not have been able to complete this Ph.D. without the generous financial and emotional support of my parents, Christine and Günter Baumann. I relied on an inheritance from my late grandmother Anna Uhly to finance part of the research and writing up. I dedicate this book to her and my other late grandmother Hildegard Baumann who called me every week to ask how my book was going.

Finally, I want to thank the wonderful Adi Lerer for her support in the process of research and writing.

1

INTRODUCTION

The start of the film *Bosta* offers an image of Lebanese society crammed into a highway traffic jam: muscular young men in a German convertible, turbaned clerics and nuns in their habits, women with headscarves and women with perms, farmers ferrying sheep on trucks, a Gulf tourist in his SUV, an elderly lady, surveying the chaos from a balcony, and a Sri Lankan maid blow-drying her hair. The broken-down bus of the main protagonists—a troupe of new-age *dabke* dancers—blocks the road. The crowd becomes ever more agitated, honking and screaming in frustration, until, in a climactic scene, a young man jumps out of his car, shouting: 'Wayn al-dawla?' (Where is the state?) Suddenly the crowd falls silent as a motorcade of policemen and black limousines smoothly glides past on the opposite lane, carrying a politician, unseen behind tinted windows. Despite its absence—or because of it—the Lebanese state establishes a hierarchy, distinguishing those who travel freely from those stuck in an eternal traffic jam.

In real life, one particular motorcade—'that pre-eminent Lebanese gauge of post-war status'—was 'the grandest of them all, stretching for hundreds of metres and bristling with anti-bomb devices, deployed atop accompanying vehicles'.[1] This was a description of the convoy of Rafiq Hariri, prime minister from 1992 to 1998 and 2000 to 2004. His social position at birth did not mark Hariri out as a future leader of his country. He was born in 1944 as the son of a smallholder in the south-

1

ern city of Sidon. While he was growing up, in the 1950s and 1960s, Lebanese politics was dominated by a few political families who represented their sectarian clientele in Lebanon's multi-confessional society. This was a period of political ferment, challenging the political elite: Hariri was an Arab nationalist youth activist in Sidon, and many of his generation entered politics as members of popular movements or militias. Yet it was not political activism that catapulted Hariri to political leadership. In 1964 he emigrated to Saudi Arabia because he could no longer afford his university studies and sought to earn money abroad. While Lebanon sank into civil war from 1975 to 1990, Hariri became fabulously rich as a construction contractor in Saudi Arabia. In the 1980s he acted on behalf of King Fahd as a 'Saudi mediator' between the factions of the Lebanese civil war. He returned to become prime minister in the post-war Lebanese republic, overseeing a neoliberal reconstruction programme. Lebanese politics at the time was dominated by neighbouring Syria, which kept troops in the country, supported Hizballah's struggle against Israeli occupation in southern Lebanon, and marginalised its opponents while keeping its allies in check through 'divide and rule' tactics.

On 14 February 2005 a bomb tore through his motorcade, killing Hariri and twenty-one others. Lebanon's growing anti-Syrian opposition immediately accused Syria of committing the crime. The United States and France supported the opposition. An international investigation was conducted by the United Nations to identify the perpetrators, and a tribunal was eventually established to try them. The assassination and the subsequent UN investigation escalated the already sweltering political conflict over Syria's role in Lebanon. Rival demonstrations of several hundreds of thousands of Lebanese congregated in Beirut, either to thank 'sisterly Syria' for its 'guardianship' or to demand an end to Syrian 'occupation'. The coalitions behind each demonstration came to be known by their dates as March 8 and March 14. The former was predominantly Shia, and later came to include a large portion of the Christian community when Michel Aoun's partisans joined, while the latter was led by Hariri's son Sa'd and included the main political movements of the Sunni and Druze communities, as well as many Christian politicians. March 14 lionised Rafiq Hariri as a defender of the Lebanese nation against Syrian encroachment. In April 2005 Syria withdrew its troops from Lebanon.

INTRODUCTION

Rafiq Hariri became even more politicised in death than in life. March 14 demonstrators were calling for *al-haqiqa*—the truth about Hariri's assassination—to pressure Syria. March 8 could hardly attack the victim of a violent crime, but they fiercely criticised his economic policies and his links to Saudi Arabia. The Lebanese debate about the billionaire businessman is highly polarised. Detractors see Hariri's economic policies as disastrous and self-serving. Although they made Hariri himself rich, they caused public debt, economic stagnation, poverty, inequality and uneven development.[2] Hariri's partisans meanwhile argue that the contractor was the only one with the vision to rebuild the country because he was not tainted by civil war violence.[3] They argue that his economic programme was a great idea but was sabotaged by the Syrian regime and its allies in Lebanon. Hariri's opponents see him as a Saudi stooge, while his supporters hail him as an anti-Syrian hero and standard-bearer of sovereignty and independence. Rafiq Hariri has exuded considerable fascination as a larger-than-life character, a 'Mr Lebanon' who either single-handedly rebuilt his war-torn country or is held responsible for many of its ills. His death was considered a threat to international peace and security, and was the first time a politician's assassination led to an international legal tribunal.[4] Amidst the fascination with the person and his violent death many commentators miss a larger story: what does the rise of a man from the geographical and social periphery to the centre of politics tell us about the wider social, economic and political transformations in Lebanon? The journalist Jerry Thompson in Orson Welles' film *Citizen Kane* retraces the life of media tycoon Charles Foster Kane. He hopes to find the meaning of 'rosebud', the millionaire's enigmatic last word, which may hold the key to his life and success. Readers who are looking for Citizen Hariri's 'rosebud' will be disappointed. This book is not a traditional biography. It does not deal with the internal life of its subject, with Rafiq Hariri's thoughts, feelings and personal motivations. Instead, it is a book about Lebanese economy, society and politics. It is not about a 'great man' shaping Lebanese history, but about what a 'great man's' political biography reveals about his country's history.

Hariri was a Saudi contractor, and his overriding goal was economic reconstruction. The primary instrument of his political influence was money, although it was by no means his only instrument—or necessarily always his most important one. As Nicholas Blanford wrote: 'For Hariri, money was a tool in negotiation as much as a plumber uses a wrench to stop a leak or a sculptor uses a chisel to fashion a block of wood.'[5] Hariri's biography thus focuses on Lebanon's political economy. While excellent studies of the post-war political economy have been written, they have often failed to bring together the functioning of sectarian politics and foreign meddling with the wider political economy of the country.[6] It is only recently that authors have started looking at how these themes work together in post-war politics, including the continuities between the civil war economy and post-war reconstruction. The works by Najib Hourani, Fawwaz Traboulsi and Reinoud Leenders are examples of this trend.[7] Traboulsi explicitly highlighted the transition from pre-war liberalism to post-war neoliberalism, while Hourani highlighted the illiberal nature of Hariri's reconstruction.[8] Rafiq Hariri was a billionaire contractor but also a Saudi envoy and the leading Sunni politician. Hariri's political biography reveals the interplay of sectarianism, international politics and political economy. My book is in a tradition of writing on Lebanon which puts the political economy at the centre of analysis.[9]

Liberal talk, illiberal walk

Rafiq Hariri framed post-war reconstruction as a return to pre-war economic liberalism. The civil war was an unfortunate interruption of Lebanon's free-market economic model:

> Perhaps the largest loss to Lebanon during the years of turmoil was the opportunity cost of wasting almost two decades of potential development … Lebanon's former open, liberal, and highly flexible market economy that constituted the financial, business, cultural, educational and health centre of the Middle East was converted into an archaic, over-bureaucratic, highly regulated, backward, and inward-looking economy.[10]

The way out was a return to liberalism:

> Our strategy was based on re-establishing and strengthening one of the fundamental pillars of the Lebanese economy, namely the free, open, liberal and democratic nature of our system.[11]

According to Hariri, the civil war had 'closed' Lebanon to the world, and he promised to open the country up again, attracting foreign investors with its excellent infrastructure and open economy. Peace with Israel seemed in the offing in the early 1990s, ushering in an era of unprecedented economic opportunity in a 'New Middle East'.[12] After independence in 1946 Lebanon had been 'the only *laissez-faire* economy in the developing world', making it 'an oddity in the post WW2 world',[13] but by 1990 Hariri's free-market rhetoric was in tune with the global neoliberal Zeitgeist. In the immediate post-Cold War era, economic wisdom seemed to have converged to a free-market 'Washington Consensus'.

Hariri's liberal rhetoric masked deeply illiberal policies. The pillars of reconstruction were the rebuilding of Beirut's city centre and currency stability. The former involved the transfer of property rights from its owners to a single development company called Solidere. State interference with property rights on this scale was unprecedented in Lebanon. A second key policy concerned the currency. Even in the darkest days of the civil war, Lebanon's central bank had maintained a floating exchange rate. From 1993 onwards it started managing the exchange rate, first appreciating the currency's value and then fixing it to the US dollar. As discussed in chapter 3, this interference in market mechanisms resulted in severe macro-economic instability as well as considerable rents accruing to Lebanese commercial banks and depositors. Markets for various consumer goods, services and raw materials were either regulated very heavily or not regulated at all. The resulting monopolies created rents for a few dominant market players.[14] The post-war economy was less liberal than the pre-war economy had been.[15] Karim Pakradouni, a pundit and political operator, has therefore argued that post-war reconstruction was not returning Lebanon to its liberal roots:

> We can see Lebanon moving backwards without reverting to the way it was. Its past is better than its future. Lebanon used to be the liberal in a region dominated by state socialism. When socialism fell, liberalism triumphed and the world turned to market economics, Lebanon began abandoning its liberal system as those in power mixed up the public and private sectors. They privatised some of the public sector to serve their own interests rather than for civil society, and seized control of the private sector to monopolise it for themselves rather than opening it up to society at large and the world.[16]

Both Hariri and Pakradouni idealise the pre-war era, which was not as liberal or monopoly-free as they suggest. The point here is that Rafiq Hariri's post-war reconstruction was no simple return to pre-war liberalism, but transformed Lebanon's political economy. Hourani called it Hariri's 'illiberal reconstruction'.[17] Despite the liberal rhetoric, Rafiq Hariri's signature economic policies, namely Beirut's reconstruction and the currency anchor, were not private-sector-driven, but relied heavily on state intervention.

Biography and 'actually existing neoliberalism'

The puzzle of post-war economic policy is the contrast between Hariri's liberal rhetoric and his illiberal economic management. Hariri's partisans argue that political opponents, such as the Syrian regime and former militia leaders, were forcing the billionaire prime minister to compromise his free-market principles. However, this does not explain why the centrepiece of Hariri's reconstruction—rebuilding central Beirut and currency stabilisation—had strongly illiberal elements. No one had forced these policies on him. The contradiction becomes analytically less troubling once we acknowledge that it lies at the heart of neoliberalism. Neoliberalism is a contested concept, rarely defined, and almost always used pejoratively as an 'anti-liberal slogan' and 'an intellectual swearword'.[18] I will therefore now define the term to show its usefulness for analysing Hariri's post-war reconstruction.

Neoliberalism is an economic orthodoxy, a 'utopian project ... for the reorganisation of international capitalism' based on the premise that the market is a superior mechanism for the allocation of resources.[19] This is the first facet of its definition, and it chimes with classical liberalism and neoclassical economic theory. Where classical liberalism often invoked the laissez-faire economy and the minimal nightwatchman state, neoliberalism seeks an interventionist state that clears the way of any impediments to the market mechanism.[20] Where there is no market to solve societal problems—say to tackle global warming—the state creates markets—for instance, emission trading. Neoliberalism therefore 'rolls back' the state in some respects, for example through privatisation and deregulation, but it also re-regulates. This includes the marketisation of the rump state itself as expressed in 'new public management' where public agencies emulate private firms. Pierre Bourdieu points out that neoliberalism weakens the 'left hand' of the state, concerned with welfare, but strengthens the 'right hand', concerned with economic management.[21] This has opened up what Neil Brenner called 'new state spaces', both of supra-national governance, such as the European Union, and sub-national governance, such as urban governance.[22]

The policies that arise from this economic ideology are not politically neutral. Through various mechanisms, such as wage repression or financialisation, the neoliberal restructuring of state and economy has increased profits and reduced wages, thus reversing the cooperative relationship between capital and labour that had marked the previous phase of 'embedded liberalism' from the 1950s to the 1970s.[23] Neoliberalism is thus not just political because it restructures the state, but also 'a political project to re-establish the conditions for capital accumulation and to restore the power of economic elites'.[24] The neoliberal economy is deeply political because it involves class struggle. Neoliberalism's twin nature as both an economic orthodoxy and a political project are the source of its contradictions, making it possible to justify illiberal and monopolistic practices with free-market rhetoric.

I define neoliberalism as both an economic ideology and a class project that restructures the state. I eschew alternative and more limited definitions. Firstly, neoliberalism as a specific set of policies: there is no single, stable list of neoliberal policies reproduced at all times and everywhere. Instead, the universe of neoliberal policy possibilities corresponds to the wider state of debate within the circles of neoliberal intellectuals, class politics and institutional legacies. There are certain policies which have been favoured by neoliberals at specific times. For instance, a first wave of neoliberal policies emphasised privatisation, while a second wave highlighted public-sector and welfare reform, corresponding to a 'roll-back' of the state in Europe and the USA in the 1980s and a 'roll-out' of neoliberal state and social forms from the 1990s onwards.[25] However, as Peck and Tickell have pointed out, these dynamics are due to wider developments in the process of 'neoliberalisation' rather than stable policy prescriptions. There is a great degree of dissent over policies within the neoliberal universe. An examination of whether all of Hariri's policies were truly neoliberal would therefore yield little insight into Lebanese political economy. A focus on the neoliberal purity of Hariri's policies would not suffice to explain the disconnect between liberal rhetoric and illiberal policies.

Secondly, analysts who define neoliberalism primarily as an ideology trace its intellectual history but fail to examine political economy. Philip Mirowski has written in great detail and with great insight about the intellectual history of the 'neoliberal thought collective' and its relationship with wider intellectual currents within neoclassical economics.[26] However, neoliberalism is not simply an intellectual exercise; it reshapes material conditions—and hence class struggle—and their institutional framework. Mirowski ascribes tremendous agency to the neoliberal thought collective. Although he writes about economic ideology, he does not analyse the actual workings of neoliberal capitalism or its politics beyond intellectual debate. With regard to Lebanon, it may not actually be possible to trace the connections of Lebanese intellectuals to the neoliberal thought collective, nor would this necessarily be the most interesting or insightful study of Lebanese neoliberalism.

Finally, post-structuralist approaches examine neoliberalism as a discourse and a rationality of government. Timothy Mitchell and Robert Vitalis, writing about Egypt in the 1990s, dissected the divergence of neoliberal rhetoric and economic reality.[27] However, neoliberalism is more than just a discourse, just as it is more than just an ideology. Other post-structuralists have focused on neoliberalism as a form of Foucauldian governmentality. Following Nikolas Rose, neoliberalism is 'a political rationality that seems to govern not through command and control operations but through the calculative choice of formally free actors'.[28] Foucauldians are not interested in grand structural transformations but the micro-sociology of new subjectivities arising from neoliberal rationality. They advocate a 'decentred' approach to the state, looking at the detail of restructuring, for instance in the health sector, revealing social struggles over welfare-state arrangements and the reformulation of identities which is not simply a top-down process.[29] It is possible to study Hariri from this perspective. The Hariri Foundation provides a case study of Foucauldian government. Its career guidance centre was training student loan recipients to conform to the job market rather than seeking to become engineers or doctors, the most prestigious professions in Lebanese society.[30] While it would be interesting to illuminate the work of the Hariri Foundation from the angle of governmentality, the Foucauldian approach—like neoliberalism-as-ideology—suffers from a neglect of political economy. Neoliberalism is first and foremost an intensification of capitalism generating class conflict and is dependent on the path of previous social struggles and institutions.

Neoliberalism involves a set of reproducible practices and discourses. Countries such as Chile after the coup against President Salvador Allende can become 'laboratories' for economic and political practices that others take up elsewhere. Theorists such as Stephen Gill have therefore described neoliberalism as a 'global market civilisation' institutionalised by international organisations such as the IMF and leading G7 industrialised states.[31] Others have described neoliberalism as a US imperial project to enrich Wall Street finance capital.[32] While this captures the hierarchies at work in the making of global neoliberalism, there is a danger of assigning exclusive agency to 'core' countries and eradicating agency at the 'periphery'. When I speak of the reproduction of global templates, I conceive of policies such as urban megaprojects as 'global phcnomcna', in their 'distinctive capacity for decontextualisation and recontextualisation, abstractability and movement, across diverse social and cultural situations and spheres of life'.[33] Neoliberal discourses and practices 'travel', but they are also always embedded in local politics. 'Actually existing neoliberalism' therefore requires 'a careful mapping of the neoliberal offensive' at local sites:

> This means walking a line of sorts between producing, on the one hand, over-generalised accounts of a monolithic and omnipresent neoliberalism, which tend to be insufficiently sensitive to its local variability and complex internal constitution, and on the other hand, excessively concrete and contingent analyses of (local) neoliberal strategies, which are inadequately attentive to the substantial connections and necessary characteristics of neoliberalism as an extra-local project.[34]

The nation-state remains the agent and the terrain of struggle for the neoliberalisation of politics, economy and culture, and local elites shape the scope, extent and limits of neoliberal globalisation.[35] Neoliberalism plays out within 'a whole complex of political models, vocabularies, organisations and techniques', which constitutes a political field of 'organisation, mobilisation, agitation and struggle' specific to a country.[36]

The biography of Rafiq Hariri is my way of mapping the neoliberal offensive in Lebanon, to see how Hariri's politics fits into the country's wider political field. Neoliberalism is a market-ideological project, but it is also a class project. So which class and which elites were pushing for neoliberal restructuring in Lebanon? What were the forms of conflict and cooperation with rival elites? What is the institutional framework within which these struggles over neoliberal restructuring are playing out? The biography of Gulf contractor Rafiq Hariri reveals the answers to these questions. Wendy Larner similarly used the career of New Zealander Mike Moore, from trade unionist and prime minister to director general of the World Trade Organisation (WTO), to analyse the embodied forms in which neoliberalism travels.[37] Rafiq Hariri's biography shows how neoliberalism came to Lebanon, and what happened once it got there. Hariri did not act alone, but assembled a network of experts on finance, economics, engineering, urban planning, law, journalism, local politics and a variety of other skills. Roger Owen, an economic historian and biographer of nineteenth-century British colonial administrator of Egypt Lord Cromer, noted that policy making is 'surprisingly social': 'You begin by looking for your subject's personal contribution to the formation of policies and ideas only to discover that the authorship of almost every one of his or her initiatives is shared with so many others that ultimate responsibility becomes difficult if not impossible to pin down.'[38]

Owen recommends biography as a method to address the different scales of nineteenth-century empire: politics, economics and society, the relationship of domestic and international politics. Because of Cromer's involvement in diplomacy, finance, administration, development and the military, the issue of how to handle the different levels of analysis 'present themselves in a somewhat higgledy-piggledy fashion in the compass of an individual life'.[39] Owen concludes: 'In a world where everything is connected to everything else, where do you start and where do you stop? The answer, in this case is that the study of a life is as good a place to jump in as anywhere else.'[40] Just as Cromer was involved in many different spheres in late nineteenth-century imperialism, so Hariri was involved in multiple spheres in late twenti-eth- and early twenty-first-century neoliberal globalisation—from diplomacy, to finance, to sectarian politics. The narrative of the individual life does not allow for parsimony or separating dependent and independent variables, but it does provide a rich narrative, which can handle multiple scales at which neoliberal politics takes place.

How does Hariri fit into Lebanon's political field? If neoliberalism is a class project, then what class was pushing it in Lebanon? Hariri was a representative of Gulf capital, which had accumulated during the oil boom of the 1970s.[41] This background conditioned his 'vision' of reconstructing Lebanon. It is hardly surprising that a contractor would regard an urban megaproject as the key to economic success. Classes are social relations, not merely quantifiable and static groups, and, as processes of accumulation change, social relations change. What we need, then, is not a neat locational map of specific classes 'objectively' identified through consumption patterns, household income or vocational background—none of these choices being neutral for the nature of the analysis—but a focus on the process of accumulation.[42] Adam Hanieh has used this perspective on class to trace the accumulation and internationalisation of Gulf capital within the different 'circuits' of capital.[43] Koenraad Bogaert looks at neoliberal class politics from a 'socio-spatial' perspective, examining the processes and contestation through which urban space is produced through urban megaprojects and the provision of social housing in Morocco.[44] Global neoliberalism provides actors with a set of practices and discourses, the reproduction of which provides the process by which we can then trace class politics. These processes can include privatisation, financialisation, fiscal austerity, urban redevelopment, public sector reform, etc.

Hariri imported several of these templates to Lebanon. The most important ones were the Solidere megaproject to reconstruct central Beirut, and the anchoring of the Lebanese pound to the US dollar. These processes created rents. For instance, property rights were reassigned to Solidere and luxury real estate was developed on the site. This resulted in land rent being appropriated by developers. Rent is a useful concept for coming to grips with class politics. Rent as 'super-profits' here is understood not as an unfortunate aberration of capitalism brought about by malfunctioning markets, but as ubiquitous in the politicised spaces that are markets.[45] Rent stands in for—and is analytically akin to—the Marxist concept of surplus.[46] Lebanese Marxist Fawwaz Traboulsi advocates a definition of class centred on the appropriation of 'social surplus'.[47] Rent appropriation is here used as an approximation. I look at how rent is being created, who appropriates it, and how it is appropriated, i.e. through which institutional mechanisms.

Hariri was in charge of rent-creation mechanisms which conformed to a neoliberal logic: reconstruction and currency stability. He placed allied technocrats at the helm of institutions such as reconstruction agencies, the central bank and the finance ministry. He thus effectively controlled those state institutions in charge of economic management. Rival political elites, such as former militia leaders, were appropriating rent by using the Lebanese state's welfare agencies as patronage instruments. They put their personnel in charge of 'service ministries' such as health or social affairs. Rafiq Hariri, however, was pursuing a very different economic logic. These competing logics—creating investment opportunities for large corporations versus state welfare as a patronage instrument—embody class struggles as mediated by the Lebanese political elite.

This account also suggests that both the state and history matter. The Lebanese state is often seen as weak, broken down and irrelevant, interesting only in the way that it apportions power between distinct sectarian groups.[48] It is considered unable or unwilling to actively shape the economy or to impose a unified national identity. However, Hariri's projects of reconstruction and currency stabilisation were associated with a high degree of state intervention. They opened up what Brenner had referred to as 'new state spaces', for instance in urban governance.[49] Hariri had to push through his neoliberal agenda against often hostile rival elites, especially former militia leaders. The patterns of conflict and cooperation between Hariri and these rival elites shaped Lebanese neoliberalism. What we need, then, to understand 'actually existing neoliberalism' in Lebanon is a historical sociology of elites, classes and institutions. These elites and institutions did not arise out of thin air. Many of the institutions that Hariri instrumentalised had been created in the 1960s and 1970s in previous attempts to build a more interventionist state. The history of elites and classes also matters. Hariri's rise was made possible by shifts in Lebanon's economic role in the world. While the pre-war bourgeoisie declined during the civil war of 1975–90, Gulf contractors such as Rafiq Hariri were entering the economy and politics. Finally, the political field is marked by a struggle over national identity and the place of different communities within it. As a businessman-politician who considered politics akin to a construction project, Hariri did not initially engage in sectarian politics. This changed over time as he sought to win elections. In Lebanon's sectarian political system, this required confessional 'leadership' and a greater attention to Hariri's Sunni community. The businessman was disciplined into behaving like a traditional Lebanese politician. This shift throws up questions about the way in which Lebanese sectarianism is being reproduced and the role of the political economy in this reproduction.

Outline of chapters

The chapters are arranged in chronological order, and are organised around five questions. What explains Rafiq Hariri's rise? This first question is addressed in the second chapter. Hariri's career reveals the wider social and economic transformation brought about by the civil war. During the conflict Lebanon lost its role as intermediary between Western financial and goods markets and the Arab East. The families that had monopolised trade and finance in the pre-war era declined in importance. A new contractor bourgeoisie of Lebanese émigrés to the Gulf replaced them as the most powerful capitalist faction. They had to deal with militia leaders who had economic agendas of their own. Hariri was just one of several such contractors. He became the most economically and politically successful of them because he enjoyed strong support from Saudi Arabia. The billionaire acted as a representative of King Fahd during the wartime diplomacy. Hariri's rise is thus also tied to the international politics surrounding the civil war.

Why did Lebanon fail to achieve sustained economic growth between 1990 and 2005? I tackle this second question in chapter 3 by looking at reconstruction from the end of the civil war in 1990 to the end of Hariri's first stint in government in 1998. I break down postwar economic policies into a series of rent-creation mechanisms, explaining how rent was created and who appropriated it: what institutional mechanisms were used by elites to create and appropriate rent. Hariri and his technocrats were in charge of rent-creation mechanisms which were following a neoliberal logic: the reconstruction of central Beirut and currency stabilisation. He used the Council for Development and Reconstruction (CDR) and the central bank respectively to realise these projects. Former militia leaders, meanwhile, were abusing Lebanon's welfare agencies as patronage resources to service their clientele. This set up the classic struggle of neoliberal state restructuring: Hariri was seeking to strengthen the agencies of economic management, while former militia leaders were bolstering the state's welfare mechanisms, even if they were plundering them for their own political ends.

Why did Lebanon fail to achieve social development? This is the first question dealt with in chapter 4. The answer explains the political economy of sectarianism. Hariri's reconstruction, his currency anchor and the former militia leaders' plundering of the meagre welfare state resulted in continued unemployment and poverty. The majority of the population remained dependent on resources controlled by Lebanese politicians. This was the economic basis of sectarian clientelism, where confessional leaders distribute resources to their own followers. These practices are central to the reproduction of sectarian identity in Lebanon. They do not just involve an abstract material exchange, but affect people's everyday life in the workplace, in hospitals and in schools. The second question the chapter addresses is: why did Hariri turn towards a more traditional sectarian leadership style in the mid-1990s? His economic project was coming under increasing political pressure from his rivals and from Syria. He therefore sought to win elections, which necessitated a more confessional leadership style. He also politically neutralised the Maqasid association, run by his Sunni rival in Beirut, Tammam Salam. His Hariri Foundation provided health and education services to the Sunni community in Beirut, directly challenging Salam's leadership claim among Beirut Sunnis.

Chapter 5 deals with the question of why Lebanon returned to political crisis after 2000. Regional tensions were affecting the country—especially the breakdown of the Israeli–Syrian peace process, the 'war on terror' following the 11 September 2001 attacks and the US invasion of Iraq. The Syrian regime was coming under pressure, and tightened its control of Lebanon. This curtailed Hariri's room for manoeuvre. One side-effect was the increasingly fierce conflict between Hariri and Syria's local allies over economic policy. Hariri continued to frame his policies in terms of neoliberal reform of an ossified economic system. Hariri also managed to stave off financial collapse in Lebanon by calling on his international allies France and Saudi Arabia to provide donor support in 2002. This was a pivotal event because it symbolised the extent to which Lebanon's economy had become dependent on the Gulf. A final chapter shows how the analysis is relevant beyond Lebanon, and how it helps us understand Lebanese politics after Rafiq Hariri's death.

Neoliberalism is here defined as both an economic orthodoxy and a class project. It is not merely a shopping list of policies, nor is it enough to simply study the intellectual history of neoliberal ideas or the new subjectivities they produce. What is required is an account of neoliberal capitalism and its political economy in Lebanon. In contrast to pre-war laissez-faire liberalism, neoliberalism actually strengthened the economic management of the Lebanese state. Defining neoliberalism this way solves the puzzle of Hariri's liberal talk and illiberal walk, his embrace of supposedly private-sector solutions under the aegis of an activist state. Gulf capital was the driving force of Lebanese neoliberalism, but Hariri had to deal with rival elites—not least former militia leaders and the Syrian regime—and work within the parameters set by Lebanon's existing institutions.

2

THE RISE OF RAFIQ HARIRI

1976–1990

Perhaps J.P. Morgan did as a child have severe feelings of inadequacy, perhaps his father did believe that he would not amount to anything; perhaps this did affect him in an inordinate drive for power for power's sake. But all this would be quite irrelevant had he been living in a peasant village in India in 1890. If we would understand the very rich we must first understand the economic and political structure of the nation in which they become the very rich.

C. Wright Mills, The Power Elite, p. 98

Rafiq Hariri's rise is puzzling. He was no militia leader, nor was he from one of the leading families that had dominated politics before the civil war. His father was a fruit-picker in Sidon, a medium-sized town in southern Lebanon. People like Hariri were not destined for high political office. The fact that he did end up as the longest-serving prime minister of the post-war era tells us something about the social and economic changes that occurred during the war. The sociologist C. Wright Mills urged researchers to employ the 'sociological imagination' by studying the interplay between individual biographies and greater social changes.[1] Biography, in this sense, is not about 'great men' shaping history but about what an individual's life journey reveals about history. Writing about 'robber baron' J.P. Morgan, Mills noted that his individual idiosyncrasies are of little interest but that his trajectory reveals the social transformation brought about by nineteenth-century American capitalism.[2] Rafiq Hariri's rise similarly provides a window into the transformation of Lebanese capitalism, politics and society. He epitomised the rise of Gulf capital to a dominant position among Lebanese capitalists. He and his technocrats were to push for the neoliberal restructuring of the Lebanese post-war economy and state.

From pre-war 'merchant republic' to civil war economy, 1943–1982

Unlike most of its Arab neighbours, the Lebanese state did not direct economic development but embraced a laissez-faire economy. The capital account was completely liberalised between 1948 and 1952, and there were few restrictions on trade. After independence in 1943, Lebanon acted as a financial intermediary between the Arab East and Western financial markets, as well as an entrepôt for Western consumer goods to the Middle East.[3] Imports created a large trade deficit. The shortfall in the trade balance was financed by large capital account surpluses created by the country's banks, tourism, transport and the real-estate sector. Private short-term capital from other Arab countries flowed into Lebanese banks and was subsequently recycled in global financial markets. Foreign direct investment went primarily into real estate in Beirut. The ability of Lebanon's liberal economy to attract capital was due to the illiberal policies of its Arab neighbours. Lebanon benefited from capital flight from Palestine in the 1948 war and from Egypt, Syria and Iraq in the 1950s and 1960s, where nationalisation drove away the bourgeoisie. The rising oil monarchies of the Gulf relied on Lebanese banks as conduits for recycling their oil money. When other Arab states started liberalising their economies in the 1980s, and when the Gulf states started dealing directly with global financial markets, Lebanon's comparative advantage evaporated. Furthermore, laissez-faire impeded structural change towards capitalist industrialisation.[4] Agriculture declined in relative importance, but growth in services outpaced industrial development.[5] Gaspard notes that, despite Lebanon's capital abundance, investment rates were low.[6] Investment was concentrated in real estate, while manufacturing received relatively less money.[7]

The national pact between the Maronite politician Bishara al-Khuri and the Sunni Muslim Riyadh al-Sulh in 1943 instituted a confessional power-sharing agreement, but also reflected the class interests of the negotiators. Out of economic self-interest Sunni and Christian merchants and financiers agreed to maintain a separate Lebanese state, an arrangement that ran counter to the nationalist commitments of Lebanon's largely Arab nationalist Sunni elites: while Sunni Muslim merchants tended to dominate trade with the Arab hinterland, their Christian counterparts conducted the majority of trade with Europe.[8] The interests of Lebanon's economic elite thus determined the country's economic openness.[9] A separate Lebanese state was the vehicle for this cross-confessional bourgeois alliance to appropriate rents from intermediation between the Arab East and Western markets. Lebanon's leading politicians were referred to as *zu'ama*. They were communal leaders, but also represented the interests of Lebanon's commercial–financial bourgeoisie. The country's major banks were controlled by a few families, as was trade. By 1974 the four biggest merchant houses were estimated to account for two-thirds of all imports from Western countries.[10] Although land ownership was less concentrated than in other Arab countries, some large landowners wielded enormous power over their domains. The market for inputs and for agricultural produce was controlled by a small number of merchant houses. Small farmers became dependent on large agribusinesses, and many were squeezed out of the sector—including Hariri's father, who had rented and owned two orange orchards before losing them.[11] The crisis in agriculture led to mass migration from rural areas to Beirut and Tripoli. The relationships between the *zu'ama* and their communal following has sometimes been characterised as a 'primordial' bond, but it contained a strong economic component.[12] The 'merchant republic' maintained a low-tax regime, and the state provided only a low level of public services such as health or education. Only 40 per cent of students were enrolled in government schools in 1973–4, 26 per cent went to schools run by charities, while the rest attended private schools.[13] Politicians manipulated education, health and jobs as patronage resources.

The *zu'ama*, who represented the interests of Lebanon's commercial financial bourgeoisie and of large landowners, faced challenges from two groups. The first were the technocrats in the institutions promoted by President Fu'ad Shihab, who had been the army commander during the brief civil war of 1958. He had kept the military neutral, and became the consensus choice as president at its end. Shihab (1958–64) and his successor Charles Hilu (1964–70) attacked the power of the *zu'ama*: they expanded the role of the state in public education and health, and extended infrastructure such as roads and electricity to peripheral areas of Lebanon. Shihabist technocrats sought a greater role for the state in the economy. They recognised that the unfettered economic liberalism of the 'merchant republic' impeded economic and social development. One of the most important measures in checking the economic power of the bourgeoisie was the foundation of the central bank in 1964. It played a central role in the collapse of Intrabank in 1966. This crisis redefined pre-war Lebanese capitalism because it exposed the underlying weakness of the Lebanese banking sector, namely the overreliance on short-term deposits. Contrary to conventional wisdom about Lebanon's 'weak' state, Shihabism did leave an—admittedly very small—legacy of 'developmental state' institutions with the ambition of confronting and disciplining capital into a more developmentalist direction. The central bank was the strongest expression of this institutional ambition.

Over the following decade Western banks captured an increasing share of Lebanese banking business. Salim Nasr estimates that the relative share of Lebanese banks in total banking activity dropped from 30 per cent in 1966 to about 15 per cent in 1975.[14] Shihabists also improved the planning capacities of the state. Shihab and his technocrats perceived economic strategy as a political question. Shihab also confronted the *zu'ama* by undermining their clientelist networks. The Shihabists lost the presidency when Sulaiman Franjiyya—himself a *za'im* and candidate of the *zu'ama*—defeated the Shihabist candidate Elias Sarkis in a parliamentary vote to become head of state in 1970. However, technocrats operating in the Shihabist tradition remained a hugely important part of the political elite in Lebanon during the civil war and the post-war era. They included President Elias Sarkis (1976–82), Prime Minister Salim al-Huss (1976–80, 1987–9, 1989–90, 1998–2000) and Finance Minister George Corm (1998–2000).

The second group challenging the *zu'ama* consisted of mass protest movements. This new urban politics grew out of a confluence of several factors. Rural crisis and migration to the cities created a large group of discontented city-dwellers opposed to the self-serving economic liberalism of the *zu'ama*. Moving to the city had removed the migrants from clientelist control by rural *zu'ama*, while urban politicians did not bother clientelising the newcomers, who continued to vote in their villages. Many migrants experienced joint political socialisation with the Palestinians in the refugee camps. The arming of the Palestinians after the 1967 Arab–Israeli war was a major factor in the outbreak of the civil war in 1975, which saw a coalition of PLO and Lebanese leftists challenge the government and Christian militias. Rafiq Hariri was himself an activist in the Nasserite Arab Nationalist Movement (ANM) in Sidon before leaving for Saudi Arabia in 1964.

The 'merchant republic' which emerged after Lebanese independence was a laissez-faire state with little state intervention in the economy. Post-war neoliberal state interventionism in property rights and currency management would have been entirely alien to the pre-war *zu'ama*. Shihabist *dirigisme* represented a challenge to Lebanon's liberal economic model and the minimal state. It is little wonder that Hariri was to take over 'Shihabist' institutional innovations to realise his policies: the central bank and the Council for Development and Reconstruction, founded in 1977 and discussed below. After the civil war Hariri would take over anti-liberal Shihabist institutions; he claimed to be returning Lebanon to a liberal economy, but actually expanded their prerogatives in order to push through his neoliberal policies, urban megaprojects and currency anchoring.

The civil war led to the loss of Lebanon's role as a financial intermediary between the Arab and Western financial markets. The looting of major banks in Beirut in 1975 spooked foreign institutions, which wound down their activities in Lebanon. In 1982 only one of Lebanon's fifteen largest banks was wholly or partially owned by non-Lebanese, compared to twelve in 1974.[15] Global developments also worked against Lebanon. The Gulf was playing a central role in the remaking of neoliberal global capitalism after the end of the Bretton Woods system in 1971. The 'oil crisis' and the subsequent oil boom of 1973–81 resulted in large petrodollar flows into the pockets of Gulf Arab monarchies. At a moment of transformation in the world economy, petrodollars became a price which the USA, as the global hegemon, was keen to capture to strengthen the status of the US dollar and the ability of Wall Street finance to serve the newly globalising financial market—

starting with the explosion of sovereign debt in the 1970s. Enormous amounts of petrodollars were being recycled by Gulf economies via investment, trade, arms purchases and construction contracts with the USA and European countries. The US–Saudi relationship was crucial in channelling Gulf petrodollars into the US financial system, especially through the purchase of US treasury bonds by the kingdom.[16] The Gulf countries became much more closely integrated into global financial markets. As Gulf oil producers grew more sophisticated in their dealings with Western finance, they stopped relying on Lebanese banks. Bahrain replaced Lebanon as the banker of Gulf Arabs.[17]

From 1975 to 1982 continued financial inflows were masking this fundamental structural change. About a third of the nation's workforce had migrated to the Gulf by 1979–80, sending $2.3 billion in remittances.[18] The oil boom increased demand for Lebanese manufactured goods in the Gulf. Inflows of 'political money' to the militias also bolstered the economy. The militias did not really alter the fundamentals of Lebanon's laissez-faire economy—for instance, a floating exchange rate and free capital movement—but their grip exacerbated the worst excesses of this form of capitalism, eventually resulting in the unfettered and predatory currency speculation of the 1980s. Militias took over most of the country's ports. The state lost revenues from customs duties, which were its main source of income. Militias came to dominate the trade in commodities such as flour, oil and gas. Remittances and militia money created new wealth, in turn creating investment opportunities in upmarket real estate along Lebanon's coast. Several banks came under the influence of militia representatives. Good relations with the militias were beneficial for banks' business because of the inflow of militia funds and because trade financing was easier if banks could liaise with militias controlling the ports.[19] International capital retreated. Lebanon's financial and merchant families internationalised their operations to Paris, London or Cyprus. The leading families remained important, but they lost the monopolistic grip on the Lebanese economy that they had enjoyed until 1975. Despite the rise of the militias, it is important to note that the state did not collapse completely, but played a stabilising function: it continued paying salaries to its employees, and the central bank tried to maintain the integrity of the financial system.

The militia leaders and their business allies were not the only ones flexing their muscles in politics and the economy. A new generation of Shihabist technocrats occupied central positions in the rump state. Elias Sarkis was elected president in 1976. He had worked closely with Shihab in the presidential palace, and had been appointed governor of the central bank in 1967. Sarkis appointed Salim al-Huss as his prime minister. As head of the banking control commission at the central bank from 1967 to 1973, Huss had worked closely with Sarkis. Both men saw a role for the state in rebuilding Lebanon after the civil war. Sarkis founded the Council for Development and Reconstruction (CDR) in 1977. The agency enjoyed unprecedented powers to direct the reconstruction of Lebanon. It would later become Rafiq Hariri's main tool for post-war reconstruction. The central bank, too, maintained a broadly Shihabist outlook. In 1978 it lifted a ten-year moratorium on new banking licences, opening the way for further restructuring of the banking sector and allowing another group of newcomers to extend their influence in the Lebanese economy: a new bourgeoisie of Lebanese émigrés who had grown rich as contractors in the Gulf during the oil boom.[20]

The Gulf oil boom following the 1973 'oil crisis' gave a major boost to the growth of a capitalist class in the Gulf. Family-owned conglomerates emerged in contracting, the provision of housing or transport to oil companies, lucrative import licences, and increasingly also through Gulf-based banks.[21] Some Lebanese became successful contractors in the Gulf. In the late 1970s and in the 1980s this new contractor bourgeoisie started buying up Lebanese banks and invested in construction in Lebanon, while seeking a political role as well. Rafiq Hariri is just the most famous example. Taha Miqati founded the Arabian Construction Company in Abu Dhabi in 1967 and enjoyed success in the Gulf. In 1982 Taha and his brother Najib founded telecommunications company Investcom, which managed to penetrate markets such as Sudan, Liberia and Yemen.[22] They also ran an analogue mobile phone network in civil war Lebanon. In 1983 Miqati bought the licence for the British Bank of Lebanon from the British Bank of the Middle East.[23] Najib Miqati later became an MP, minister, and even prime minister. 'Issam Faris is a Greek Orthodox from rural north Lebanon.[24] After an early career in Abela, one of the country's most powerful trading houses, he built up his own group of businesses in 1975. His contract-ing firm Ballast Nedam received a string of lucrative contracts in Saudi Arabia. In 1983 Faris opened Wedge Bank in Lebanon with a new licence from the central bank.[25] He employed former central bank governor and president Elias Sarkis as its chairman. There was a whole new contractor bourgeoisie of Lebanese expatriates in the Gulf, who were investing in Lebanese banks and real estate. Rafiq Hariri was thus part of a wider trend. Hariri's post-war policies served the interests of this class. He sought to open Lebanon to foreign investors by building 'world-class infrastructure' in Beirut and to ensure investor confidence by anchoring the Lebanese currency on the US dollar. These policies followed global neoliberal templates of urban governance and currency stability. Foreign investors were primarily from the Gulf. Rafiq Hariri turned Lebanon into an outlet for Gulf capital.

Rafiq Hariri in Saudi Arabia and early stages of return to Lebanon, 1964–1982

Rafiq Hariri was born in Sidon in 1944. Hariri's father, Baha' al-Din, owned an orchard and rented another from an 'unsympathetic land-lord'.[26] After a particularly bad harvest he lost both orchards. This was a major blow to Rafiq Hariri that was to shape his outlook and his early political activism.[27] Baha' al-Din Hariri was reduced to the status of a labourer, and Rafiq would join him in his school holidays to work in the orchards. His father had thus fallen victim to the crisis that swept Lebanese agriculture, in which large landowners and the monopolists of inputs and marketing would squeeze small producers. Rafiq Hariri joined Sidon's most influential urban protest movement, the Nasserite Arab Nationalist Movement (ANM). It was led by the Palestinian George Habash and Muhsin Ibrahim. A fellow activist from that time described Hariri as 'a doer' who was reliable and fully committed.[28] Hariri participated in demonstrations, handed out pamphlets and assisted clandestine operations, including smuggling George Habash out of Syria, where he had been imprisoned.[29] Hariri received his early political education in the ANM. He also built up contacts with people he would later recruit for his post-war political project. The most important one was Fu'ad Siniura, who came from a prominent Sidon trading family and would go on to run Hariri's banks before becoming acting minister of finance. The two young men were classmates at school and fellow activists in the same ANM cell.[30]

After completing secondary school Hariri moved to Beirut to study accounting at the Arab University. However, he was unable to finance his studies, a problem made all the more acute by the birth of his first child to his first wife, Nida.[31] In 1964 Hariri moved to Saudi Arabia, where he first worked as a teacher.[32] In 1973 Hariri was working as an accountant for a Saudi contracting company when oil prices sky rocketed. Input prices shot up as well, pushing the business into bankruptcy. Yet the position allowed Hariri to learn the ropes of contracting, handling all aspects of the business. He then struck out on his own, founding a contracting company with his cousin. They fulfilled small subcontracts for his former boss. This was part of a wider gold rush in Saudi Arabia at the time. Hundreds of thousands of small-scale contracting and trading enterprises were registered in the 1970s and 1980s, creating a highly competitive environment.[33] Hariri's company fell victim to another oil shock in 1975. Hariri faced a heavy debt burden; he was down and out, and had to give up his apartment, but continued to chase his dream of a big contract.

Hariri kept up appearances, dressing smartly and mingling with Western contractors. His big break came when Nasir al-Rashid, an engineer who had won a contract from King Khalid, had difficulties completing a project in 1976.[34] The American company that had promised to build three tower blocks in Riyadh pulled out in the last minute. Al-Rashid approached Hariri, who managed to persuade an Italian company to take on the project. The commission Hariri received for this contract was enough to settle his outstanding debts. King Khalid asked al-Rashid and Hariri to tackle another highly ambitious contract: the Masara Hotel in the resort of Ta'if, to be completed in only ten months. Hariri procured the French construction company Oger as the contractor, overcoming the management's initial reluctance to tackle the high-risk project. A contract for $112.5 million was signed in January 1977.[35] The contract was fulfilled in record time and with little regard for cost. Without Hariri's drive and energy, the project would have been impossible to realise. Crown Prince Fahd was said to have been deeply impressed by al-Rashid and Hariri's feat, and they received a string of highly lucrative contracts. Hariri was also rewarded with a Saudi passport, a rare perk for a foreigner. Citizenship bestowed tangible monetary benefits because non-Saudis were legally obliged to rely on Saudi citizens as middlemen to obtain certain contracts.[36] In January 1978 Hariri established Saudi Oger to manage projects in the kingdom, and in 1979 he bought the French mother company. In summary, Hariri's business success was due to a combination of his personal abilities and the mechanics of Saudi royal patronage. The young Lebanese businessman originally struggled to get a break in Saudi contracting. Only through his association with Nasir al-Rashid did he gain access to highly lucrative royal contracts. His relationship with King Khalid and Crown Prince Fahd was still purely commercial, and appears not to have been political yet.

Rafiq Hariri became a philanthropist in his native Sidon in 1977. He made a major donation to his former school, run by the Sidon Maqasid association.[37] In 1979 he founded his own philanthropic association, the Islamic Institute for Culture and Higher Education. In 1979 Hariri opened a branch of his Oger company in Lebanon in order to build the Kfar Fallus centre near Sidon. He would later repeat this pattern of engagement in Sidon local politics on a national scale.[38] Rather than displacing the city's notable families or militias, he sought to win them over by using patronage. His financial means were far superior to those of established local actors. Hariri also placed allied technocrats in municipal administration and clientelised the Sunni mufti of Sidon. The Bizri family, among whose members were the leading *zu'ama* of the city, eventually became Hariri allies. He enjoyed a more tense relationship with Mustafa Sa'd and his son 'Ussama, who were leading the Sunni-dominated leftist and popular movement in Sidon.[39] Hariri also started investing in the economy. In 1981 he bought a 73 per cent stake in the Mediterranée Investors Group (MIG), which owned Banque Mediterranée in France and Lebanon as well as some other interests.[40] Khuri had steered the bank into trouble by speculating in the silver market. Hariri provided the necessary capital to keep it afloat. However, in 1983 Hariri eased Khuri out of the chairmanship of MIG, reportedly because he had hidden the true extent of the bank's troubles from Hariri. Fu'ad Siniura became chairman and general director of Banque Mediterranée in France and Lebanon. Hariri also obtained a licence to open the Saudi Lebanese Bank in 1981.[41] After his initial business success in Saudi Arabia between 1976 and 1978, Hariri turned his attention to business opportunities in Lebanon.

Rafiq Hariri and the clean-up of Beirut, 1982

Rafiq Hariri was not unique: he was one of several Lebanese who had emigrated to the Gulf and had accumulated great wealth as contractors there. Several of them returned to Lebanon to invest in construction and finance and to engage in the country's politics. They used the economic and political opening that the civil war represented. Not only was the political dominance of the *zu'ama* broken, the shift of Lebanon's economic role allowed the new contractors to buy up assets from the pre-war bourgeoisie and from international investors, who were fleeing the country. However, Rafiq Hariri was by far the most successful member of this class, both in civil war diplomacy and as prime minister. What distinguished him from the other contractors was the strong diplomatic support that he received from King Fahd of Saudi Arabia. Other new contractors also built strong relations with members of the Syrian regime or with the US administration, but no other country relied on a businessman to represent its interests in Lebanon in the way that Saudi Arabia used Hariri. Up until the Israeli invasion of Lebanon, Hariri's relations with the monarch had been commercial rather than political. He used the clean-up project of Beirut by his company Oger Liban to show the king that he could be politically useful in Lebanon. Only afterwards did Hariri become the 'Saudi mediator' between Lebanon's warring parties, taking on the role of 'Saudi man in Lebanon'.

Israeli forces invaded Lebanon in June 1982, linked up with the Lebanese Forces, and proceeded to besiege West Beirut where the PLO leadership was stationed. After weeks of shelling, PLO chairman Yasser Arafat eventually had to withdraw his forces and go into exile in Tunisia. Bashir Gemayel was elected president by the Lebanese parliament in a vote held under Israeli guns. However, Gemayel fell victim to a bomb attack on 14 September 1982. His brother Amin was elected president on 21 September. The Israeli invasion left massive destruction in its wake. Oger Liban went to work in Sidon to clear away debris, survey the war damage, reinstate public utilities, and give emergency aid to refugees.[42] Hariri decided to do the same in Beirut, thus assuming a national role, rather than just a local one. Hariri put the Oger engineer Fadl Shalaq in charge of the clean-up of Beirut, giving him a blank cheque to use funds from the Hariri-owned Saudi Lebanese Bank.[43] The work involved clearing barricades and sandbags, removing rubble and securing dangerous buildings, while French forces were clearing landmines. The style of project management was typical of the early Oger projects. Relentless speed was combined with a disregard for cost. The number of daily truckloads transported to landfill was raised from 135 to 1,000, and 286,646 cubic metres of rubble were removed in only thirty days.[44] Cost quickly escalated from the $5.9 million estimated at the beginning to an eventual $27 million.[45]

Hariri lacked the political connections necessary for undertaking the project in a city riven by divisions between militias, the Lebanese army and Israeli occupiers. He therefore solicited support from leading Beirut politician Sa'ib Salam, a Saudi ally. Salam supported the clean-up, an arrangement that was beneficial to both men. For the Beirut *za'im*, the Oger project provided a platform from which to restate his claim to leadership of Sunni Beirut. At the project launch on 5 September 1982 Salam thanked Hariri, 'the son of great Sidon', in the name of 'heroic Beirut'.[46] He stressed that Hariri was working together with Maqasid, a charity headed by Salam. Hariri, in turn, required political support for the clean-up. As Shalaq put it: 'The real question was not: "why Sa'ib Bek"? But "who but Sa'ib Bek?"'—referring to Sa'ib Salam by his honorific title.[47] Salam ensured the support of the governor and the mayor of Beirut, and also arranged a meeting between Shalaq and Nabih Birri, the militia leader in charge of Beirut's predominantly Shia southern suburbs.[48] Hariri started the project without King Fahd's help, and only approached the king once it was under way, lobbying him vigorously through numerous channels.[49] The fact that he needed intermediaries at all suggests that Hariri still had a primarily commercial rather than political relationship with the Saudi monarchy at this point. An important intermediary was Hariri's new Beirut ally Sa'ib Salam.[50] Hariri was trying to show the king that he could be politically useful in Lebanon. The king did indeed recompense Hariri. The posters on Oger's trucks initially publicised the 'Project of

Cleaning Beirut, courtesy of Rafiq Hariri, Oger Liban 1982'.[51] Once Fahd had been brought on board, they were replaced with posters advertising the clean-up as a donation by the Saudi king.[52]

Why did Rafiq Hariri return to Lebanon? He cherished a political and economic 'vision' for Lebanon. Foreign Minister Elie Salem described this aspect of Hariri's motivation in his memoirs:

> Hariri was a dreamer, but with a difference: he often realised his dreams. … When I visited Hariri in his new residence [in Saudi Arabia], he seemed to be living more in his native Sidon than in Riyad. Here he was, one of the busiest entrepreneurs in the world, and yet he still followed the course of Lebanese politics with the passion of one who wanted to get involved and change it. To him, the solution to the Lebanese crisis was not unlike a project: it could be contracted out and successfully completed on time.[53]

The vehicle for Hariri to realise his vision was his alliance with the Saudi king, which opened the doors to Lebanon's political elite. Yet it would be wrong to assume that Hariri was entirely selfless in his political engagement; he also had economic reasons to return to Lebanon. He had experienced the shocks of the Saudi oil economy, and had lived through bankruptcies in 1973 and 1975. The only way to avoid the vagaries of business was to build up a direct, close and firm relationship with the Saudi king. This was particularly important in 1982, when falling oil prices severely hit Hariri's contracting business in Saudi Arabia. Gulf contractors were forced to diversify after the easy, rent-fuelled construction bonanza of the 1970s came to an end. One of the prime strategies of diversification was internationalisation through investment in other Gulf states, in industrialised countries or in Arab countries. This was the 'internationalisation' of Gulf capital which Hanieh talks about in his book on Gulf capitalism.[54]

The economist Marwan Iskandar wrote at the time that Hariri had earned profits of no less than $750 million on 'cost-plus' contracts between 1979 and 1982.[55] Under cost-plus arrangements, contractors are reimbursed for all their outlays. The risk for the contractor is thus minimal and there is no incentive to control cost. In 1982 cost-plus contracts were prohibited in Saudi Arabia in order to cut government expenditure in the face of falling oil prices. Iskandar writes that Hariri had to cut his workforce by 40 per cent. Hariri was opening up new sources of revenue by diversifying into Lebanese finance and construction. Furthermore, Hariri's political usefulness to King Fahd ensured continued access to royal contracts. The importance of direct access is illustrated by the episode of a major Saudi hospital contract in 1984. The health minister, Ghazi al-Qusaibi, was a Saudi technocrat who insisted that the tender follow correct procedure. However, the minister was sidelined and was unable to gain access to Fahd to make his case. Qusaibi's marginalisation was reportedly due to pressure from Rafiq Hariri, who was bidding for the contract.[56] In frustration, the health minister penned a poem addressed to the ruler and published in the newspaper *al-Jazeera*:

> Between you and me, there are 1,000
> informers cawing like crows,
> So why do I need to continue talking or
> singing?
> My voice will be lost and you will feel
> its echo.
> Between you and me there are 1,000
> informers who are lying.
> You were cheated and you were pleased with the cheating,
> But in the past you were not like this,
> admiring false things.[57]

Al-Qusaibi was subsequently sacked. Through the clean-up in Beirut Hariri had shown that he could be politically useful in Lebanon. By 1984 the lucrative contracts that Oger had received included the Royal Diwan, the Council of Ministers, and the buildings for the Secretary General and the Majlis al-Shura in Riyadh.[58]

Support for the Gemayel project, 1982–1984

Hariri's wealth and his access to the top table at which Lebanon's future was negotiated depended on his alliance with the Saudi king. In turn, the scope and limits of Saudi Arabia's influence in Lebanon were set by two factors: economic power; and relations with Syria, the dominant Arab power in Lebanon. Saudi foreign policy is also deeply influenced by the kingdom's alliance with the USA. Washington's relationship with Damascus therefore cast a long shadow on Saudi–Syrian relations. The US–Saudi relationship is often reduced to 'the deal': the provision of security by the USA in exchange for Saudi oil. However, the relationship goes deeper. The USA has been deeply implicated in Saudi state-building since the first oil concession in 1932 through the American oil company ARAMCO.[59] In turn, Saudi Arabia played a central role in channelling petrodollars into the American financial system in the 1970s. Rachel Bronson argues that US–Saudi relations are 'thicker than oil' and included an ideological affinity: in its Cold War struggle the USA relied on the conservative monarchy to confront communism and Arab nationalism in the Middle East.[60] This meant that relations were especially cordial when the Cold War confrontation was at its peak. The early 1980s was such a phase of intensified superpower conflict, known as the 'second Cold War'.[61] King Fahd had been lukewarm on US détente with the Soviet Union and was enthusiastic about President Reagan's escalation of the Cold War confrontation. The two countries cooperated in various Third World interventions, most famously in Afghanistan. In Lebanon, both the USA and Saudi Arabia supported the political project of President Amin Gemayel. Syria opposed Gemayel's withdrawal agreement with Israel, bringing the USA and Syria into conflict and straining Saudi–Syrian relations.

While Saudi Arabia was a conservative monarchy, Syria was a 'revolutionary republic'.[62] While the kingdom was a close US ally, Syria stood in the Soviet camp. Both Arab states were opposed to Israel but Saudi Arabia considered Soviet communism an equal or even greater threat. This explains Saudi support for Afghan fighters against the Soviet invasion in 1979, an issue entirely alien to the Damascus regime. Damascus and Riyadh reacted very differently to the Iran–Iraq war in the 1980s. While Saudi Arabia saw the Iranian revolution as a threat, Syria regarded it as an opportunity to strengthen the front against Israel. Syria was the only Arab country to support Iran, while the Arab monarchies in the Gulf rallied around Saddam Hussain's Iraq. Yet all these differences mask a high degree of cooperation based on joint Arab and Islamic identity.[63] Most importantly for our story, in 1978 Saudi Arabia decided to reject the Camp David Accord between Israel and Egypt, joining the rejectionist camp of Arab states.[64] The Saudi aim appears to have been to remain within the 'Arab consensus', to prevent further Soviet infiltration of the Middle East, and to move the consensus towards an eventual negotiated peace with the Jewish state.

The means by which Saudi Arabia and Syria exerted influence in Lebanon differed greatly. While Syria could project military force into the neighbouring country, Saudi Arabia used its superior financial means to influence Lebanese politics. Syria itself was also becoming reliant on Saudi financial support because of rising military expenditure and the escalating economic cost of state-led import substitution. However, Syria set clear limits to 'riyalpolitik' in Lebanon. The kingdom's chief concern was to square its close alliance with the USA and solidarity with Syria as an Arab and Islamic state. Between 1982 and 1984 this was impossible because Reagan was confronting Assad as a Cold War adversary.

From 1982 to 1984 Saudi Arabia supported Amin Gemayel. He was the brother of Bashir Gemayel, the Lebanese Forces leader who had allied with Israel to expel the PLO from Beirut and have himself elected president in August 1982 with Israeli support. His assassination the following month was followed by the Sabra and Shatila massacre and the succession of his brother to the presidency. Amir Gemayel concluded a withdrawal agreement with Israel on 17 May 1983, removing the prima facie reason for the Syrian military presence. This raised Assad's ire because it hindered his goal of containing Israeli influence in Lebanon and preventing separate Arab peace agreements with the Jewish state. The Reagan administration supported Gemayel in order to undermine Soviet influence in the Middle East, represented by the Syrian regime. Lebanon became a 'major theatre of surrogate Cold War confrontation'.[65] Damascus mobilised its local allies in a rejectionist coalition against the 17 May agreement: Walid Junblat's Progressive Socialist Party (PSP), Sulaiman Franjiyya's Marada militia and Nabih Birri's Amal. Whether Saudi Arabia supported or opposed the 17 May accord is in dispute, but the kingdom's diplomacy seemed designed to persuade the Syrians to accept the agreement.[66]

Gemayel used the army as his power base to extend his control over the whole Lebanese territory and confront militias allied to Syria. The Lebanese Forces and the army were working together. The USA bolstered the army's capabilities through major arms sales, and shelled PSP positions from the aircraft carrier *New Jersey* in December 1983. Saudi Arabia expressed its misgivings about the actions of Gemayel's army, but subsequently acquiesced to them.[67] The third aspect of the

Gemayel project was control of the levers of the economy. Amin Gemayel had already built a reputation as 'Mr. Ten percent'.[68] Gemayel sought to control key government institutions, in effect 'Kata'ibising' the state—in reference to the Kata'ib Party founded by Gemayel's father, Pierre. As Hourani has shown, Gemayel founded the Council of Foreign Economic Relations (COFER) as a 'super-ministry' and sought to either take over or sideline the CDR.[69] Furthermore, he placed his confidant Roger Tamraz at the head of Intra Invest, the state holding company that had taken over the remnants of Yussuf Baydas's business empire in 1966. The economy was the main avenue for Saudi influence in Lebanon, and Gemayel initially accepted Saudi capital inflows chan-nelled by Hariri. On a visit by Gemayel to Riyadh in November 1982, King Fahd reportedly obliged him to keep Lebanon open to Saudi investments in return for Saudi support.[70]

Hariri's diplomatic role grew from 1983 onwards, while other Saudi representatives were sidelined. In April 1983 the Saudi ambassador, 'Ali al-Sha'ir, was recalled to Riyadh and promoted to the position of infor-mation minister.[71] Ambassador al-Sha'ir had previously been the most influential Saudi actor in Lebanon. Apart from his diplomatic role, he had also been the main distributor of Saudi patronage in Lebanon.[72] The recall paved the way for an increase in Hariri's role. He acted as a junior mediator during the Shuf war in September 1983. The Israeli withdrawal from the area had precipitated fighting between Junblat's PSP and the Lebanese Forces, supported by the Lebanese army. Prince Bandar bin Sultan had been appointed as a mediator between the Americans and the Syrian regime that June, and was now leading the Saudi diplomatic effort for a ceasefire in the Shuf. For security reasons Bandar only met the different parties in Damascus, while Hariri liaised with them inside Lebanon.[73] Hariri played only a junior role in the negotiations, but his involvement in the diplomacy signified a major increase in his stature.[74]

The ceasefire agreement was followed by a national reconciliation conference, a dialogue supported and facilitated by the Syrian regime. Hariri brokered an agreement that Geneva would be the location, and helped bring the delegates there in late October 1983. He presented himself as 'the real voice of King Fahd'.[75] The Lebanese foreign minis-ter, Elie Salem, later claimed in his memoirs that he was so impressed by Hariri's performance that he urged President Gemayel to appoint Hariri prime minister. Gemayel declined.[76] The conference could not resolve the impasse over the 17 May agreement. The Lebanese president, together with the USA and Saudi Arabia, embarked on another round of diplomatic initiatives to persuade Assad to accept the agreement. Hariri supported the mission by American envoy Donald Rumsfeld at the end of 1983, and tried to broker a 'security plan' for Beirut in January 1984.[77]

The Gemayel project received a fatal blow on 6 February 1984, when Amal and the PSP launched an all-out attack on the army in Beirut, pushing it out of the western part of the city. The next day the US marines, who had first arrived in August 1982, withdrew from Lebanon. America and the Saudi kingdom had been unable to either defeat Syria or convince it to accept the 17 May agreement. All that was left for Saudi Arabia was to negotiate a ceasefire between Gemayel and his opponents. Hariri was deeply involved. He toured Damascus, Beirut and Larnaca, but it took a visit by Crown Prince 'Abdallah on 24 February to persuade Syria to agree to a ceasefire. On 29 February Gemayel travelled to Damascus and formally renounced the 17 May agreement. The Lausanne conference of March 1984 once again brought all Lebanese actors together, but this was merely a show of Syria's unassailable position in Lebanon. Hariri was once again present in a junior capacity. By now he had become deeply involved in the diplomacy of the civil war.

Saudi support for Gemayel's project went hand in hand with increased Saudi investment in Lebanon. This paved the way for Hariri's investments in Lebanese finance and construction. In February 1983 he took control of the top positions of Banque Mediterranée.[78] He also engaged in three construction projects with the backing of President Gemayel: Beirut's city centre; the northern littoral; and the southern suburbs of the capital. All three projects were premised on Gemayel's success because they relied on army control of the areas under construction and on political support from the president, for instance through his influence on the CDR as the agency in charge of government construction contracts. As early as 1983, Rafiq Hariri started drawing up plans for reconstructing Beirut's city centre. The area had been the heart of commerce, trade, government administration, culture and transport before the war. In 1975 it became a battleground and a virtual no-go area. The area remained at the heart of Hariri's reconstruction policy and the centrepiece of his 'vision' for Lebanon during and after the war. In January 1983 Oger tore down Suq Nuriya and Suq Tawil.[79] Oger painted the facades in the Mara'ad area in the first half of 1983 and built a prototype block of houses in Suq Tawil in the winter of 1983–4. Hariri also prepared a model of the reconstructed city and showed it to Gemayel.[80] In mid-July 1983 the army, backed by the Lebanese Forces, engaged in an eight-hour battle to evict Lebanese war-displaced from Wadi Abu Jamil, an area of the city centre.[81] The eviction of the displaced was a prerequisite for reclaiming the area's real estate.

Another Hariri project carried out in conjunction with Gemayel was the development of the littoral north of Beirut. This had long been one of Gemayel's pet projects.[82] In July 1983 Rafiq Hariri won the contract to execute the plan. His partner was Joseph Khuri, an engineer from Gemayel's home town, Bikfaya, who was considered close to the president.[83] The third project was the development of luxury housing in the southern suburbs. Hariri's plans for gentrifying the area necessitated the displacement of the predominantly Shia refugees, who were supporters of Nabih Birri's Amal movement, a move that would politically benefit Gemayel.[84] As early as October 1982 Oger Liban appears to have coordinated the clean-up of southern Beirut with the Lebanese army. While the military was tearing down 'informal' and 'illegal' housing in southern Beirut, Oger was removing rubble and roadblocks.[85] In 1983 Oger presented a plan for the area, developed in coordination with Gemayel's Committee for the Development of the Southern Suburbs:[86] high-value tourism and luxury residences were to be developed in areas close to the sea and the beaches.[87] This was the same logic of value-creation as in the city centre. Yet the predominantly Shia inhabitants of the area interpreted the resettlement plans by the Maronite president and the Sunni contractor as an attack on their community.

Relations between the Saudi contractor and the president were not entirely smooth.[88] In August 1983 Hariri intervened on behalf of the head of the CDR, Muhammad 'Atallah, in a dispute with President Gemayel. 'Atallah was an economist from Hariri's home town, Sidon, and had been appointed by President Sarkis in 1977. The technocrat objected to the blocking of CDR contracts he had awarded and the sidelining of the CDR by Gemayel's 'super-ministry', the COFER. 'Atallah was opposed to Gemayel's 'Kata'ibisation' of the state and sought Hariri's support. In August 1983 'Atallah resigned in protest and left Beirut to 'holiday' as Hariri's guest in southern France. Hariri then reportedly raised the issue at a meeting with Gemayel, while also conveying a message from King Fahd concerning the pending Israeli withdrawal in the Shuf mountains. The episode illustrates how Hariri managed to mix his role as 'Saudi mediator' and his own business interests. After all, the CDR was the central agency in charge of reconstruction and awarding contracts such as the one for the northern littoral, which Hariri had secured.

Hariri had to abandon his Beirut construction projects when Syria's allies defeated the Lebanese army in West Beirut on 6 February 1984. The city centre became a battle zone again.[89] The Oger team withdrew to Paris to continue its planning activities. At the end of 1984 Oger presented a second plan for the southern suburbs, but it was not implemented until after the war.[90] The national unity government of April 1984 included the pro-Syrian warlords Birri and Junblat. The state was subsequently 'de-Kata'ibised', and agencies that had been Gemayel's power base were dismantled.[91] The Ministry of State for the South was specifically created for Birri, who also gained the right to countersign all payments made by the CDR.[92] This marked the rising influence of Syrian-allied militia leaders in the Lebanese state. However, Birri and other militia leaders were less interested in dismantling the state than in taking it over and restructuring it in their own interest, namely as a resource for patronage. This was in contrast with the pre-war *zu'ama*, who had sought to keep the welfare functions of the state minimal. This also ran counter to Hariri's neoliberal logic of state restructuring in the post-war era, which centred on strong economic agencies that would ensure a friendly 'business climate' to attract investors and make Lebanon 'competitive' in a new Middle East. These competing logics and the struggle over state restructuring between Hariri and the militia leaders shaped the neoliberal reconstruction of Lebanon's post-war economy, as explained in chapters 3 and 6.

International politics, 1985–1990

Gemayel's defeat in February 1984 represented a failure of US and Saudi policy in Lebanon. Over the next few years Rafiq Hariri spearheaded a Saudi shift towards Syria. The businessman accepted Syrian predominance in Lebanon and supported Damascus's efforts at imposing a settlement on the country's warring parties. This culminated in the 1989 Ta'if accord, which was made possible by a US–Syrian rapprochement brokered by Saudi Arabia. Hariri had been an important but junior player in the Saudi mediation efforts between 1983 and 1984; senior princes and King Fahd had held the reins of Saudi Arabia's Lebanon policy. This changed in 1984, when top US and Saudi decision-makers turned their attention to the Iran–Iraq war. Hariri thus gained greater leeway for mapping the path of Saudi policy in Lebanon. This was also due to the declining influence of two other poles of Saudi influence in Lebanon. The Sunni *za'im* Sa'ib Salam was marginalised after the defeat of the Gemayel project. He was excluded from the 'national unity' cabinet headed by Tripoli *za'im* Rashid Karami, assembled in April 1984. In 1985 Salam moved to Switzerland, leaving Rafiq Hariri as the most influential 'Saudi man' in Lebanon.[93] The other pole of Saudi influence was the embassy in Beirut. The influential Saudi ambassador 'Ali al-Sha'ir had already been transferred back to Riyadh in April 1983. On 17 January 1984 the Saudi consul Hussain Farrash was kidnapped, and throughout the summer of that year repeated protests and attacks by Shia groups such as Islamic Jihad prevented the re-opening of the Saudi embassy.[94]

The long and tortuous process towards the signing of the Syrian-brokered 'militia agreement' continued through 1985. Hariri moved his centre of operations to Damascus: 'Hariri, however, sensing where the power was, spent more time in Damascus than in Beirut. In Damascus he could move freely and meet radical leaders who had offices in Damascus as well as in Beirut, and he hoped through Syrian influence to curb their activities.'[95] Hariri built up close relations with Syria's vice-president, 'Abd al-Halim Khaddam, who was in charge of the 'Lebanon file' and was putting together an agreement between Syria's allies Birri and Junblat. What was missing was a Christian party to the accord. One of Hariri's most important contributions to the militia agreement was to bring Elie Hubaiqa, one of the warlords of the

Lebanese Forces militia, to the fold. Hariri is said to have paid Hubaiqa and the other parties large sums of money.[96] Hubaiqa had previously been considered 'Israel's man'. His volte-face in turning towards Syria cannot be explained with reference to Saudi financial inducements alone. The militia leader was also involved in a power struggle with other Christian leaders, especially his rival for the Lebanese Forces leadership, Samir Geagea, and President Amin Gemayel. Hubaiqa probably calculated—incorrectly—that an alliance with Syria would pave the way to dominance in the Christian sector. This suggests that Hariri's cash was not decisive in winning over Hubaiqa, but it ensured that Hariri—as a Saudi representative—was able to sit at the table when the post-war order was being hammered out. Much of the agreement was said to have been negotiated in Hariri's flat in Damascus.[97] The tripartite agreement was defeated in January 1986, when forces under the control of Geagea and Gemayel defeated the Hubaiqa loyalists. Syria had failed to impose a settlement on Lebanon. The period from 1986 to 1988 was one of stalemate in which Gemayel remained a lame-duck president, while Syria managed to deepen its control of Lebanon—for instance by redeploying troops to Beirut—but proved unable to impose a settlement.

Another aspect of Saudi involvement in Lebanon at the time was its conflict with Iran. The two countries were engaged in an ideological contest that pitted a conservative monarchy against a revolutionary republic. Both appealed to Islamic ideology for legitimacy. Saudi support for Saddam Hussein's war against the Islamic Republic and the kingdom's invitation of the US navy to the Gulf to protect shipping from Iranian attack exacerbated tension.[98] Lebanon became an arena for the Saudi–Iranian conflict. The kingdom was forced to close its embassy due to attacks by radical Shia groups allied with or at least sympathetic to the regime in Tehran. The extent of Hariri's involvement in Saudi Arabia's confrontation with Iran in Lebanon is unclear. Investigative journalist Bob Woodward claims that Saudi Arabia helped the CIA to carry out a bomb attack on Shia cleric Muhammad Hussain Fadlallah in March 1985.[99] Fadlallah survived, but eighty people were killed and 200 wounded. According to Woodward, Saudi Arabia denied any involvement and, as a distraction, provided Fadlallah with the details of the operatives who had carried out the attack.[100] Saudi Arabia subsequently offered Fadlallah $2 million in cash to act as an 'early warning system' against attacks on Saudi and American facilities. Fadlallah is said to have accepted the payment in the form of food, medicine and education expenses for some of his people. Hariri's biographer Nicholas Blanford presents a different version. According to his informant, it was Hariri who offered the money to Fadlallah. In return, the cleric would help calm Shia unrest in Saudi Arabia's Eastern Province. According to Blanford's source, Fadlallah turned the money down, 'suspecting a bribe'.[101] The conflicting and unreliable accounts by investigative journalists shed little light on Hariri's exact involvement in the 'intelligence politics' of the time. What is clear is that the philanthropic Hariri Foundation became a target for attacks. According to Blanford, Hariri's offices were attacked with rocket-propelled grenades the day after he first met Fadlallah. Allegedly, Amal leader Nabih Birri wanted to discourage Hariri from preferring any Shia representatives over himself.[102] In May 1986 Hariri Foundation general secretary Fadl Shalaq was briefly kidnapped.[103] Throughout 1986 Hariri Foundation offices were attacked by unknown assailants.[104]

Gemayel's presidency was coming to an end in September 1988. The identity of the next president was the subject of intense diplomatic activity in the months before he was to step down. Hariri was in the midst of these efforts. In this context, the then-Lebanese ambassador to the United States, 'Abdallah Bu Habib, relates a revealing episode about Hariri's money politics and his relations with King Fahd.[105] In August 1987 Hariri suggested to Bu Habib that he would pay Amin Gemayel $30 million to hand over power to Johnny 'Abdu, the Lebanese ambassador to Switzerland. If Bu Habib helped convince Gemayel to step down, Hariri would send King Fahd to Damascus to win Assad's approval. Another $500 million would suffice to disarm the militias and get the Syrians to withdraw from Lebanon. 'Abdu and Gemayel later claimed that they did not take Hariri's offer seriously, while King Fahd was said to have been so incensed by Bu Habib's revelation that he refused to speak to Hariri for three months.[106] Bu Habib's account makes Hariri look naively unaware about what money can and cannot achieve in Lebanese politics. It suggests that Hariri managed to buy access to decision-making processes but could not determine their outcomes. Money was an important interest of

Lebanon's politicians and militia leaders, but not necessarily the most important one. Secondly, the episode reveals the nature of the relationship with Fahd. Hariri would speak as 'the voice of Fahd' but seems to have enjoyed great discretion over the means with which to pursue Saudi goals. As Elie Salem put it:

> Hariri had real power ... when Hariri was talking it was King Fahd talking. He would come up with ideas that were very forceful and say that this is what King Fahd wants. And what Fahd wants is what Hariri tells him. Fahd, of course, was not interested in the details.[107]

It is therefore hard to unpick what was Fahd's initiative, and what Hariri came up with himself, only gaining approval after the fact.

The deadline of Gemayel's term was preceded by frantic US–Syrian diplomacy, but no consensus candidate was found. In the two months running up to the election the Americans had sought Saudi help to find a compromise candidate, and Hariri was vetting presidential hopefuls in Paris.[108] Within the last minutes of his presidency, Gemayel appointed army commander Michel Aoun prime minister and hence interim president. The period between 1988 and 1990 saw competing administrations led by Aoun and the rival prime minister Salim al-Huss, who enjoyed Syrian backing. The end to the civil war proceeded in two steps: first, the Ta'if conference in 1989, at which Syrian dominance in Lebanon was cemented and the confessional power-sharing formula was adjusted; and secondly, the Syrian military defeat of Aoun in 1990. Syria silenced or expelled its opponents in Lebanon. The process was based on US–Syrian rapprochement and an agreement on Lebanon, which was brokered by Saudi Arabia and built on Hariri's diplomatic efforts since 1985. Syria and the USA had been moving closer to each other's positions since 1987, with Syria realising that the power of the Soviet Union was waning and Washington understanding that it needed Syria to help it achieve its policy objectives in the Middle East, especially a negotiated Arab–Israeli peace agreement. Ta'if was 'an agreement between, and managed by, the US and the Syrians through the Saudis'.[109] The parts of Ta'if dealing with Syrian–Lebanese relations bore great resemblance to the 1985 tripartite agreement.[110] The end of the Cold War and of the Iran–Iraq war allowed the USA to turn its attention to the Lebanon conflict. The American aim was to put Syria in a position to regulate Hizballah, the Shia militia that had developed an effective resistance capability to Israeli occupation in South Lebanon. Saudi Arabia saw Ta'if as an opportunity to achieve its long-term goal to include Syria in a conservative 'consensus' solution to the Lebanese and the Arab–Israeli conflicts.

In October 1989 an Arab League 'troika' consisting of the kings of Morocco and Saudi Arabia and the Algerian president called on all surviving Lebanese MPs to assemble in the Saudi resort of Ta'if. Hariri was intimately involved in organising the conference, and arranged for the deputies to be flown to the Saudi city.[111] The Ta'if agreement consisted, firstly, of an adjusted power-sharing formula that strengthened the Sunni prime minister and the Shia speaker vis-à-vis the Maronite president. Secondly, it legitimised the presence of Syrian troops in Lebanon. The troika had acquired Syrian approval of the agreement and presented it as a fait accompli to the deputies.[112] Hariri was deeply involved in liaising with Damascus and Washington and persuading the deputies to accept the agreement.[113] The deputies renegotiated some details of the power-sharing formula, but its fundamentals were not altered. Saudi influence has been credited with achieving the strengthening of the position of the Sunni prime minister at Ta'if.[114] The Saudis thus bolstered the position that Hariri was to occupy just three years later.

While Aoun still claimed to be prime minister, and hence the legitimate acting president of Lebanon, Saudi Arabia and Syria moved to get a new president elected. Hariri was one of the driving forces behind the election of René Mouawad, a traditional politician from the Syrian-controlled north. In Lebanon, parliament elects the president. It therefore fell to the surviving MPs, elected in 1972, to choose a new head of state. On 5 November 1989 Hariri flew the deputies on his private aircraft to Quli'at airbase near the Syrian border, where they elected Mouawad. The USA, too, accepted Mouawad. Hariri provided the president with an armour-plated Mercedes and offered him the use of his Oger building in Beirut.[115] However, Mouawad was assassinated the same month, possibly by a Syrian regime fearful that the new president might negotiate with Aoun rather than fight him.[116] Within twenty-four hours a new president was elected by fifty-three deputies, whom parliamentary speaker Hussain Hussaini gathered in a Syrian intelligence building in Shtura in the Biqa'. The new man was Elias Hrawi from Zahle. He was willing to confront Aoun. Once again, Hariri's plane had carried the deputies to the vote.[117] Hariri provided Hrawi with living quarters and offices in an apartment block in Beirut and contributed to staff costs, accommodation, logistics, communications, armoured cars and security equipment.[118] The fact that the 'Saudi man in Lebanon' supported the logistics of electing two presidential candidates who were ready to work with Syria and then contributed financially to their expenses underlines the Saudi–Syrian understanding over Lebanon.[119] According to Syrian vice-president 'Abd al-Halim Khaddam, the Syrian regime was for the first time seriously considering him for the post of Lebanese prime minister.[120]

General Aoun rejected both Mouawad and Hrawi, but he had failed to build bridges with the USA and now lacked international allies to confront the Syrians. This gulf became particularly acute when Iraq invaded Kuwait in August 1990. Aoun refused to break with Saddam Hussain—who was his major backer—while Syria joined the US-led coalition against Iraq. In November 1990 Syrian jets bombed the presidential palace in Ba'abda, where Aoun had been holed up. Assad could not have moved against the general without US approval.[121] Aoun fled to the French embassy, and finally went into exile in Paris, paving the way for Syria's unfettered domination of Lebanon. Aoun's eviction from Ba'abda illustrates the extent of US–Syrian concord over Lebanon.

Political economy, 1985–1990

The second half of the 1980s was a highly dramatic time for the Lebanese economy. Reduced militia funding and remittances after 1982 resulted in currency collapse and hyperinflation. The period was marked not just by conflicts between international powers and their proxies but also between different political and economic elites battling to shape the post-war economic order. This meant that Hariri engaged in conflict and cooperation with militia leaders, their business allies, and with Shihabist technocrats. Sectarian politics, international politics and the political economy were intricately intertwined.

Between 1982 and 1984 Hariri had tied his construction plans closely to the Gemayel project. His business interests were thus aligned with his diplomacy on behalf of Saudi Arabia. After Gemayel's failure in 1984 Hariri had to abandon these projects, and came to accept

Syrian dominance in Lebanon. Just as he was helping negotiate the militia agreement in Damascus in 1985, he started doling out financial benefits to Syria's militia allies. Hariri reportedly paid Elie Hubaiqa to persuade him to join the militia agreement.[122] There is also evidence that he supported the business interests and patronage vehicles of Walid Junblat and Nabih Birri. Junblat's Sibline cement company was having difficulties financing the completion of a cement works. Rafiq Hariri extended a loan to Sibline in November 1985, and became a major shareholder in the company in 1987.[123] The loan was granted while the negotiations for the militia agreement were taking place. Rafiq Hariri also sponsored Birri, for example with a loan of LL500 million extended to the Council of the South in July 1987 for road construction in the West Biqa' and the south.[124] The council had been created as a patronage vehicle for Birri in 1984. These loans are examples of the way in which Hariri distributed financial benefits to Syria's allies in support of his diplomatic efforts. Other examples include payments to Lebanon's General Security directorate.[125]

At the same time as Hariri turned to Syria's allies, he entered into conflict with Amin Gemayel's business network. These Christian businessmen were opposed to the influx of Gulf capital personified by Hariri. The confessional ownership of the largest banks had changed. Clement Moore Henry calculates roughly that in 1974, 62 per cent of lending of the top fifteen banks came from banks with Christian-majority ownership and 18 per cent from 'non-Christians', with the rest being 'indeterminate'. By 1982 lending by 'Christian-owned' banks was down to 47 per cent of total lending, the share of 'non-Christian' banks had risen to 36 per cent, while indeterminate banks stood at 17 per cent.[126] The established 'Christian' bourgeoisie had lost its influence during the civil war. Kata'ib and the Lebanese Forces were trying to restore their sect's dominance in the economy. This benefited businessmen linked to Kata'ib and the Lebanese Forces rather than the pre-war bourgeois families. The most prominent business ally of Amin Gemayel was Roger Tamraz. As chairman of state holding company Intra Investment Company (IIC) Tamraz spearheaded Gemayel's effort to control the Lebanese economy. Tamraz proceeded to marginalise Gulf interests in the holding company, and also alienated shareholders from Lebanon's pre-war economic elite.[127] Tamraz went on a buying spree using Bank al-Mashriq as the main vehicle to extend control over large parts of the Lebanese economy.[128] Intra became 'part of the Phalangist [i.e. Kata'ib] infrastructure'.[129] In particular, Tamraz's attempts to gain control of Lebanese flag carrier Middle East Airlines drew the wrath of his opponents.

The beginning of 1985 not only marked the beginning of Hariri's drift to Damascus but also saw the start of economic conflict between Hariri and Gemayel. In January the chairman of one of the Hariri banks officially announced the cessation of reconstruction projects in the city centre and the southern suburbs, complaining about the unhelpful stance of the Gemayel government.[130] In February 1985 Saudi Arabia reportedly used the slide of the Lebanese pound to pressure Gemayel. The currency had crashed from LL8.89 to the dollar at the end of December 1984 to LL11.72 at the end of January. In February Hariri offered Saudi aid of $500 million to Gemayel, but reportedly imposed two conditions:[131] the removal of Roger Tamraz from Intra; and the repeal of a legislative decree issued by President Gemayel in October 1983, which prohibited foreign investors from holding more than 49 per cent of Lebanese banks.[132] The latter measure was designed to curtail the influence of Gulf investors in Lebanese finance. By the end of February the pound had further deteriorated to LL16 to the dollar, and Saudi aid had not actually been disbursed.

The context of these political battles was the collapse of the Lebanese currency. The exchange rate had remained relatively stable until 1984, but then dropped from LL5.89 to the dollar in May 1984 to around LL500 in 1989. Because of the expulsion of the PLO in 1982, the amounts of militia money flowing into Lebanon declined markedly.[133] The end of the oil boom in the Gulf reduced the number of Lebanese migrants there to 65,000 in 1987, and remittances declined to an estimated $300 million, while demand for Lebanese exports also declined.[134] The large trade deficit could no longer be offset by capital inflows. At the same time the government budget was in constant deficit: militias controlled the ports and the state could not recover customs revenues, while government expenditure remained high due to continued salary payments, weapons purchases by Gemayel, and ministers using their office for patronage.

These structural conditions were the underlying cause of the currency collapse, but speculation played a big role in the dynamics of decline.[135] An IMF report in 1988 held that such speculation was welcome because it helped establish the market price of the currency.[136] However, as Gaspard shows, the timing of individual episodes of currency devaluation can only be explained with reference to coordinated rounds of speculation by key investors with little relation to market fundamentals.[137] Lebanese banks faced strong incentives for speculation. Their traditional business of providing letters of credit for the import trade had collapsed, investment in agriculture and industry remained unattractive, and banks were burdened with bad loans.[138] Coordinating speculation against the Lebanese pound was relatively easy. The banks used loans to create the pound liquidity required to buy US dollars. If a declining currency was a safe bet, then profits could be realised by selling foreign-currency holdings and repaying the original loan. The dollar counterpart to this speculation was provided by central bank intervention in the foreign-exchange market and liquidation of foreign asset holdings by Lebanese.[139] Although most Lebanese participated in this game, and speculation became something of a national sport, the main beneficiaries were the members of the cartel that was driving the speculation. Ordinary Lebanese saw the value of their savings, salaries and wages wiped out.

The central bank tried to rein in speculation using two mechanisms: First, the sale of treasury bills to 'mop up' liquidity in Lebanese pounds, reducing the currency available for speculation. At times, banks flatly refused to buy treasury bills, showing they were more powerful than the central bank.[140] The second mechanism was an increase in reserve requirements and a reduction in the value of foreign capital positions that banks were allowed to hold.[141] In response, Lebanese banks simply shifted their currency trading abroad, speculating with funds held in offshore accounts that were known as the 'Europound market'.[142] The governors of the central bank can broadly be identified as operating within the Shihabist tradition. Michel al-Khuri (1978–84) was both from a notable family—his father was Lebanon's first president, Bishara al-Khuri—and was considered a Shihabist, having been appointed governor by Shihabist president Elias Sarkis.[143] Khuri defended the independence of the central bank on several occasions, and was critical of the Tamraz empire and of Gemayel's profligate spending on arms purchases from Western countries.[144] His successor, Edmond

Na'im, was a less independent figure. He was appointed in 1985 and was a compromise candidate between Gemayel's camp and the militia leaders—including Junblat and Birri—who were in the national unity government.[145] Despite claims that Na'im lacked sufficient banking competence and charges that he was too close to the militia leaders, the central bank continued its attempts to rein in speculation.[146] Eventually, the central bank confronted the Tamraz empire, refusing to bail out the failing Bank al-Mashriq in 1988. Gemayel had stepped down and Tamraz had lost political protection.

Khuri went on to build an alliance with Rafiq Hariri. According to 'Abdallah Bu Habib, Hariri promoted Khuri's candidacy to succeed Gemayel as president in the summer of 1988.[147] The cooperation represented an alliance between a Shihabist technocrat from a notable family and the prime representative of Gulf capital. Hariri explained Khuri's appeal thus: 'Shaykh Michel is the son of a former president; he is congenial and smart; people respect him for that and even the Syrian vice-president 'Abd al-Halim Khaddam wears his blue suit when he meets him.'[148] Khuri returned to the post of central bank governor between 1991 and 1993, and was considered Hariri's man.[149] Under Khuri's watch the central bank embarked on a policy of managed currency appreciation, driving up interest rates and thus shielding the currency from speculators—an achievement that had eluded him in the 1980s. This was one of the pillars of Rafiq Hariri's post-war policy, as discussed in chapter 3.

Hariri's philanthropy[150]

Most of Hariri's political and economic schemes were being discussed in smoke-filled back rooms out of the limelight. What brought the name Rafiq Hariri to wider public attention was the Hariri Foundation. Its student loan programme benefited roughly 32,000 young Lebanese between 1983 and 1996.[151] Hariri presented the programme as completely non-political.[152] Yet philanthropy was highly political in Lebanon. In the absence of effective state provision of education and health services most Lebanese relied on charities for access to such services. Lebanese politicians used philanthropy as patronage. They sought to control existing charities or build their own. Charity tended to run along confessional lines, both because local associations were providing for their confessional community and because politicians represented 'their' communities. Schools in particular tended to recruit among their co-religionists. Philanthropy thus had several political effects: a political–economic effect of material exchange between patron and client; and a cultural effect of reproducing sectarian identity. Because of this linkage of political economy and political culture, philanthropy is an arena in which it is possible to turn 'economic power' into 'symbolic power', the power to confirm or transform the vision of the social world, of maintaining or subverting the social order.[153] So did Rafiq Hariri's philanthropy reproduce or transform sectarian clientelism?

Hariri's earliest charitable work in Lebanon was the Islamic Institute for Culture and Higher Education, which he established in his home town, Sidon, in 1979. Run by Hariri's sister Bahiya, the association started giving scholarships, albeit on a small scale. It provided loans for 176 students in higher education between 1979 and 1981.[154] The aim of the foundation was the spread of knowledge and education 'in Lebanese Islamic society in general and in Sidon in particular'.[155] Yet Hariri also seems to have been genuinely interested in going beyond the confessional patronage that was the norm in Lebanon. He started building an educational and health centre in the village of Kfar Fallus in cooperation with the Jesuit-founded St Joseph University (USJ) as well as the American University of Beirut (AUB) and the English-language International College.[156] The complex was consciously placed at an intersection of areas where different confessional groups were concentrated, 'a meeting point for all the Lebanese family'.[157] It was within easy reach for Sunni, Shia and Christian populations in southern Lebanon. Kfar Fallus was damaged by the Israeli invasion in 1982. It was eventually destroyed by the Lebanese Forces and the Israeli proxy militia under General Antoine Lahd in 1985, which aimed at cementing homogeneous sectarian 'cantons'. The destruction provoked strong protests from the president of St Joseph.[158]

The scale of Rafiq Hariri's philanthropy increased exponentially after the Israeli invasion of 1982, the period when he assumed an important diplomatic and economic role in Lebanon. The student loan programme was an act of charity, but also followed a political rationale.

In the spring of 1983 Rafiq Hariri charged Fadl Shalaq, who had overseen the clean-up of Beirut in September 1982, with putting the programme together.[159] In June 1983 Hariri first started promoting his philanthropy publicly in a TV interview. The interview was clearly a publicity stunt: a taped version was passed on to Lebanon's Central News Agency without the knowledge or permission of the TV producer or company.[160] Hariri's very public foray into philanthropy was part of a bid for the post of prime minister. The dramatic gesture of providing education to thousands of students was bound to increase the stature of Hariri, an outsider to the political scene. By October 1983 he was being considered as a possible candidate for the post.[161]

Hariri Foundation representatives consistently claimed that it was open to Lebanese from all sects and regions and that no *wasta* (intercession) was needed to obtain a loan.[162] The foundation sought to project an image of rational planning rather than sectarian favouritism. Applicants were assessed in exams put together and administered by AUB.[163] The dates of these exams were published in national newspapers.[164] In preparation of the student loan programme, Shalaq's team of experts toured the country and surveyed the obstacles that would-be university students were facing: lack of personal funds and foreign-language skills, and a preference for prestigious courses such as medicine and engineering that far outstripped demand in the labour market.[165] Based on this initial survey, the Hariri Foundation paid AUB and other centres in Lebanon and abroad to provide language training and to establish a career-guidance centre. The Hariri Foundation put a strong emphasis on 'Western' education. Hariri Foundation general director Shalaq explained that the foundation wanted students to obtain culture 'from its truthful source, and this source is today in Western Europe and in America and Canada'.[166] Cost considerations meant that the original policy of sending two-thirds of Hariri Foundation students abroad—primarily to North America and Europe—had to be abandoned.[167] By 1989–90 slightly less than three-quarters were studying in Lebanon.[168] Yet the focus remained on a Western-style education: the AUB and the English-language Beirut University College—later to become the Lebanese American University—were the Lebanese institutions with the highest number of Hariri Foundation students.

Hariri played a central role in saving the AUB during its existential crisis in the 1980s. In 1982 acting AUB president David Dodge was kidnapped by a pro-Iranian group, and in January 1984 AUB president Malcolm Kerr was assassinated. The collapse of the Lebanese pound eroded professors' salaries, and the university had trouble retaining staff. This is when Hariri stepped in. His student loan and language-training programme pushed up the number of students able to pay university fees. Hariri helped pay the salaries of professors, employees, administrators and workers at AUB. He also instituted a faculty development programme to train promising academics, and provided a new building.[169] Hariri was invited to join the university's board of trustees. In Washington, the US government was consulted over Hariri's aid to the university.[170] Hariri was thus saving an institution that was spreading 'American values'.[171] His action also helped reproduce the great inequality between well-endowed English- and French-language institutions—such as AUB, St Joseph University and International College—which fostered Lebanon's future economic and political elite, and poorer institutions such as the Lebanese University and the Arab University.

Despite repeated claims that the student loan programme selected students regardless of confession and regional background and that no *wasta* was required, recruitment during a sectarian civil war could not be disentangled from the confessional context. Hariri charged Fadl Shalaq with setting up a programme to help Lebanese students in March 1983.[172] Shalaq's memoirs and various newspaper reports about the Hariri Foundation suggest that students were primarily recruited with the help of Sunni Muslim religious and social organisations. When the programme started recruiting students, Shalaq asked the shaykhs of north Lebanon's 'Akkar region to publicise the Hariri Foundation student loans in their Friday prayers.[173] In the Western Biqa', too, the Hariri Foundation appears to have recruited through local shaykhs.[174] In Sidon and southern Lebanon the Hariri Foundation recruited students through Hariri's own Islamic Institute of Culture and Higher Education.[175] In Tripoli the Hariri Foundation worked with the Association of Islamic Youths and other Sunni Muslim organisations.[176] 'Akkar, Tripoli, Sidon and the Western Biqa' are all predominantly Sunni Muslim areas of Lebanon. Christians were not excluded from applying to the Hariri Foundation, but it was simply much easier for Sunni Lebanese to access it. Hariri's initiative of opening an office at St Joseph University in East Beirut only partially mitigated the situation, but was a symbolic gesture towards the claim to non-sectarian recruitment.[177] Staff at the Hariri Foundation were predominantly Sunni Muslim and drawn from the peripheral regions of Lebanon[178]—most prominently Fadl Shalaq himself. By 1985 the number of staff had grown from four to seventy.[179] Professionalism seems to have suffered from expansion. By 1990 a survey of 400 Hariri Foundation students at AUB recorded 84.5 per cent of respondents complaining that they had received unprofessional services from the foundation's staff.[180]

Although the majority of Hariri Foundation aid recipients appear to have been Sunni Muslim students, it is noteworthy that members of other sects also benefited from student loans to a considerable degree. Yet paradoxically, the mechanisms by which non-Sunni students received loans appears to have bolstered non-Sunni sectarian leaders. The best quantitative assessment of the beneficiaries of the Hariri Foundation is Hilal Khashan's survey of 400 recipients of student loans at the AUB, conducted between October 1990 and January 1991.[181] Khashan found that 62 per cent of respondents were Sunni, compared to 18 per cent Shia, 11 per cent Druze and 10 per cent Greek Orthodox.[182] There were no Maronite Christian respondents in Khashan's sample, probably because travelling to predominantly Muslim West Beirut to attend AUB was simply too dangerous for these students. Only 31 per cent of respondents told Khashan that their application had been processed 'on its own merits', while 69 per cent said that it had been processed 'through a connection'. This belies Shalaq's assertion that the Hariri Foundation did not work through *wasta*. Khashan cites an interview in 1991 with an unnamed Hariri Foundation official:

> Political scholarship applications have priority over regular applications: The former are processed favourably and expediently. Community leaders, influential businessmen, friends and acquaintances also press top Hariri officials to consider their requests. More often than not, Hariri officials acquiesce to pressures placed on them. On one occasion, a community leader imposed upon the Foundation a list of 400 applicants after the application deadline.[183]

Of those students who had used intercession, 40 per cent said that a political leader had helped them, while another 40 per cent cited a militia leader as the contact. What is interesting is the way that the different confessional groups applied. A slight majority (55 per cent) of Sunni recipients said that they had used contacts, while the corresponding number reached around 90 per cent among all other confessional groups. Non-Sunnis thus almost exclusively relied on *wasta*. Sunni students also performed at a higher academic standard than their non-Sunni counterparts, suggesting that their selection had been more oriented on academic criteria. In short, non-Sunni students tended to receive Hariri Foundation scholarships through intercession by militia leaders or politicians from their sect.

The evidence thus suggests the following pattern: the student loans of the Hariri Foundation primarily but not exclusively benefited Sunni Muslim students from poor peripheral regions of Lebanon, often recruited through religious charities or mosques. Non-Sunni students tended to gain acceptance through intercession by their community's militia leaders or politicians. In some ways, it is hardly surprising that Hariri recruited mainly Sunni Muslim students: he started his foundation in the midst of a sectarian civil war; pre-existing personal networks of the staff made it easier to recruit from Sunni communities; and leaders from other communities would have eyed Hariri's attempt to serve 'their' communities as an infringement. Recruitment of the Hariri Foundation happened in a particular political context. As former foreign minister Elie Salem's memoirs reveal, Hariri was already being thought of as a possible prime minister when he started the student loan programme.[184] Support from the political, social and religious leaders of the Sunni community was indispensable for his ambitions, because prime minister was the highest political position open to a Sunni. Distributing student loans via Sunni social and religious organisations was a means of drawing them into a clientelist network. Rather cleverly, however, Hariri expanded his network in a way that was not threatening to established communal leaders. He chose not to compete directly against established Sunni leaders but offered a service that few of them were able to provide and none of them could offer on such a grand scale. Hariri's relationship with the Maqasid association is indicative here. The Maqasid was the patronage instrument of the Salam family in Beirut. Rather than opening health centres or schools in Beirut or providing student loans in competition with the charity run by Tammam Salam, Hariri helped finance the Maqasid's own university scholarship programme.[185] Hariri had gained access to the leading group of Sunni politicians by virtue of his close relations with King Fahd. By drawing Sunni social and religious organisations into his clientelist net, he was laying the groundwork for eventually assuming the highest political post reserved for a member of his community.

If Hariri was trying to reap the political benefits of supporting Sunni students, why did he deny that his foundation followed a sectarian logic? The civil war and militia violence had discredited sectarianism. Hariri's claim to non-sectarian aid was a means of distinguishing his philanthropy from the sectarian violence of militia leaders and the inefficiency of *zu'ama* patronage. Hariri was trying to have his cake and eat it, to clientelise Sunni communal leaders while remaining above sectarian politics. This inherent contradiction in Hariri's attitude to sectarianism persisted throughout his political career. The source of his funding enabled him to embrace a non-sectarian discourse. This contrasts with other Sunni charities such as the Maqasid association: it had been founded by Beirut's Sunni notables, and its financing depended on the privileged position of the city's Sunni bourgeoisie. As such, it had to reflect both the confessional outlook and the ideological proclivities of Beirut's Sunni community, especially during the phase of Nasserite mobilisation. In contrast, the Hariri Foundation was financed by Hariri's personal wealth and King Fahd. At times, Hariri was in charge of directly distributing the Saudi King's charitable donations to the Lebanese.[186] Running the foundation was hugely expensive, and one newspaper report from 1986 put the cost at $30–40 million annually to pay for 12,000 students.[187] The proportions of Hariri's personal wealth and Saudi financing for the Hariri Foundation are unclear, but King Fahd's support was acknowledged at several points.[188]

Khashan's study suggests that non-Sunni students who received support from the Hariri Foundation had used intercession from militia leaders or politicians of their sects. This had a paradoxical effect: the cross-confessional element of Hariri Foundation aid actually strengthened the sectarian militia leaders and politicians from whom Hariri was trying to distinguish himself. He may not have had a choice: the allocation of student loans may have been a form of protection money paid to hostile militias. Alternatively, the Hariri Foundation may simply have been unable to convince suspicious Christians, Shia and Druze to apply to a 'Sunni' foundation, while non-Sunni communal leaders would have seen Hariri as a threat to their position had he tried to circumvent them. However, once again there is likely to be a deeper political reason: Hariri's main means to influence the diplomacy of the civil war was the provision of financial benefits to militia leaders, politicians and members of the Syrian regime. Allocating quotas to student loans was one form of benefit.

The political rationale of the student loan programme is thus clear, but it also chimes with Hariri's personal experience. At secondary school he had benefited from a local Maqasid association scholarship.[189] Hariri had emigrated to Saudi Arabia in 1964 because he was unable to finance his studies. His activism with the Arab Nationalist Movement is said to have imbued him with a deep concern for social issues. The creation of an enormous loan programme for students who would otherwise be unable to pursue higher education must have filled Hariri with a great sense of personal satisfaction, which the fact that it also furthered his political agenda is unlikely to have reduced. As Fadl Shalaq put it, talking about Hariri's motivation for setting up the student loan programme:

> Like any good person. There are selfish reasons, altruistic reasons, political reasons. He liked the big bang: he comes into Beirut, he cleans the whole city. He liked big projects, he had big ambitions. So I know that in, '84 he told me: 'You just put anybody who finished high school into university.' That's what I did. Why did he do it? It's a mission. Because he grew up in a poor family. He never forgot his roots. So he felt he had an obligation. Of course this satisfied his political ambition. So if you are a sceptic you say he did it for political reasons. If you are a believer in Hariri, you say it was because he was a good person. I think it was because he was a good person. I don't say he was a saint but I don't think anybody else can do such a dear thing.[190]

Rafiq Hariri's rise from political outsider to prime minister

Rafiq Hariri first became prime minister in 1992. The fruit-picker's son had risen to become head of government. Hariri's rise is an important milestone in the history of Lebanese capitalism. It is crucial for understanding the political economy of post-war neoliberalism. Hariri represented the rise of Gulf capital and the decline of Lebanon's domestic bourgeoisie. It also represents the replacement of the pre-war economic liberalism, which ensured the dominance of a few families in trade and finance, with post-war neoliberalism, which was dominated by Gulf contractor Rafiq Hariri heading a much more interventionist state.

Power sharing in pre-war Lebanon was a deal not just between 'the Maronites' and 'the Sunnis' as communities, but a cross-confessional compact of the country's bourgeoisie. Lebanon, as an entity separate from other Arab states, was able to act as the banker and entrepôt for increasingly statist Arab republics and the emerging oil monarchies of the Gulf in the 1950s and 1960s. The economic success of Lebanese liberalism depended very much on being the only laissez-faire economy in the region. A few families monopolised trade and finance, and their political dominance also ensured the continuation of a laissez-faire economy and a minimal state obsessed with sectarian quotas. The minimal state would not disturb trade and financial flows, politicised patronage or monopolistic structures. This approach stands in contrast to the neoliberal strengthening of the state in the post-war era.

Hariri was part of a new and rising class of Lebanese émigrés to the Gulf who had become successful contractors, and had risen to become the dominant capitalists in Lebanon, replacing the families that had monopolised banking and trade prior to 1975. They could do so because Lebanon lost its role as intermediary between Arab and Western financial and goods markets—the source of wealth of the pre-war bourgeoisie. Their rise was not without obstacles, nor did they rule alone. Shihabist technocrats were holding out in the shells of state institutions such as the central bank or the CDR, and at times they supported the new contractors—for instance, by providing banking licences. The old families, meanwhile, did not completely disappear, but their monopoly on the economy was broken. Many found an arrangement with the militias; others took their wealth out of Lebanon. The new militia leaders were promoting their own business allies, such as Gemayel crony Roger Tamraz. As Najib Hourani has pointed out, the contest between the Hariri network and the Tamraz network is one of the many overlooked but crucial episodes of the 1980s in Lebanon.[191]

The war was fought not just over sectarian voting shares or the relative influence of foreign powers, but also over the post-war economic order, what Reinoud Leenders has called the 'spoils of truce'.[192] Rafiq Hariri was not the only Gulf contractor to push into Lebanon in the 1980s. Najib Miqati and 'Issam Faris were other examples, and they would also seek political careers. Hariri was the most politically successful of them all because he enjoyed strong backing from Saudi Arabia: he was the Saudi man in Lebanon. Whether his role was crucial in helping end the civil war is debatable, but what is without doubt is that he did have a seat at the table by virtue of Saudi support. No other Lebanese contractor could make such a claim. This is also why Hariri's position after 1990 remained so closely tied to Saudi Arabia. Syria had emerged as the dominant outside power in Lebanon in 1990. Hariri's pragmatic acceptance of Syrian dominance in Lebanon had helped pave the way for US–Syrian and Saudi–Syrian rapprochement over Lebanon in 1989 and 1990. The Saudi–Syrian relationship would remain crucial for Hariri's position in Lebanon.

After the civil war Rafiq Hariri claimed that the conflict had disconnected Lebanon from the global economy, converting it into 'an archaic, over-bureaucratic, highly regulated, backward, and inward-looking economy.'[193] Najib Hourani has shown that the 'militia economy was never outside larger processes of financial globalisation'.[194] Hariri's own rise belies the idea of a closed economy. The fundamentals of the laissez-faire economy did not change, with no restrictions on capital flows and a floating exchange rate. There were inflows of militia funding, investment from the Gulf and the Lebanese diaspora. There were outflows of drugs, and Lebanon became one of the centres of the illicit arms market. This was hardly a closed economy. The militia system was highly predatory, and after 1982 it became unsustainable. The coordinated rounds of speculation against the Lebanese pound were a way of feeding on the carcass of the economy, at the expense of ordinary Lebanese. Hariri's rhetoric does not present an accurate picture of the economy, it provides a foil for his post-war vision. Lebanon's economy was not 'over-bureaucratic' or 'highly regulated', but Hariri presented it in these terms in order to prevent Lebanon from ever becoming thus. Neoliberal recipes are a cure for excessive state intervention in the economy, so Hariri had to identify such intervention as the disease in Lebanon, even if that characterisation of the civil war economy is absurd. The 'overregulated' civil war economy was the *bête noire* of Hariri's neoliberal 'vision' of post-war Lebanon.

Neoliberalism is an economic orthodoxy, but also a political project for the benefit of capital—in this case Gulf capital—which strengthens the economic management functions of the state and weakens its welfare functions. Hariri wanted to make Lebanon competitive in the global economy by rebuilding Beirut's city centre to a world standard to attract international investors. He had, together with Amin Gemayel, already started planning for reconstruction in 1983, even putting together a model of the city centre. It is hardly surprising that a construction contractor from Saudi Arabia would identify a construction project as the key to economic success. Neoliberalism strengthens the state in order to implement 'market-conforming' solutions. Hariri strengthened the state in the post-war era. He needed capable and empowered agencies to push through Beirut's reconstruction and the anchoring of the exchange rate. This stands in sharp contrast to the laissez-faire state of the pre-war era. Hariri did not design new institutions from scratch, but took over the shells of Shihabist institutions: The Council for Development and Reconstruction was to reconstruct Beirut and the central bank was to manage the currency. These institutional histories are crucial for understanding 'actually existing neoliberalism' in Lebanon. Although Shihabist institutions had been created to curb Lebanese pre-war liberalism and end laissez-faire, they were the ideal instruments for Hariri to shape post-war neoliberalism. The exact shape of Lebanese neoliberalism, its scope, extent and limits, then depended on the patterns of conflict and cooperation between Rafiq Hariri and his technocrats, on one hand, and former militia leaders, the military and intelligence establishment, and the Syrian regime, on the other. This is the story of the following chapters.

3

RECONSTRUCTION

1992–1998

The economic record of Rafiq Hariri's governments from 1992 to 1998 is mixed at best. The initial reconstruction boom resulted in an average annual real GDP growth rate of 7.2 per cent from 1993 to 1995, but this rate dropped to a lacklustre 2.1 per cent from 1996 to 1998.[1] Investment rates were respectable, but this is hardly surprising given the scale of wartime destruction. Unemployment and poverty remained high, and the benefits of growth were distributed highly unequally. His detractors paint Hariri as a rapacious capitalist whose self-serving policies were the cause of economic failure.[2] Defenders of Hariri's record argue that his policies were essentially sound but that they were torpedoed by militia leaders and the Syrian regime.[3] The discussion is framed in highly personal terms, with detractors denouncing Hariri's greed and supporters praising his 'vision' to move beyond the militia economy. The key to understanding Lebanon's post-war political economy is not the person of Rafiq Hariri per se, but the wider social forces and the institutional environment within which he was acting.

The way to unpack Lebanon's post-war political economy is to break the main policies of the governments from 1992 to 1998 into different rent-creation mechanisms, to see who appropriated rent, and how it was appropriated—which institutions were involved in rent-creation and who controlled them. Neoliberalism is a useful concept to analyse post-war reconstruction. 'Actually existing neoliberalism' involves borrowing global neoliberal templates and implementing them in a specific local context. Hariri reproduced two neoliberal templates in Lebanon: a large-scale urban development project to reconstruct central Beirut; and anchoring the currency on the US dollar. These policies came straight out of the neoliberal toolbox. In chapter 2 I set out the historical sociology of Lebanese classes and elites, and how Hariri fits into it. Gulf capital had replaced the pre-war bourgeoisie as the dominant faction of capital. Hariri had to contend with rival elites, namely former militia leaders. They were seeking to control state welfare agencies as a source of patronage resources for their clientele. In this chapter I conceptualise the three policies—reconstruction, the currency anchor and welfare agencies—as rent-creation mechanisms. I look at the way rent was created, who appropriated it, and how it was appropriated—in other words, what institutions were involved. Rent creation and appropriation helps us come to grips with the shape, scope and limits of Lebanese neoliberalism as well as its economic effects: slow growth and continued social crisis. The latter is the topic of chapter 4.

What is rent, and why is the concept useful?

Neoclassical economic theory has a very limited conception of rents, which are simply defined as excessive profits earned from government intervention in the market.[4] Further costs arise because firms invest in rent-seeking rather than production.[5] Yet this conception of rent is based on the ideal of the perfectly functioning market. Since this ideal is never achieved, rents are ubiquitous in capitalism as it exists, especially during the process of capitalist development when property rights are being reassigned to enable capitalist accumulation. If markets are regarded as social relations rather than just neutral reflections of the impersonal forces of demand and supply, then an account of the creation and appropriation of rent by different classes and elites under different institutional arrangements provides a framework for analysing a country's political economy.[6] The first step of the analysis looks at how rent is created, the second at who appropriates it. It is also necessary to look at the decision-making within the institutions that govern the rent-creation mechanism to see whether those who benefit are actually also the instigators of the policy.

A focus on rents also avoids value-judgements about 'corruption'. Rent-seeking is often described as a type of corrupt behaviour, but the ubiquity of rents suggests that they are not simply an outgrowth of graft or bribery. Both academics and journalists have described Hariri's actions as corrupt.[7] Corruption is commonly defined as 'the abuse of public office for private gain'.[8] This definition is seemingly simple; however, the line between public and private, between state and society, is not a clear-cut demarcation but is itself constantly negotiated. Narratives of corruption thus reveal the contestation of where the line should be drawn. The reassignment of property rights inherent in capitalist development means that the economic development process is constantly open to challenges over the legitimacy of property rights, debates which engage with questions of legality and morality. I will therefore not address the question whether Rafiq Hariri was corrupt or not because the ways in which rent was created and appropriated are analytically more important than legality or morality.

Rent creation I: the reconstruction of central Beirut

The first mechanism to be discussed here is reconstruction. The flagship project of this process was the reconstruction of the commercial centre of Beirut. This followed a neoliberal template.[9] The declared goal was to increase Beirut's competitiveness through 'world-class' infrastructure that could rival other regional metropoles. This would attract international investors to the Lebanese capital. Hariri's promise was to make Beirut once again the economic entrepôt to the Middle East. This focus on the high-end luxury market was highly profitable; but it also created an elite playing field segregated from the rest of the city, and thus typical of the kind of spaces produced by neoliberal urbanism. The reconstruction was not just neoliberal in its economic logic of 'competitiveness' but also in the way it created rents for a select few. Property rights in Beirut's city centre were being transferred to a single real-estate development company called Solidere, listed on the Beirut stock exchange. This was 'accumulation by dispossession', wealth distribution through a transfer of property rights.[10] Urban development was oriented on the needs of investors rather than Beirut's citizens. In order to cut through red tape, oversight by munici-pal or national government was kept to a minimum. The state played a central role through initial legislation, project facilitation through the Council for Development and Reconstruction (CDR), and by reducing risk and cost for investors. The neoliberal state, acting through strong state agencies such as the CDR, is a very different beast from the pre-war laissez-faire state, in which urban planning was minimal. As Rachel Weber has highlighted, the state plays a central role in the neoliberal value extraction from the city.[11]

Property rights in central Beirut were transferred to Solidere in exchange for shares for the original owners.[12] Solidere was the vehicle for extracting rents. The rationale for the expropriation was the com-plex web of ownership rights, with both owners and tenants having claims to properties, some dating back to Ottoman times. The number of owners is therefore variously estimated to range from 100,000 to 150,000 tenants and landowners.[13] The original owners received $1.17 billion in shares as compensation, while another $650 million was raised through a public issue in January 1994, which was oversub-scribed by 142 per cent.[14] Over 90 per cent of original property own-ers accepted the deal and took the shares.[15] Once the company had gained control of the area, it pursued the maximisation of profit by more than doubling the density of the city centre and the floor space.[16] This drastic increase in density necessitated the demolition of much of the area's historical fabric. Schmid estimates that the original fabric was totally cleared on around 80 per cent of the area covered by Solidere: 'In the end, far more buildings were demolished during the recon-struction than had been destroyed during the civil war.'[17] Those parts of the city centre that were indeed restored were those that already had the highest density.

The imperative of profit maximisation drove the planning and development efforts. Solidere's public-relations brochures included several pledges to serve wider societal goals: reintegrating the central district in metropolitan Beirut and strengthening links with neigh-bouring areas; preserving the area's historical core; and providing cultural centres such as a national library.[18] Yet the question of which parts of the historical fabric to restore was decided along economic lines, and the Solidere master plan has been criticised for not achieving the area's integration with the surrounding neighbourhoods. Instead, roads and flyovers act as barriers to adjacent areas.[19] The road network gives a clue as to whose needs Solidere was to serve: an eight-lane highway 'quasi wormholes the airport to the downtown', rendering the poorer quarters of southern Beirut invisible to the gaze of the tourist or businessperson arriving in the city.[20] As expressed in an information brochure by Solidere: 'In the modern financial centre planned on the sea-front, national and international companies operating in the region will have a prestigious location for their headquarters or local branches. This centre will be equipped with sophisticated infrastructure facilities and be easily accessible from the city and the airport.'[21] The other functions of the Solidere area were to be residential, commercial, tourism, culture and recreation, as well as governmental. In all these domains the aim was to cater for the high-end and luxury segment of the market, be it hotels, retail, or residential developments. It was this potential to capture the lucrative end of the market that was to attract international investment. This deference to the need of international investors is a typical feature of neoliberal urban planning that creates 'elite playing fields'.[22]

Much of the investment in and demand for tourism services, retail and luxury apartments comes from the Gulf or the Lebanese diaspora, a wealthy portion of which derives its income from the Gulf. The profits are realised by investors in Solidere and by developers who bought plots to pursue their own projects. Solidere pursued the neoliberal goal of making Beirut 'competitive' in the global marketplace. This was to be achieved by providing 'world-class' infrastructure (and thus making Beirut the same as elsewhere), but also making Beirut seem unique in its history and culture. This commodification of 'heritage' was expressed in Solidere's slogan describing Beirut as an 'ancient city of the future', suggesting that the Solidere project stood in a long trading and financial tradition stretching back to Phoenician times.[23] This is the 'place marketing' typical of neoliberal urban development. Solidere echoes large-scale urban development projects such as New York's Battery Park or the London Docklands.

The state played a vital role in reducing investors' risks. In order to recompense Solidere for the infrastructure work in the area, the

Lebanese government agreed in 1994 to sign over the area of land reclaimed from the sea by converting the Normandy landfill that had sprung up during the war. Critics raised concerns that the government might have overpaid the company, considering that the land it gained was worth much more than the infrastructure work.[24] Leenders estimates that Solidere's profit is set to amount to $662 million.[25] Furthermore, Solidere benefited from substantial tax breaks: dividends to shareholders, capital gains from the sale of shares, as well as Solidere income itself were exempt from tax for ten years following incorporation in 1994.[26] Most original owners did not benefit from receiving Solidere shares. Some property owners complained that their properties were undervalued, with one claiming that the property, which had been valued at $800 per square metre of built-up area in 1992 fetched $15,000–20,000 in 2007.[27] Other property owners complained that their shares were issued late, when the secondary market had already been established. By April 1995 only 2.6 million of a total 11.7 million shares had been distributed to original owners.[28] This meant that they missed a peak in share prices at $173 in August 1994—up from $100 at issue.[29] The share price subsequently plunged, and hovered between $3 and $10 from 1997 to 2004.[30] The state bore much of the cost of reconstruction, and the original property owners did not share in the land rents realised by developers. Furthermore, the mechanism by which property was expropriated illustrates one of the contradictions between neoliberal orthodoxy and practice: while one of the main functions of the liberal state is to defend property rights, Solidere represented an enforced, rather than a voluntary, transfer of such rights.[31] The interventionist neoliberal state enabled new forms of accumulation by dispossession.[32]

The single most important state institution for the reconstruction effort was the Council for Development and Reconstruction (CDR). Founded in 1977 by President Elias Sarkis and his prime minister, Salim al-Huss, the CDR was a 'Shihabist' vehicle for reconstruction. In order to insulate the CDR from interference by the old bourgeoisie or the militia leaders, it was given wide-ranging powers:[33] to draw up studies and propose laws; issue administrative licences and authorisation, and thus bypass other public bodies, including municipalities; supervise all reconstruction projects under its care; and—crucially—

to procure financing for all its projects, either from Lebanon or abroad, while being exempted from advance oversight by the court of accounts.[34] President Amin Gemayel sought to gain control of the CDR in 1983, leading to conflict with its chairman, Muhammad 'Atallah. Hariri intervened in the dispute on 'Atallah's side in August 1983.[35] Hariri was at the time already benefiting from CDR contracts, such as the contract for the northern littoral known as the Linord project.[36]

After the war, the billionaire contractor was looking for an institutional vehicle to control government spending on reconstruction. The CDR was to be this vehicle. In Law 117 of 1991, the CDR was given the power to establish and supervise real-estate companies such as Solidere. In June 1991 Hariri protégé Fadl Shalaq was appointed to head the CDR. Shalaq had previously been an employee at Hariri's engineering company Oger, before being charged with overseeing Oger's clean-up of Beirut in 1982 and setting up the Hariri Foundation student loan scheme in 1983. When Shalaq became telecommunications minister in 1995, he was succeeded as president of the CDR by Nabil al-Jisr, another former Oger employee.[37] Parliamentary supervision of the CDR's work was made more difficult because its budget remained outside the official government budget, which had to be submitted to parliament for approval.[38] The CDR was the agency in charge of the majority of government expenditure on reconstruction. It was also tasked with setting up the real-estate companies by which rent creation occurred in prime urban spaces such as Beirut's city centre.

Neoliberal urban megaprojects share certain governance features, as noted by Swyngedouw and his collaborators.[39] They override established urban governance structures—such as municipalities—citing the 'exceptionality' of their projects 'on the basis of different factors: scale, the emblematic character of the operation, timing pressures, the need for greater flexibility, efficiency criteria, and the like'.[40] Participation of 'stakeholders' is not formalised, but occurs through 'cooptation and invitation'; 'the projects are therefore closely associated with the interests of particular coalition sets (and their clients); they are usually self-referential, closed circles that consolidate their power while preventing access to others'. There is a strong reliance on experts 'at the expense of a diminishing role of the public in general and of traditional organised groups in particular, with a consequent loss of democratic accountability.'[41]

These elements are also found in the Solidere project, which was to overcome the 'exceptional' situation created by the civil war, described thus in a Solidere information brochure:

> Located at the historical and geographical core of the city, the vibrant financial, commercial and administrative hub of the country, the Beirut Central District came under fire from all sides throughout most of the 16 years of fighting. At the end of the war, that area of the city was afflicted with overwhelming destruction, total devastation of the infrastructure, the presence of squatters in several areas, and extreme fragmentation and entanglement of property rights involving owners, tenants and leaseholders. In addition, the Normandy garbage dump, formed in the course of the war in the absence of an alternative dumping site, posed health and environmental problems.[42]

According to Solidere, only a real-estate company with wide-ranging powers to appropriate, plan and market the space in the city centre could deal with this situation. The Solidere project was seen as a reproducible model for urban regeneration to be followed elsewhere, as this quote from Angus Gavin, the leader of the planning team responsible for the city centre master plan, shows:

> Solidere pioneers a growing trend toward less government involvement, more direct private investment and the incorporation of a broader community of 'stakeholders' in the urban regeneration process. ... This institutional framework takes forward to a new frontier the initiative of the private sector in large-scale urban renewal and reconstruction. It may offer the basis of a new model for application in other urban renewal projects elsewhere in the world. Many urban regeneration agencies are now seeking to reduce public sector funding and increase direct private sector involvement in such projects, while at the same time broadening the appeal to a wider range of both community and investment interests. The pioneering concept behind Solidere carries with it a great responsibility to the people of Beirut and a twofold discipline: the rigours of the market place and a commitment to a comprehensive Master Plan.[43]

Of course, this praise for the private sector glosses over the fact that the Lebanese state was heavily involved in the project, reducing the risks faced by Solidere. Gavin himself embodies the reproduction of neoliberal urbanism. Before joining Solidere he had been principal urban designer and development manager at the Docklands project in London, which has been cited as an inspiring urban model for Solidere.[44]

Law 117 also stipulated that no individual shareholder was allowed to own more than 10 per cent of all shares. In January 1994 Hariri subscribed to 7 per cent of total shares.[45] Another major investor was Nabil Bustani, representative of one of the pre-war bourgeois families. He took $50 million worth of shares.[46] The company was set up via a 'board of founders', which included a large number of representatives of Saudi business.[47] Solidere is headed by a board of directors, chaired by Nasir al-Shama', formerly head of operations and maintenance at Saudi Oger. The board of directors also included Bassil Yarid, who had been a legal adviser to Hariri and board member of Hariri's Banque Mediterranée since 1985. Board member Sami Nahas was a representative of the Maqasid association, which had been a major landowner in the city centre. Muhammad Ghaziri was the representative of the municipality and also a member of the Maqasid board. He had been an ally of Beirut Sunni za'im Sa'ib Salam, but moved closer to Hariri in the 1990s.[48] The other board members had various contracting interests, including the major Solidere investor Nabil Bustani. Solidere was thus very much in the hands of Hariri and a network of allies among Saudi businessmen, Lebanon's pre-war bourgeoisie, and former employees.[49]

Another important aspect for understanding how this control was established is to look at the gestation of Law 117 of 1991. Hariri had to win over parliament and the property owners of the area to gain approval for the law. He had the support of major figures such as leading Beirut politician Sa'ib Salam, who was flown in on Hariri's private jet, briefly abandoning his self-imposed exile in Switzerland, to attend the official ceremony initiating Beirut's reconstruction in 1994.[50] Another major constituency that Hariri had to win over were the awqaf (sing. waqf), endowments belonging to the different religious communities. Awqaf enjoy special legal status and face restrictions on selling land, although historically they have behaved pragmatically to get around restrictions on sale.[51] Hariri lobbied the awqaf and managed to gain their agreement to his plans.[52] Schmid reports that the Maqasid and the Christian awqaf were won over by granting them higher compensation than 'normal' property owners, but Solidere did not manage to convince the Sunni Muslim awqaf islamiyya.[53] The person who was lobbying both parliament and the awqaf was Bahij Tabbara, a legal adviser to Hariri.[54]

Traditionally, urban planning and regulation had been minimal in Lebanon, reflecting the country's laissez-faire economy.[55] Solidere represented the privatisation of planning, and led to the almost complete marginalisation of the municipality and the governorate (*muhafaza*) of Beirut. According to the original legislation of 1977, the CDR could override the local authorities. Solidere was charged with planning the city centre, with little input by the governor (*muhafiz*) or the president of the municipal council (*ra'is baladiyya*) of Beirut. Solidere was thus only accountable to the CDR, and both institutions were headed by Hariri protégés. In order to prevent any opposition from the *muhafaza* of Beirut, Prime Minister Hariri appointed a former Oger employee as *muhafiz* in November 1995.[56] Hariri thus ensured that there would be no significant opposition to Solidere from the city authorities. The neoliberal post-war state was thus more interventionist than its pre-war laissez-faire predecessor. While the former had supported capital through non-interference in the economy, the latter was actively supporting the 'private sector' through 'public–private partnership'.

The reconstruction of central Beirut was typical of neoliberal urban 'renewal': rents were created and privatised to benefit a small elite; much of the cost was borne by the state; and the 'exceptionality' of the project allowed this small elite to control the institutions in charge of the reconstruction process.[57] At the same time, the specific political conditions, such as the need to share rent with rival elites, shaped the institutional and economic outcome of the project. What was the role of Rafiq Hariri, the individual? The answer to this question tells us something about agency in the reproduction of neoliberal urban space. A closer look at Hariri's role confirms Larner's suggestion that individual biographies can help us trace the ways in which neoliberalism 'travels'.[58] Hariri presented himself as the individual who had had the 'vision' of rebuilding Beirut:

> I am the man behind the idea to rebuild central Beirut. In 1975 I was just a small poor guy, working in Saudi Arabia, so I did not really know how Beirut was then. We do not want to rebuild Beirut as it was. It lacked a lot of things in 1975. Communications, roads, electricity, and other things were not that good. Instead we want Beirut to be a city of the 21st century. We might see an agreement with Israel coming out of the negotiations [following the Madrid conference of 1991]. We should be prepared for it. But we cannot be prepared with the capital as it is now.[59]

Hariri claimed the 'vision' to prepare Beirut for the competitive marketplace, which the 'new Middle East' (minus the Arab–Israeli conflict) was going to be.[60]

The idea of reconstructing Beirut as a neoliberal city originated not from Rafiq Hariri alone but from the network of Lebanese and Saudi businessmen around him. Hariri had started planning the reconstruction of central Beirut in 1983 (see chapter 2). When the area reverted back into a conflict zone in February 1984, Oger withdrew its planners to Paris. At the head of this group stood the engineer Charbel Nahas, who had started working for Oger during the post-invasion clean-up of West Beirut in 1982. According to Nahas, a debate about the shape of reconstruction was already taking place in 1985 and 1986.[61] He and his team of planners based their proposal for reconstruction on the interaction of three actors: a collection of several real-estate funds charged with sorting out the complicated claims to property rights of existing owners and tenants; a public agency in charge of the overall management of the project; and developers who were going to invest in the area. Crucially, the programming of the plan was based on two principles: first, that the reconstructed city centre provides a space which would help unify a fragmented society; and secondly, that the reconstruction would be used to put in place necessary infrastructure, such as the core of a mass transit system, including metro stations.

The actual outcome was different: the sole real-estate company, Solidere, took charge of the reconstruction project, and the goal of profit maximisation created a segregated space rather than one that is integrated into and serves the wider urban fabric. According to Nahas, the impetus for focusing on profit came from within Hariri's network: a group of Saudi and Lebanese businessmen around Hariri regarded Nahas's proposal—focused as it was on public needs—as an obstacle to profit maximisation through high-end luxury real estate. Nahas's account of competing visions of the city illustrates the social background from which a neoliberal vision of Beirut emerged: the reconstruction of central Beirut was not primarily oriented on the needs of the city's inhabitants but those of a small elite of Gulf-based businessmen around Hariri. Urban space was to be commodified and marketed to international capital—especially Gulf capital. After Rafiq Hariri's death, Charbel Nahas would emerge as one of the most trenchant critics of his son Sa'd. According to one author, the format of Solidere was based on a model created in Saudi Arabia for the renovation and reconstruction of areas surrounding the holy sites in Mecca.[62] The example of the cities that had emerged in the oil-rich countries of the Gulf served as the benchmark for Beirut's reconstruction.[63]

Former militia leaders were forcing Hariri to share the rent from reconstruction. The strongest example of this was the more than $200 million in compensation paid to displaced persons living in the area, variously estimated to be 18,000 or 21,000.[64] Since most displaced people in central Beirut were Shia families originally from southern Lebanon, Amal and Hizballah acted as representatives of their interests.[65] Amal leader and parliamentary speaker Nabih Birri thus strengthened his position as someone who could channel benefits to his supporters. In 1995 Birri also managed to get his brother Yassir appointed to the board of the CDR. This is likely to have played a role in the contract to build the coastal road from Beirut to the south in 1996, which was criticised by MPs for being overvalued and given without competitive bidding. The companies to benefit were Ittihad Contracting, Geneco and Qassiun. Randa Birri, wife of Nabih, owned a 20 per cent stake in the first, Rafiq Hariri's brother Shafiq owned the second.[66] The highway is thus an example of the way in which well-placed contractors benefited from contracts. Birri could extract a share of the reconstruction rent due to his ability to act as a 'spoiler' for reconstruction, using both his position within the troika and the popular support he could mobilise.

Solidere was not the only real-estate company that was founded. Other ones were Linord on the Metn coast north of Beirut and Elissar in southern Beirut. As discussed in chapter 2, all three projects had been started with Hariri's participation after the Israeli invasion in 1982 but had to be abandoned because Hariri's political ally at the time—President Amin Gemayel—was defeated by Syrian-allied militias. A fourth project, in Sidon, had already been started during the civil war but was only carried out thereafter.[67] Linord works along similar lines to Solidere to facilitate rent extraction for investors: the state recompensed the company for the cost of land reclamation by giving it property rights over reclaimed land; planning is in the hands of Linord and oriented on maximising profit, while the area is deliberately separated from the surrounding social and physical fabric in order to market its 'exclusivity'.[68] The idea behind Elissar, located along the littoral in southern Beirut, was the same as Solidere and Linord: to create rent in a prime location, this time by transferring land use from 'informal' and 'illegal' settlements to tourism, recreation and luxury residential developments. Yet Hariri's plans were held up by having to contend with Amal and Hizballah. As Mona Harb has shown, the two movements were not opposed to the project in principle, but sought to gain a share of the rent and, importantly, to direct benefits towards their predominantly Shia constituency in the area.[69]

Neoliberal urbanism in Lebanon went beyond large-scale projects, also benefiting smaller developers. High-end tower blocks were proliferating across Beirut in the 2000s. Marieke Krijnen and Mona Fawaz examine the urban governance of these projects.[70] The process of obtaining a permit for these buildings was highly informal. This was not due to a laissez-faire approach, but was the outcome of the Building Law of 2004, which had been written with input by developers themselves, and allowed for ad hoc decision-making for 'exceptional' projects. The committees deliberating on building permits were not governed by hard-and-fast rules but were given great leeway, which worked in favour of developers. Like Solidere, these projects could cite 'exceptional circumstances' to circumvent democratic checks and balances. Developers were benefiting from a permissive environment in which private interest and favours were prevalent, and where Dubai-style glitz was the overriding aspiration for urban planners. Najib Hourani looks at the property regime adopted in the post-war reconstruction. This framework, supported by the World Bank and IMF, conformed to neoliberal tenets and resulted in property speculation and the restoration of class power based on finance and real estate.[71] This facilitated 'reconstruction' not only by Solidere but also in areas controlled by Hariri's rivals. Hourani gives the example of the shopping areas of Verdun, financed by the Shia diaspora and facilitated by Nabih Birri. Marieke Krijnen and Christiaan De Beukelaer meanwhile show that the mechanisms of gentrification in Beirut are similar to those seen elsewhere, but also display distinct characteristics, such as the important role of the diaspora.[72] Looking at the other end of the social spectrum, Mona Fawaz notes that neoliberal urbanism has curtailed the 'right to the city' of informal urban dwellers.[73] Neoliberal urbanism in Lebanon was not confined to Solidere and not all of it was directed by the Hariri network. However, the upmarket tower blocks which were proliferating across Beirut were mini-Solideres which were similarly enabled by a neoliberal state. Solidere thus had been an inspiration for wider trends of gentrification and curtailing the right to the city.

Rent-creation mechanism II: the currency anchor

The second main tenet of Hariri's economic policy was to anchor the Lebanese currency to the US dollar. This was done by providing attractive interest rates on government debt, bought up mainly by Lebanese commercial banks, who were in turn drawing in Lebanese pound-denominated deposits. The managed appreciation and subsequent pegging of the Lebanese currency was to ensure the currency a stability that had eluded Lebanon since the mid-1980s and to foster investor confidence. The anchor was supposed to be a pillar of economic stability, but the fixed exchange rate also led to severe macro-economic imbalances. One effect was the stabilisation of the currency, another was the explosion of government debt, a third was a slowdown of economic growth through 'crowding out' of credit to the private sector by government borrowing, and the fourth was the revival of Lebanon's banking sector. The anchor followed a neoliberal logic: currency stability was to bolster investor confidence in Lebanon's economy, making it more competitive. Pegging a currency to the US dollar has become a common policy response to the extreme volatility induced by financial globalisation.[74] The policy is also very dangerous, as the rigidities of currency pegs could induce the very financial crises they were supposed to prevent. This is exactly what happened in Lebanon.

The currency anchor was a rent-creation mechanism. It led to a transfer of wealth from the state—and thus ultimately the Lebanese taxpayer—to banks and depositors. Since bank ownership and deposits were extremely concentrated, wealth was subsequently also concentrated. This was a major break with pre-war laissez-faire capitalism. Post-war neoliberalism did not simply turn back the clock to the pre-war period; it transformed the economy. The central bank and finance ministry managed the currency much more actively than they had done previously. The state thus ensured new forms of accumulation in ways it had not in the pre-war period. This once again shows that the interventionism of the neoliberal state is different and potentially more intense than that of the liberal state. Public debt had been virtually unknown in pre-war Lebanon. The *zu'ama* who acted as representatives of Lebanon's commercial–financial bourgeoisie kept the state provision of public services minimal. During the civil war, militias seized the ports and their customs points, the main source of government revenue. The state continued paying salaries to its employees, and thus started slipping into debt. Yet, when Hariri came into office, public debt was under control. The government had regained some ability to collect customs and taxes, and a currency crisis in 1992 had induced runaway inflation, thus slashing the value of Lebanese-pound-denominated debt. Under the Hariri government debt skyrocketed from 50.7 per cent of GDP in 1993 to 109.1 per cent in 1998, the year that Hariri stepped down as prime minister.[75] This level of public debt would have been unthinkable in the pre-war merchant republic. The government financed its debt by selling Lebanese-pound-denominated treasury bills, which were primarily bought up by domestic commercial banks. Only from 1999 onwards—after Hariri had left office—did the government make a sustained effort to finance the debt by issuing foreign-currency bonds termed Eurobonds. Between December 1993 and December 1998 banks held between two-thirds and three-quarters of all Lebanese-pound-denominated debt at any one time.[76] The vast majority of these banks were Lebanese.

During the 1980s, and into 1993, Lebanese banks had often been reluctant to buy up treasury bills, and had to be coerced into doing so by requiring them to invest nearly 80 per cent of their pound deposits in government bonds, while interest rates were 'arbitrarily set' by the Ministry of Finance and the central bank.[77] Yet from May 1993 onwards the central bank turned to carrots rather than sticks to market government debt instruments. It started weekly auctions for treasury bills, apparently allowing the forces of the free market to determine interest rates. Yet two conditions had to be met to encourage banks to keep buying the bonds. The first was the convertibility of the Lebanese pound to the US dollar. The value of the Lebanese pound rose from LL2,420 to the US dollar in September 1992—just before Hariri became prime minister in October—to LL1,507 in December 1997, where it has remained fixed ever since.[78] This convertibility made investment in T-bills an attractive proposition, because the spread of treasury-bill interest rates over comparable foreign currency investments elsewhere made for enormous profits. The reference rate that is usually used is the London Interbank Offered Rate (LIBOR). In theory, the spread of treasury bills over LIBOR is supposed to reflect the currency risk: the risk that the Lebanese currency would be devalued, thus devaluing the treasury bills the investor holds. However, two studies published by the IMF suggest that the market by which interest rates on treasury bills were determined was anything but free. One study finds that the 'pass through' from international benchmark interest rates to rates on Lebanese government bonds is lower than expected, considering that Lebanon puts no restrictions on capital exchange. The author explains this with reference to 'a home bias effect resulting from a dedicated Lebanese investor base'.[79] The second study finds that interest rates on government bonds reflect macro-economic fundamentals but not to the degree that one would expect. The authors therefore speculate that 'socio-political conditions' play a role in determining Lebanese interest rates.[80] Since the play of the free market does not seem to have determined the value of interest rates, it is worth having a closer look at the 'socio-political conditions' and 'home bias' that influenced Lebanese bond markets.

The central bank maintained high interest rates on treasury bills to keep them attractive for investors.[81] Before 1993 interest rates would shoot up when investors were speculating against the currency, but would then come down again when the Lebanese pound stabilised. From February 1993, however, interest rates remained high, both when the pound was under pressure and when it was not. When the pressure on the pound was particularly high, interest rates could shoot up to dizzying heights. Central bank intervention in foreign-exchange markets also propped up the pound. Appreciating the value of the currency through high interest rates carried considerable cost for the Lebanese treasury, which overpaid on debt servicing. Gaspard calculates that between 1993 and 2002 the weighted annual yield on Lebanese-pound-denominated treasury bills averaged 18 per cent but estimates that 9 per cent would have been a more realistic rate, enabling savings of $8.5 billion.[82] He adds excess interest payments of $1 billion and a 'corruption' rate, estimating that the Lebanese government overpaid a total of $16 billion on its debt between 1993 and 2002.[83] This overpayment was the primary cause of the explosion in Lebanese government debt. Gaspard further calculates that 38 per cent of cumulative government expenditure totalling $56 billion between 1993 and 2002 went to interest on public debt.[84] This is the biggest chunk, dwarfing expenditure on investment at a mere 16 per cent. Debt dynamics derived from currency stabilisation rather than from the costs of reconstruction. Hariri defended the policy, arguing that criticism was 'based on a hypothetical calculation of the financial cost of such a fixed exchange rate policy on the Lebanese Treasury' which were 'purely theoretical'. He argued that 'the stability of the Lebanese Lira represents a critical component of the confidence in the Lebanese economy both domestically and internationally' and had led to capital inflows and low inflation. Incongruously, Hariri also claimed that the policy kept interest rates low. 'Consequently, and irrespective of the theoretical cost that some may wish to attach to this policy, it remains a crucial factor in the successes achieved since the end of 1992.'[85]

Government debt management allowed the central bank to appreciate and then effectively peg the currency to the US dollar: it created artificial demand for Lebanese pounds, thus drawing in Lebanese pound deposits. This led to a reduction in the 'dollarisation' of the Lebanese economy: foreign-currency deposits' share of total deposits fell from 86.8 per cent in September 1992 to 54.7 per cent in March 1997, before rising again to 63.7 per cent in November 1998.[86] Of course, this 'de-dollarisation' was somewhat artificial because it depended not so much on the economic success of the country as on the continued ability of the central bank to maintain high interest rates and roll over government debt. Yet notice the circularity—and fragility—of this confidence game: the convertibility of Lebanese pounds to US dollars depended on the government's ability to roll over debt. But the willingness to roll over debt depended on convertibility because, as Charbel Nahas put it, 'the Lebanese pound is another dollar that is better remunerated'.[87] The way in which confidence was maintained is the central puzzle of Lebanon's post-war political economy, and it requires not just an economic explanation but a sociological and political one.

Anchoring an exchange rate to the US dollar is a common response by developing countries to the neoliberal globalisation of finance that has occurred since the early 1970s. Financial globalisation resulted in an enormous increase in global capital flows and greater financial volatility as 'hot money' started circulating the globe and could be withdrawn at short notice. 'Good policies' such as macro-economic balances or accumulating foreign-exchange reserves could help prevent these crises, but even developmental 'star pupils' such as South Korea and Malaysia were hit by financial crisis in 1998, demonstrating the limits of domestic policy in insulating countries from the volatility induced by financial globalisation.[88] Lebanon was no star pupil. The militia economy of the 1980s had seen currency collapses brought on by coordinated rounds of speculation. The currency anchor was therefore important for the Hariri government to signal stability to foreign investors. Fixing the exchange rate to the US dollar is dangerous because the anchor can itself exacerbate macro-economic imbalances. The economists Nouriel Roubini and Brad Setser summarise the dangerous effects of fixed or semi-fixed exchange-rate regimes in general:

> Governments often believe that their exchange rate peg is the pillar of their macroeconomic policy framework, the anchor of financial stability, and the source of their economic success. Consequently, they defend a peg that comes under pressure. ... While higher interest rates increase the return on some local financial assets, their negative impact on the government's budget and on the health of the financial system as well as the risk that higher rates will lead to a politically unacceptable slowdown in economic activity all can undermine the credibility of an interest rate defence. Governments often respond to pressure on the exchange rate in two additional ways: They sell their reserves to defend the exchange rate and increase their issuance of debt denominated in a foreign currency, often the dollar. Such debt is a form of indirect foreign-exchange intervention: By increasing the supply of local dollar-linked or dollar indexed debt, the government hopes to persuade its own citizens to opt for local dollar-linked assets rather than move their funds abroad.[89]

This is precisely what happened in Lebanon. The anchor was an article of faith for Hariri and his technocrats, which they presented as the foundation of Lebanon's post-war 'success'. However, it resulted in high interest rates, which crowded out private-sector investment, and skyrocketing government debt. As will be discussed in chapter 5, the government then switched to selling US-dollar-denominated Eurobonds, the very mechanism that Setser and Roubini had identified as a typical method for keeping the exchange rate anchor going in the face of macroeconomic imbalances. Roubini and Setser were writing on financial crises in general, but regarding Lebanon they noted that 'Lebanon remains a crisis waiting to happen' due to 'its extraordinary debt burden, fixed exchange rate, and dependence on domestic banks to finance the government' as well as the government's inability to reduce the budget deficit—the latter being Hariri's main concern after 2000.[90]

The effect of overborrowing has been a transfer of wealth from taxpayers to banks and depositors. This has already partly taken place in the form of interest payments, and partly it has been deferred to the future repayment of the debt, or an economic crisis following default. Only then will the full cost of the debt have been realised at the expense of Lebanese citizens. Lebanese commercial banks benefited from government overborrowing. Banks were able to build up their assets by lending to the government: about a third of the spectacular growth in bank assets of 387 per cent between 1992 and 1998 was due to T-bills.[91] The total interest that banks earned from T-bills amounted to $6.3 billion between 1994 and 1998. Profitability was restored. Banks' net profits amounted to 2.2 per cent of GDP between 1992 and 1998.

The banks were not the only beneficiaries of rent created by the currency anchor. They financed lending to the government by drawing in Lebanese-pound-denominated deposits. Their profits therefore derived from the interest-rate differential between T-bills and these deposits. Depositors earned handsomely from high interest rates: during Hariri's tenure as prime minister from October 1992 to December 1998, the average rate on Lebanese-pound-denominated deposits fluctuated between a low of 11.1 per cent and a high of 19.1 per cent.[92] In order to understand the distributive effects of the rents flowing to depositors, we need to have a closer look at the structure of deposits, which are extremely concentrated. According to a report from 2002, 0.6 per cent of the number of accounts were holding more than 40 per cent of total deposits.[93] The effect was that the enormous rents derived from government borrowing benefited a small group of investors. This depositor structure is key to understanding how confidence was maintained. The constant inflow of Lebanese-pound-denominated deposits created the capital account surplus required to maintain the value of the Lebanese pound.

Rafiq Hariri's network was firmly in charge of the institutions that were managing government debt. In March 1993 the CDR presented the Horizon 2000 plan to the public. It included projections on the macro-economic framework, which was to govern reconstruction over the next ten years. Hariri had provided $5 million to finance the $6.9 million contract to the American Bechtel corporation, which put the plan together on behalf of the CDR.[94] This was even before Hariri was prime minister and shortly before his protégé Fadl Shalaq became head of the CDR. The Horizon 2000 plan was based on the assumption that reconstruction would 'kick-start' the economy and lead to rapid growth. According to Horizon 2000, real GDP growth was to reach 9.0 per cent annually from 1995 to 1998; government debt was to peak at 90.9 per cent in 1999 and then decline rapidly.[95] In reality, government debt reached 131 per cent of GDP in 1999 and continued growing. The plan also contained overly optimistic projections for government budget deficits, the level of interest rates, and subsequent interest payments by the government. Hariri and his technocrats seemed to believe that physical reconstruction of infrastructure would suffice to 'kick-start' the economy and outgrow debt. Hariri stood to gain financially in either case: in the case of growth he would have had ample investment opportunities, but in its absence he could fall back on rents derived from high interest rates on government debt.

In 1999 Hariri published a defence of government borrowing. He argued that he had been faced with three options in 1992: waiting for foreign aid; not incurring a deficit and following a prudent fiscal policy but forgoing reconstruction; or investing heavily in reconstruction and thus kick-starting the economy—but incurring debt, which would be made up by strong economic growth later.[96] However, he conveniently glossed over the fact that he and his technocrats did *not* expect massive debt: Horizon 2000 underestimated the rise in debt. Interest payments on government debt between 1995 and 2004 ended up being 1.9 times higher than the Horizon 2000 projections had suggested.[97]

Hariri's 'vision' of the financial sector also did not come true. In his scheme, the financial sector was to channel foreign investment to Lebanon. Angus Gavin, one of the chief planners of the Solidere project, put it thus:

As a re-emerging business centre, Beirut will find its new opportunities somewhat different from those that stimulated the growth of other centres in the region during the Lebanese war. In the past, growth depended on the recycling of oil revenues from the Arab world for investment in the West. New opportunities will no longer depend on the historic outflow of petro-dollars, but for managing the growing inflow of capital that needs to be directed toward investment sectors and identified projects—initially within Lebanon and later, in a new order of security and cooperation, throughout the region. Compared with other competing centres, Beirut is well placed to benefit from such emerging opportunities.[98]

Lebanese banks did not become an intermediary for foreign-investment inflows to the Middle East. Instead, they became an intermediary between depositors and the Lebanese government, which was offering high interest rates to bolster the currency.

The central bank is crucial to understanding government debt management. It was powerless to prevent coordinated rounds of currency speculation by Lebanon's banks in the 1980s. This predatory speculation was unsustainable. In the post-war era a new system of accumulation was required, within which the appropriation of surplus would be stabilised and put on a more sustainable footing. Government overborrowing was such a mechanism. But before it could be put into place, the central bank had to emancipate itself from both speculating banks and the militias. The tension between the central bank and militias came out in March 1990, when Walid Junblat backed interior minister Elias al-Khazin in a dispute with central bank governor Edmond Na'im. Al-Khazin was said to have used central bank funds to overpay on the printing of new passports.[99] A compromise was struck, but the episode illustrated the greater ability of the central bank to stand up to the militias than had been the case during the 1980s.

Michel al-Khuri, whose time as central bank governor (1977–84) had been marred by militia pressure on his institution, returned to the post from 1991 to 1993. According to 'Abdallah Bu Habib, Khuri had been Hariri's candidate to succeed Gemayel for the presidency in 1988, and thus was a Hariri ally.[100] It was under Khuri that Lebanon was put on the path of debt: from May 1993 the central bank started auctioning treasury bills rather than fixing the price. It was from this moment onwards that government borrowing was put into place. This was central to the new system of accumulation. The benefit was that

banks and depositors would share in the rents created by overborrowing and would have no incentive to speculate against the Lebanese
pound, as had happened during the civil war. The previous bout of
speculation occurred in 1992, and had played a role in bringing Hariri
to power. Prime Minister 'Umar Karami stepped down in May after the
collapse of the value in the Lebanese pound had led to trade union
protests. The crisis was caused both by an inflationary rise in public-
sector wages and speculation against the pound, which has been interpreted by some as a politically motivated attempt to destabilise the
currency and thus disrupt the upcoming parliamentary elections.[101]
When Hariri became prime minister in October, the currency immediately recovered.

In an earlier part of this chapter two studies published by the IMF
were cited, which could not explain the movement of Lebanese interest rates with reference to the indicators that investors usually respond
to in a free market. Instead, they pointed to 'a home bias effect' and
'socio-political conditions'.[102] In order to understand how this came
about, how it was sustained and who benefited from it, it is necessary
to examine the institutional mechanisms that governed the treasury-
bills market. In August 1993 Riyadh Salameh became governor of the
central bank. When his appointment was announced in May 1993,
Beirut papers reported that Salameh had previously managed Hariri's
personal finance portfolio at Merrill Lynch in Paris.[103] Hariri thus not
only placed former employees at the head of the institutions in charge
of reconstruction but also his personal banker at the head of the central
bank. Another central institution for controlling the mechanism of
government borrowing and overborrowing was the finance ministry.
Formally, Hariri assumed the post himself, but he installed Fu'ad
Siniura as the man in charge at the rank of minister of state. Siniura had
of course been Hariri's classmate in Sidon, a fellow activist in the
Nasserite ANM, and had played a central role in running Hariri's banking concerns.[104] Siniura had enjoyed a close working relationship with
Michel al-Khuri between 1977 and 1982 when he was head of the
Banking Control Commission (BCC) while Khuri held the governor-
ship of the central bank for the first time.[105] Siniura had assumed the
post after Salim al-Huss—who had been Siniura's professor at AUB—
had stepped down as head of the BCC to become prime minister and

had recommended his former student for the position of BCC president.[106] In 1982 Khuri had to bend to political pressure from prime minister Shafiq Wazzan, who demanded that Siniura's contract not be renewed.[107] Siniura and Khuri therefore had a history of fighting off political interference from *zu'ama* and militia leaders in central bank affairs. It is easy to see how the experience of helplessly watching the speculation against the Lebanese pound shaped the desire by Khuri and Siniura to seize the levers of monetary and fiscal policy.[108]

Monetary and fiscal policy were coordinated in regular meetings between Hariri as prime minister, Siniura as acting finance minister and Riyadh Salameh as central bank governor.[109] According to Siniura, the decision to stabilise the exchange rate and to prevent political shocks from disrupting it was based on a consensus between Hariri, Siniura and Salameh:

> At that time it was a decision that was taken collectively by the three of us so that we can guarantee, first of all, long-term sustainability of such a movement, that we have stability in the foreign exchange market, and at the same time to account for the situation within Lebanon … because of other shocks that may take place.[110]

Hariri and his allies had obtained control of monetary and fiscal policy which had eluded the central bank during the civil war. Michel al-Khuri was a Shihabist technocrat who allied himself with Hariri. Fu'ad Siniura had worked with al-Khuri at the central bank from 1977 to 1982, and was a Hariri employee and acting finance minister. Finally, Riyadh Salameh had been involved in managing Hariri's wealth. In short, allies and employees of Hariri managed Lebanon's monetary and fiscal policy. They put the rent-creation mechanism of government overborrowing into place. Hariri did not himself develop the policy, but the Hariri technocrats Siniura, Khuri and Salameh did.

While the central bank and the government were the sellers of treasury bills in the market, they were faced with the banks as buyers. In the 1980s the relationship between the two parties had been acrimonious with regard to treasury bills (the banks did not want to buy them), speculation against the Lebanese pound (the central bank could not protect the currency against bank speculation) and banking failures (with banks taking excessive risks). The monetary and fiscal regime under Hariri reconciled the commercial banks with the central bank. High interest rates opened up the prospect of high returns without having to speculate against the Lebanese currency. On the contrary, the rent flow to the banks through high interest rates on government borrowing even managed to stabilise the currency. This way, Hariri would not have to face the political cost of speculation against the pound, which had brought down the government of 'Umar Karami in 1992.

The central bank was dealing with only a few key players in an increasingly concentrated banking sector.[111] In January 1993 parliament passed a law that encouraged the concentration of banking, providing tax breaks and concessional loans for mergers or acquisitions.[112] A flurry of mergers and acquisitions followed. Another factor in the concentration of banks was that the biggest players took a larger share of the market. The share of total assets in the banking sector held by the top five banks rose from 36.1 per cent in 1992 to 44.4 per cent in 1998.[113] The rate of growth was largely determined by how ready banks were to buy up treasury bills. The six largest holders of treasury bills in 1998 accounted for 55.1 per cent of all treasury bills held by Lebanese banks and received 53.5 per cent of the interest between 1994 and 1998.[114] Conspicuous among them were Hariri's Banque Mediterranée, Bank Audi and Banque Libano-Française. Banks that did not join the treasury-bill rally lost their leading positions in Lebanese banking.[115]

The banks had to finance the purchase of treasury bills by drawing in deposits. The deposit structure is highly concentrated, with 0.6 per cent of the accounts holding more than 40 per cent of total deposits, according to a report published in 2002.[116] The depositors were not simply anonymous participants in a free market. First of all, economic elites had a far greater ability to benefit from government overborrowing than ordinary Lebanese citizens because they had the necessary savings to deposit in Lebanese banks. The collapse of the currency and hyperinflation from 1984 to 1987 had wiped out the savings that ordinary Lebanese had held in their bank accounts. Continued high unemployment and stagnating incomes meant that most Lebanese did not have the means to benefit from high-interest treasury bills.[117] Meanwhile, those Lebanese who had managed to preserve or build up their wealth during the civil-war period were looking for investment opportunities in the early 1990s. Former militia leaders had amassed great wealth during the civil war through control of trade within Lebanon as well as illicit dealings in drugs or weapons.

A 2008 report on Lebanese government debt published by the IMF suggests that the Lebanese diaspora were the biggest investors in deposits.[118] Wealthy members of the Lebanese diaspora include remnants of Lebanon's old bourgeoisie who were able to return their money to Lebanon. It also includes those involved in commerce in West Africa and the Gulf contractor bourgeoisie. The report also points to the reason why non-Lebanese foreign investors tend to shy away from investing in Lebanese treasury bills: high 'information cost' and the fact that the market in government bonds effectively 'freezes' in times of stress. Non-Lebanese did not understand how the market works and no one is willing to buy Lebanese government bonds when a crisis occurs.[119] Most non-Lebanese investors therefore tended to avoid Lebanese government bonds. Those foreign investors who did deposit funds in Lebanese banks or who bought up treasury bills directly either sought to diversify their portfolios—hence investing only small portions of their overall funds—or were able to 'manage' the political risk. Wealthy Syrians fall into this category, as do non-Lebanese banks acting on the instruction of Lebanese clients.[120] In summary, there was a class of very wealthy Lebanese—which included Hariri—who owned banks or were large depositors and who effectively mediated between global financial markets and the market in Lebanese government debt. The central bank had to keep these investors happy.

Rent-creation mechanism III: service ministries, military and intelligence

Neoliberal capitalism did not reign supreme in Lebanon. Hariri came in as a political outsider, and had to contend with rival political factions with very different economic agendas. They included the remnants of the pre-war *zu'ama*, former militia leaders, Hizballah, and the military and intelligence establishment. While Hariri was the 'Saudi man' in Lebanon, these rival forces were to varying degrees all beholden to the Syrian regime. They followed a different economic logic to Hariri's brand of neoliberalism. That does not mean that they were fundamentally opposed to neoliberalism, but it meant Hariri had to cater for their self-enrichment and their need for patronage resources to feed clientelist networks. He had to share rents with them. As Elizabeth Picard has pointed out, the economic beneficiaries of the militia economy were more than happy to invest in Hariri's schemes, giving them a stake in their success.[121] Furthermore—and this is the topic of the following section—Hariri's rivals were using 'service ministries' such as Education, Health and the Ministry of the Displaced as patronage instruments. This ran counter to the neoliberal logic of welfare, which variously embraces 'trickle down' or safety nets for the most vulnerable, all the while employing market incentives in the management of poor populations. Hariri pandered to his rivals' economic needs, but they were neither able nor willing to push for a radical economic alternative to Hariri's neoliberalism.

Government spending on 'service ministries' rose under Hariri. The World Bank calculated that government expenditure on community and social services—which includes education, health, and social welfare—reached 7.8 per cent of GDP in 1997, while expenditure on military and security reached 6.5 per cent.[122] Expenditure on wages and salaries for the whole government reached 10.3 per cent of GDP in 1997. While these figures are high, they should be put in the context of spending on public debt transactions—the cost of rent-creation through government debt management—which reached 14.5 per cent of GDP in 1997. The provision of welfare is of course not a 'rent'; it is the waste and political use of social welfare as a patronage instrument that constitutes the rent element. There are indications of overstaffing by providing jobs to supporters and fraudulent practices to benefit private interests. These issues are widely discussed in Lebanon, and anecdotal evidence crops up in several reports. Pupil–teacher ratios in public schools stood at 8:1 compared to 17:1 in private schools in the 1990s.[123] Overstaffing is one reason for the discrepancy, with reports of teachers receiving salaries without actually working. In the health sector, private hospitals overcharged public social security funds while 'political pressure' prevented the Ministry of Health from investigating the abuses.[124] There is also evidence of ministers channelling social benefits to their constituencies rather than those who need them most. Nisreen Salti and Jad Chaaban compared data on the geographic distribution of government social expenditure with the distribution of Lebanon's poor.[125] They found that public investment expenditure on infrastructure projects related to social outcomes between 1995 and 2004 did not match the distribution of poverty: Beirut received 16 per cent of total public investment expenditure while being home to only 2 per cent of Lebanese living in poverty, while the Biqa' received only 6 per cent but was home to 13 per cent of the poor. Similarly, they compared the number of recipients of social assistance given out by the Ministry of Social Affairs (MOSA) to the number of poor people. They found that 10.5 per cent of Beirutis living in poverty were receiving benefit, compared to only 1.7 per cent of the poor in North Lebanon and Nabatiyya, and 2.8 per cent in the Biqa'. This suggests that political factors, rather than need, were the basis for allocating funds.

The most obvious case of the political use of service ministries were the Council of the South and the Ministry for the Displaced. The former was controlled by former militia leader Nabih Birri, the latter by former militia leader Walid Junblat. The level of expenditure by these bodies is hard to ascertain because they are excluded from the regular government budget—just as the CDR is.[126] Birri was heavily reliant on access to the state for patronage. As early as 1984 he used his first foray into cabinet office to control the newly created Ministry of State for the south and to gain influence on the CDR.[127] Picard argues that Birri used the Council of the South to channel benefits to his followers during the war.[128] After the civil war he became speaker of parliament, a position that had been beefed up at Ta'if. He retained control of the Council of the South, which conducted reconstruction projects among Birri's Shia constituency in South Lebanon. However, patronage appears to have been more important than efficiency, and the council's efforts at rehabilitating infrastructure in the South in response to the Israeli withdrawal in 2000 were slow.[129] Birri also had many civil servants among his supporters. He therefore resisted efforts to cut government staff or to reduce government salaries. Right from the moment that Hariri became prime minister, Birri sought to rein in the billionaire's ability to reshape the state, blocking his demand for exceptional powers.[130] Birri and Hariri also clashed on issues such as pay rises for the public sector.[131] In October 1993 an ally of Nabih Birri—Samir Azar—took over the presidency of the finance and budget committee, which has a say on where spending is allocated.[132] While Hariri controlled the finance ministry, Birri's influence in the finance committee enabled him to at least influence the government's budget and financial policies.

The Ministry of the Displaced was established in the early 1990s to support the estimated 500,000 people who were displaced during the civil war, with an estimated 75 per cent of them living in poverty.[133] Walid Junblat headed the ministry from October 1992 to December 1998, when Hariri was prime minister. The Fund for the Displaced—which controlled the purse strings for the ministry—was headed by former Oger employee Antoine Andraus. After Junblat lost his post in 1998 a report by his successor accused him of corruption and paying 'political money' to maintain support.[134] Other former militia leaders or powerful zu'ama who headed service ministries were Elie Hubaiqa at Electricity and Water (1993–8) and Social Affairs (1992–4) and Sulaiman Franjiyya, who held several posts, such as health minister (1996–8).

Finally, the military and intelligence establishment appropriated government funds. This group was firmly under Syrian control. Any loyalists of General Michel Aoun, who had conducted a brief and ill-fated 'war of liberation' against Syria in 1990, had been purged from the army. The new army commander, Émile Lahoud, was a reliable Syrian ally who used the trust placed in him by Damascus to reconstitute the army as one of the few unified national institutions in a society otherwise rife with sectarian factionalism. A certain percentage of militiamen were admitted into the army. The number of soldiers increased from 21,000 in 1990 to 45,000 in 1995, and 72,000 in 2002.[135] Government expenditure on military and security fluctuated somewhat but reached 6.5 per cent of GDP in 1997.[136] Hariri and the finance ministry complained about increasingly generous perquisites being provided to the top brass.[137] Lebanon had never been a militarised society compared to other Arab states. However, there was a frequently expressed longing, going back to President Shihab, a former general, for a strong army that would overcome society's internal weakness and disunity. Ever since Shihab's time army commanders have dreamed of repeating the trick of transitioning from military to political leadership. Michel Aoun had tried to become president but he failed, while Lahoud would be elected president in 1998. Michel al-Murr, defence minister and interior minister from 1994 to 2000, was another staunch ally of the Damascus regime.[138] He was a contractor, but had associated himself first with Gemayel and later with the Syrian regime. He was so well trusted by Damascus that the regime put him in charge of the most important ministries for disciplining the Lebanese population—and controlling the electoral process. Finally, Faris Buwayz, foreign minister from 1992 to 1998, was a close ally to his father-in-law Elias Hrawi, and as such considered reliable by Syria.[139]

Hariri's rivals could have vetoed his economic policies. Lebanese post-war neoliberalism therefore depended on the patterns of conflict and cooperation between them. Between 1990 and 2000 the relationship remained largely cooperative, not least because the two sides' foreign backers—Saudi Arabia and Syria—were in accord. However, even at this stage Hariri and his ministers were expressing increasing frustration about the side-payments they had to cede to Birri, Lahoud and others. Meanwhile, Lahoud's election with Syrian support signalled a tougher line towards Hariri's attempts at controlling the levers of the Lebanese economy.

The political sociology of neoliberal rent-creation

Rafiq Hariri and his technocrats were defending their policies with liberal rhetoric. Growth was to be private-sector driven; macroecononomic stability was to attract foreign investors; the state acted not as a producer or wealth redistributor but a facilitator in creating a friendly business environment—not least through providing world-class infrastructure. Yet Hariri's policies and the way they were realised through the takeover of key economic institutions by the Hariri network made Lebanon less liberal.[140] The establishment of Solidere rode roughshod over the rights of property owners. Lebanon had maintained a free-floating exchange rate even in the darkest days of currency collapse in the 1980s, but under Hariri's watch the exchange-rate regime was altered into a highly managed—and highly costly—dollar peg. Both policies clearly benefited Hariri personally, via his share in Solidere and ownership of Banque Mediterranée. Viewed from this perspective, Hariri was no free marketer but instituted politicised oligopolies. This was no return to the pre-war laissez-faire state.

The contradictions between free-market rhetoric and a state that intervenes in the interest of monopolistic capitalists is not unique to

Lebanon but is at the heart of neoliberalism. David Harvey defined neoliberalism as both a type of free-market economic orthodoxy and a reassertion of class power by capital.[141] Capital asserts itself by assaulting the economic and political rights of labour, and by creating new modes of accumulation, for instance financialisation, privatisation or debt. The neoliberal 'roll-back' of the state requires a strong state which directs the restructuring process and defeats any societal opposition. Marxist political sociology recognises that markets are never 'free' but always express social relations and are therefore deeply political. We must therefore not study idealised visions of market freedom, but the politics of how markets are constructed. This is even more important because neoliberal theorists themselves stress the importance of capturing the state in order to construct markets.[142] Viewed from this perspective, Hariri's takeover of the economic agencies of the state also conformed to neoliberal theory and practice. This was, in turn, distinct from pre-war liberalism.

International financial institutions such as IMF and the World Bank are commonly identified as driving forces behind neoliberal reforms in Arab countries that switch from statist development to neoliberalism, for instance Egypt and Jordan in the 1980s and 1990s. Financial crises and the conditionality of structural adjustment pushed regimes dominated by small and unaccountable elites around a ruler into neoliberal restructuring. State elites remain in charge of the process, balancing the need for economic restructuring with the requirement for regime maintenance. For instance, regime cliques make sure that the domestic bourgeoisie remains dependent on state largesse or they privatise to trusted 'cronies'. In so far as this process actually strengthens authoritarian rulers, it can be referred to as 'authoritarian upgrading'.[143]

In Lebanon the IMF and World Bank did not play a dominant role, and there was no strong presidential clique directing neoliberal restructuring. Instead, Gulf capital, personified by Rafiq Hariri, was the driving force of neoliberalism, the rents of which he had to share with rival elites. Adam Hanieh was the first researcher to point to the phenomenon of Gulf capital.[144] The oil boom in the 1970s had spurred the accumulation of capital in the Gulf Cooperation Council (GCC) states, diversifying from contracting into finance, retail and some industrial production. Hanieh further saw that Gulf capital was 'internationalising'. Profitable investment opportunities within individual GCC countries were insufficient to absorb the capital that had been accumulated, so Gulf capital was expanding its horizon, investing across the GCC and the wider Arab world. The return of Lebanese-born Gulf contractors to their native country from the 1980s onwards was part of this process of internationalisation. Their passports may have been Lebanese—although Hariri also holds Saudi citizenship—but the capital they were importing to Lebanon was from the Gulf. This new Gulf-based contractor bourgeoisie replaced the pre-war commercial–financial bourgeoisie as the dominant capitalist class in Lebanon. This was due to a shift in Lebanon's role in the capitalist world economy and the loss of its function as financial intermediary between Arab East and Western financial markets. The families who had controlled finance and commerce during the pre-war era had lost influence relative to the newcomers who derived their wealth from contracting in the Gulf. Rafiq Hariri was not the only exponent of this class, which also included Najib Miqati, 'Issam Faris and Muhammad Safadi. The appearance of new capitalist factions is not a phenomenon unique to Lebanon. Lebanon's new contractor bourgeoisie arose from the oil boom in the 1970s, but elsewhere it was neoliberal market reforms that created new capitalists in liberalised sectors such as telecommunications, construction and the media. Well-known examples elsewhere include Carlos Slim in Mexico, Thaksin Shinawatra in Thailand and Silvio Berlusconi in Italy. Some of these businessmen famously entered politics, just as Hariri did.

Neoliberal policies did not spring solely from Hariri's personal vision, but were developed by a network of technocrats drawn from among employees of his banks and his engineering firm, Oger. Hariri had to deal with former militia leaders, a newly empowered military and security establishment, remnants of the pre-war bourgeois families and *zu'ama*, and remnants of Shihabist bureaucrats, which forced him to negotiate and compromise his neoliberalism. Most of all, he was faced with a Syrian regime which had emerged as the clear winner of the Lebanese civil war and which had sidelined all opposition to its dominance. The ruling clique in Damascus divided the Lebanese factions in order to rule over them, never averse to themselves personally profiting from reconstruction.

The shape of neoliberalism—how rent is created, appropriated and shared—depends on the relative power of classes and elites who pursue competing economic interests, and the institutional framework within which this competition takes place. Classes, elites and institutions possess specific histories in different countries. They create what Zubaida has referred to as a specific 'political field' within different 'nation' states.[145] This field also includes particular national discourses and 'political cultures', such as Lebanon's sectarianism. These institutional pathways have no unchanging essence, but they are 'sticky', reproduced over long periods of time. To understand the politics of Lebanese neoliberalism we must combine an analysis of both the modes of accumulation and governance of neoliberalism, which are being constantly reproduced across the globe, and the locally specific political field with its history. Analysts who focus on the worldwide reproduction of neoliberal forms miss the variation of these forms within a specific polity. Those who argue that Lebanon's politics is *sui generis* and unchanging, determined by sectarianism and the laissez-faire merchant ethos inspired by the Phoenicians, miss the profound economic and political changes that neoliberalism has brought about: the emergence of Gulf capital with new political and economic players, and the centrality of the state in fixing the exchange rate and enabling Solidere. None of these profound changes can be explained with reference to timeless sectarianism or the country's merchant ethos.

Solidere followed the neoliberal template, but was also embedded in local and regional politics. The reconstruction of central Beirut has a specific history, linked both to Hariri's personal experience and his embeddedness in the networks of Gulf capital. Hariri was a contractor himself, so the idea of basing economic reconstruction in post-war Lebanon on the reconstruction of physical infrastructure came naturally. His vision was based on the fallacy that physical buildings would create a sufficient basis for a new system of accumulation. Instead, the Lebanese economy was integrated into the rentier system of the Saudi oil monarchy, and Lebanon became an outlet for Gulf capital. While Hariri's personal vision for reconstructing Beirut was important, the network of Saudi and Lebanese businessmen around him was crucial in shaping the reconstruction project. It was their desire to maximise profits by realising the maximum land rent from the reconstructed city centre that determined the contours of the Solidere project: the transfer of property rights to a private developer and marketing the city centre to international (especially Gulf) investors. Rafiq Hariri put technocrats who were former employees of his construction companies at the head of the institutions in charge of reconstruction. In order to realise the project he had to provide side-payments to established political elites who could have exerted a veto over the project, and Hariri had to bring them on board.

The Hariri technocrats were developing and implementing neoliberal economic policies. They had the legal knowledge to develop the framework for Solidere, the engineering expertise, managerial capacity and urban planning expertise to run the CDR and Solidere, and the financial expertise to run the finance ministry and central bank. Since the state is central in neoliberal restructuring, globalising bureaucrats are crucial for the process.[146] Hariri brought globalisers to the state apparatus from within his own companies. The Hariri network mobilised different forms of capital.[147] Hariri brought the financial capital into the mix, while the technocrats possessed the cultural capital to speak with confidence and competence about the economy. They flaunted their degrees from prestigious American and European universities, as well as employment with Hariri's firms, with the IMF or American and European banks. They were expressing Hariri's policies in terms of neoliberal buzzwords of private-sector-oriented growth, public–private partnership, friendly investment climate, achieving macro-economic stability, and the trickling down of wealth. They spoke the language of neoliberalism as an economic orthodoxy. They had allied themselves with the Gulf capitalist Rafiq Hariri, who was using neoliberalism to assert the power of this faction of capital in the Lebanese economy. Together, they colonised Shihabist state institutions and repurposed them to serve their goals.

The Hariri protégés came from a variety of confessional backgrounds, not only from his own Sunni community. This accords with Wallerstein's observation that the 'cadres' of economic management are recruited according to 'universal criteria'.[148] This trend becomes even more obvious when we look at the 'second generation' of Hariri protégés who came to the fore after 2000 and are discussed in chapter 5. The most senior first-generation technocrats did share Hariri's background as Sunni Muslims from outside Beirut: Fu'ad Siniura, Fadl Shalaq, Nabil al-Jisr and Farid Makari. In some cases the connection stems from a strong alliance built over many years, such as Fu'ad Siniura from Sidon. More importantly, however, this was a group of people who were more open to attach themselves to someone like Hariri—a Sunni from Lebanon's periphery. Christians and Sunnis from Beirut were more likely to ally with local political leaders from their own community, which represented the centre of power in Lebanon at the time. Beirut Sunnis would rather attach themselves to one of the powerful political families of the capital than a newcomer from Sidon. Similarly, during the sectarian civil war Christians would have been wary of throwing in their lot with a Sunni Muslim businessman. When Hariri then became prime minister and was looking for loyal personnel to promote to government positions, he drew from the repository of trusted experts he had built up since the late 1970s. In short, these dynamics are not necessarily evidence of Hariri's sectarian mindset, but show how structural factors shaped these choices.

My argument brings the political economy back into the analysis of Lebanese politics. The civil war was not only fought about the relative power of sects or foreign powers but was also over Lebanon's economic future. Elite conflict was therefore not solely conditioned by confessional identity or foreign alliances, but also competing economic agendas. The most important new set of actors were Gulf capitalists. Rafiq Hariri was pushing for their interest in new investment opportunities. His main allies in this effort were technocrats who had worked in his construction and banking concerns. Former militia leaders, the military and security establishment, and remnants of Shihabist technocrats and *zu'ama* had different economic agendas, as did the Syrian regime. Gulf capital had not been a combatant in the civil war, but it readied itself during the war to benefit from post-war reconstruction. Hariri never maintained his own militia, and the resumption of hostilities after the failure of the May 17 Agreement in 1984 was a setback for the Saudi contractor's plans to rebuild central Beirut. He therefore engaged in diplomacy to end the civil war and positioned himself to play a central economic and political role in the post-war era. Yet he still had to deal with the actors who had fought and had eventually made peace: former militia leaders and the Syrian regime.

My approach of looking at the post-war economy through the lens of businessman–politician Rafiq Hariri also gives new relevance to the study of the Lebanese state, which is usually ignored in analyses of Lebanon's political economy.[149] Yet it is not just weak, absent and irrelevant; it was central to the neoliberal restructuring of post-war Lebanon. The property transfer that enabled Solidere required a legal basis from parliament and a strong CDR. The currency anchor required a strong central bank insulated from predatory encroachment by militia leaders. The Lebanese state did not completely 'break down' in 1975 only to be resurrected in 1990. Presidents were still elected, salaries were paid, and the central bank remained intact, although the state could no longer fulfil other key functions. The key institutions restructuring the economy of post-war Lebanon had pedigrees going back to the civil war or pre-war era. The CDR as the main vehicle of 'public–private partnership' with Solidere had been founded by Shihabist technocrats in 1977. They had given the institution extraordinary powers in order to insulate it from militias and *zu'ama*. Gulf capitalist Rafiq Hariri took it over in the post-war era and strengthened its prerogatives. He used the CDR to facilitate the reconstruction of central Beirut, a project conceived during a lull in the civil war in 1983. Similarly, militia leader Nabih Birri first joined the government during the 1984 'national unity cabinet'. The Council of the South was created and became a patronage vehicle for Birri. He relies on access to state funds to finance much of his clientelism, in contrast with Hariri, who used personal wealth, and Hizballah, which uses funds from Iran, donations and various overseas activities in Africa and Latin America. Both the CDR and the Council of the South were set up in the midst of civil war. An explanation of the restructuring of state and economy after 1990 thus requires an account of state institutions in a period when the state had supposedly 'broken down'.

4

SOCIAL CRISIS AND HARIRI'S SECTARIAN TURN

1998–2000[1]

In 1993 Rafiq Hariri faced an angry crowd outside his villa. The Popular Congress of Islamic and National Forces was protesting at the closure of one of its dispensaries. The protestors shouted that Hariri should have done more to prevent it. The Congress was an umbrella organisation of Sunni groups which had come together in 1984, when the Shia Amal movement and the Druze PSP had defeated Beirut's Sunni militias. Days later, several Congress officials were arrested by plain-clothes police. Contemporary commentators had the following to say about the occasion:

> On the one hand, it seems to confirm the impression that Mr Hariri has yet to impose his leadership on the Lebanese Sunni community, in particular the Sunni 'street'. The demonstration in front of Mr Hariri's house, the criticism of the prime minister, and the detention of Congress officials, all point to a pattern of relations marked by tension and a struggle for influence rather than by the traditional pattern of interaction between patrons and clients in Beirut politics. Secondly, on a wider level, it points to a vacuum in the upper echelons of the Sunni leadership. The fact that Mr Hariri was so openly challenged indicates the precariousness of his position as a communal leader.[2]

By 1999 this picture was reversed. In that year Hariri opened no less than six health centres in predominantly Sunni neighbourhoods of

Beirut. He was putting his commitment to the Sunni community into 'brick and mortar'.[3] This chapter explains Hariri's shift from reluctant communal leader to Sunni politician.

Sectarianism is not an unchanging given, but is constructed and reproduced. Furthermore, it is situational. Reference to sectarian identity is appropriate in some contexts but not others. In order to correctly explain Hariri's form of sectarianism, we need to characterise the exact way in which his leadership became more specifically Sunni. In what contexts did Hariri find it appropriate to use sectarian discourses and practices? When did he find it inappropriate? How did his sectarian leadership differ from that of other politicians, and how does this relate to his class interest as a Gulf contractor? Once we know how Hariri's leadership became more sectarian, we need to explain why this turn came about. The answers to these questions allow us to explore the ways in which neoliberal capitalism reproduced sectarianism in Lebanon.

This poses questions for the relationship between neoliberal capitalism and sectarianism. Does neoliberalism reproduce or transform particularist identities? It will not be possible to give a generalised answer to this question from the Lebanese case. This is due to several reasons. First, neoliberalism is highly contradictory as both a class project and an economic orthodoxy. The needs of economic elites to stay in power may require them to mobilise particularist identities in a way that contradicts the universalist claims of neoliberal economic theory. This is further complicated by the fact that 'actually existing neoliberalism' is shaped by the specifics of local politics. The defining feature of Lebanese politics is sectarianism. Secondly, sectarian identity is constructed and situational. This means that different actors may embrace sectarianism in some contexts but not in others. Having included these caveats, I will go on to argue two points in this chapter. Firstly, Hariri's economic policy reproduced the poverty and inequality that forms the economic basis of sectarian clientelism. Second, Hariri's 'sectarian turn' in the late 1990s was due to electoral politics: he needed to bolster his parliamentary representation to push through his economic policies. Clientelism along confessional lines was a form of 'neoliberal populism' designed to appeal to voters across class lines.

SOCIAL CRISIS AND HARIRI'S SECTARIAN TURN: 1998–2000

Social crisis in Lebanon

Hariri's neoliberal policies resulted in continued poverty and deprivation. Overborrowing hurt the private sector and undermined growth through 'crowding out', which occurs when government uses up scarce credit and pushes up interest rates, making credit unaffordable for many private businesses.[4] Evidence on the demand side also illustrates that Lebanese businesses were suffering from a lack of credit. A World Bank study of small and medium enterprises (SMEs) in 1995 found that lack of bank services was the greatest concern, followed by lack of infrastructure.[5] While Hariri's policies addressed the latter issue through reconstruction, government overborrowing actually exacerbated the lack of credit. The World Bank survey showed that bank loans accounted for only 11 per cent of firms' working capital and 19 per cent of investment capital, while personal savings and profits were the main source of financing.[6] Another study commissioned by Lebanon's Economic and Social Council in 2002 identified monetary policy and the resultant lack of credit as one of the main obstacles to growth of SMEs.[7] Like deposits, credit was highly concentrated. In December 1998 less than 1 per cent of beneficiaries accounted for almost half of all credit.[8] This suggests that the credit that was available went mostly to large-scale projects rather than SMEs. Credit was also highly concentrated in terms of sectors, with services receiving the bulk of lending. In 1998 trade and services accounted for 44.8 per cent of total credit, construction took 21.9 per cent, while the share of the 'productive sectors', agriculture (1.5 per cent) and industry (excluding construction, 12.6 per cent), was much smaller.[9] This unequal distribution of credit also shaped the structure of the economy. The share of services in GDP rose from 60.9 per cent in 1994 to 71.7 per cent in 2005. In contrast, the share of agriculture fell from 12.0 per cent to 7.3 per cent and manufacturing from 27.1 per cent to 21.0 per cent.[10] The scarcity of credit was a major factor in stifling growth among SMEs and in the agricultural and industrial sector, which are the biggest job creators in Lebanon.

The difficulties of SMEs and of agriculture and industry were causing unemployment, poverty and deprivation.[11] Unofficial unemployment estimates exceeded 25 per cent.[12] The structure of employment is shaped by Lebanon's service-based economy. About a third of total employment in Lebanon was non-waged in 1997, with only 1 per cent skilled manufacturing labour.[13] A large section of non-wage labour occupies a precarious position, such as taxi drivers, small shop owners or street peddlers. Because demand for regular wage labour among the unemployed and those in precarious service jobs outstrips the supply of regular waged labour jobs, those who can provide such employment—in the public or private sectors—enjoy strong patronage power; 42 per cent of household income is derived from sources other than wages.[14] Non-wage income consists of interest and rent (19 per cent of total income), property sale (7 per cent), assistance—such as financial assistance from family or relatives or grants (9 per cent) and a residual category including pensions or inheritance (7 per cent). These data allow us to gauge households' vulnerability to clientelism. Savings, deposits and investment are concentrated among a very small section of Lebanese. Similarly, property sales are only an option for people of relative wealth. Hence, income from interest or rent and from property sales—comprising about a quarter of total income— are virtually irrelevant to Lebanon's poorest households. Similarly, waged employment is scarce and unavailable to many. The share of 'assistance' for these poor households is thus likely to be higher than the 9 per cent average for all households. Much of this will derive from remittances. Emigration has traditionally been a solution to Lebanon's unemployment problem, and the resultant remittances amounted to 36.4 per cent of GDP in 1992, which fell to 7.2 per cent in 1998 due to the falling value of remittances.[15] However, many poor or deprived families relied on financial support from charities connected to politicians. Charity to the poor is therefore a means of patronage for Lebanese politicians.

This is particularly true for those households who live in poverty or deprivation. The first post-war assessment of poverty was a UN-ESCWA report of 1996, authored by Antoine Haddad. He estimated that 28 per cent of Lebanese families were living below the poverty line, with a monthly income below $618 per month.[16] The report went largely unnoticed until the autumn of 1996, when Walid Junblat used its findings to embarrass Hariri.[17] Haddad's expertise became an instrument for Junblat to pressure Hariri. The prime minister, in turn, was keen to counter the suggestion that poverty was a major problem or indeed that his policies were the cause for its persistence. Hariri therefore initiated a more rigorous study of deprivation in Lebanon conducted by the UNDP and the Central Administration of Statistics (CAS), resulting in the 'mapping of living conditions' survey of 1997.[18] It was conducted by social scientists who were considered independent of Hariri such as Kamal Hamdan and Adib Na'ma. In the absence of reliable household income data, the report looked at unsatisfied basic needs, namely housing, water and sewerage, education, and income-related indicators. It found that the basic needs of 32.1 per cent of Lebanese households went unsatisfied, confirming the findings of the earlier ESCWA study—much to Hariri's discomfort.

The government did not formulate a coherent policy to reduce poverty, but counted on 'trickling-down' effects. In a statement to the World Summit for Social Development in Copenhagen in 1995, Lebanon's national report explained the Hariri government's stance thus:

> Lebanon has a liberal economic system, where the role of the state is limited to formulating the legal, institutional, and infrastructural framework necessary for economic growth. … Therefore plans to combat poverty and unemployment do not appear as independent stand-alone plans, but form part of the overall comprehensive framework of the reconstruction and development plans, which place priority on ensuring the demands of economic growth.[19]

The idea that a 'rising tide' of growth lifts all boats is a classic neoliberal claim.

The most important state instrument to pay for public services and to redistribute income is progressive taxation. In December 1993 a new tax law was passed, drafted by the finance ministry controlled by Hariri. It followed the classical neoliberal prescription of 'a broad tax base with moderate marginal tax rates'.[20] Neoliberal tax reforms revolve around cutting direct taxes (e.g. income tax), expanding indirect taxes (e.g. value-added tax (VAT)) and a decline in customs tariffs. Low corporate taxes were to improve international competitiveness and encourage investment, and low personal income tax was to reward personal ambition and encourage wealth creation. VAT was a tax that was easily administered, and was to replace high customs and excise charges, which curtailed free trade. Hariri cut direct taxes to

3–10 per cent for corporate tax and 2–10 per cent for personal income tax.[21] Significantly, treasury bills were exempted from the 5 per cent capital gains tax. While cutting direct taxes, the Hariri government increased indirect taxes. Customs and excise remained the biggest contributor to government revenue at 43.1 per cent in 1998, compared to only 7.2 per cent from taxes on incomes and profits—a share which is minuscule compared even to other Middle Eastern countries, where income tax generally represents a smaller share than in industrialised countries.[22] Hariri pushed for raised revenue from telecommunications (7.0 per cent of revenue after being virtually non-existent in 1996) and administrative fees (8.5 per cent, up from 2.1 per cent in 1996). These revenue increases were achieved against strong opposition from Nabih Birri, who was trying to protect his popular constituency from rises in surcharges on petrol, cigarettes, mobile-phone use and fees on passports.[23] In the end, Birri managed to prevent policies such as the introduction of VAT and fee rises at the state-run Lebanese University. The overall effect of cutting direct taxes and raising indirect taxation was to make income distribution even more unequal. According to one analysis of Hariri's tax law of 1993, the distributive effect of lowering direct tax rates was neutral but the rise in indirect taxes tipped the balance towards a regressive tax system.[24] Hariri's fiscal policy allowed the rich to keep their wealth, while disproportionately affecting low-income households.

Even in times of severe fiscal crisis, Hariri preferred to raise duties on petrol or mobile-phone usage and introduce VAT than to raise tax rates on top income earners. Low taxes have proved a blunt instrument to attract foreign investors, who tend to look for other incentives first before being swayed by low tax rates.[25] Nor did corporate tax spur investment by domestic firms, because they were hampered by the effects of crowding out. Furthermore, Hariri's government demanded in 1994 that businesses pay taxes that had remained unpaid between 1971 and 1991.[26] This led to protests from the business community and penalised the lower rungs of the pre-war bourgeoisie who had been unable or unwilling to relocate their businesses abroad during the war. In conclusion, the extremely low rate of income tax conformed to the class interests of wealthy Lebanese such as Hariri.

Reconstruction did not benefit those who were economically disadvantaged. This was obvious in the spending of the institutions under

Hariri's control. In the Horizon 2000 study of 1993, which Hariri had commissioned and which supposedly formed the basis of the CDR reconstruction plan, social infrastructure was to receive 27.8 per cent of total spending from 1993 to 2002, while the productive sector—industry and agriculture—was to receive 11.5 per cent.[27] However, CDR figures show that physical infrastructure received 81.6 per cent between 1992 and 2001, leaving little for social infrastructure (12.3 per cent) and the productive sectors (1.5 per cent).[28] The shift in spending priorities away from social concerns and towards physical infrastructure benefited contractors, and illustrates Hariri's disregard for social issues. Uneven development also had a regional aspect, which was not addressed by Hariri's policies. The flagship projects of reconstruction, such as the airport or Solidere, were based in the capital while deprivation is greatest in rural areas. The 1997 mapping of living conditions survey found the incidence of deprivation to be highest in rural areas and lowest in Beirut and its suburbs.[29] Those aspects of reconstruction that did address poverty and deprivation tended to be concessions to Nabih Birri, who represented a more popular constituency. Examples include compensation for the displaced in the Solidere area as well as Amal and Hizballah's mediation with inhabitants of the Elissar project area. As Harb and Sawalha note in their works on Elissar and the displaced respectively, these interventions strengthened Birri's position vis-à-vis his constituents.[30]

Welfare ministries were strengthened, and did receive more funding, but they remained inefficient because former militia leaders were abusing them as patronage sources. Rather than an improvement in services, there tended to be merely an increase in employment. The government's share in total employment rose from 8 per cent in 1970 to 11 per cent in 1997.[31] The high incidence of unemployment and the scarcity of waged employment turned government jobs into a patronage resource. Government spending on wages and salaries rose from 6.6 per cent of GDP in 1992 to 9.2 per cent in 1998.[32] The expansion of government employment helped to keep down unemployment, but evidence of overstaffing and granting funds according to political criteria rather than need suggests that it did not necessarily improve the performance of government agencies. Overstaffing was therefore a form of rent-creation and rent-sharing.

While the provision of public services was expanded after the war, the majority of Lebanese remained reliant on resources controlled by political and economic elites. An expansion of public education took place in the post-war period but an enormous gap remains in educational opportunities, especially between the quality of private and public education. A study by the Ministry of Education showed that only 50.4 per cent of students enrolled in public schools achieved an acceptable level of academic competence, compared to 64.8 per cent in free private schools and 77.1 per cent in private fee-paying schools.[33] Poorer households rely on free education: 57.4 per cent of students enrolled in public schools in Beirut and its suburbs in 1995 came from poor households, as did 61.3 per cent of those in free private schools. There is therefore scope for patronage by providing education, either by building schools, giving scholarships or providing access to schools of philanthropic associations, most of which were run along confessional lines. In 1994/5 14 per cent of students were enrolled in private non-fee-paying schools, while 56 per cent were attending fee-paying private schools.[34] The impact of educational opportunities is particularly high with regard to university education. In 2004 50.3 per cent of Lebanese university students were in public education at the Lebanese University.[35] Yet an education in fee-paying universities such as the AUB or St Joseph University enabled students to gain higher-paid jobs and increase the chances of finding work abroad. In a highly competitive labour market education was the main means of reproducing or improving social status. This anxiety went beyond the poor and reached deep into the middle class, which was struggling to send its children to private universities. A similar picture emerges in the health sector. In 1997 60.4 per cent of Lebanese residents were not covered by health insurance.[36] Furthermore, health insurance does not cover all health costs, and households have to contribute large out-of-pocket payments.[37] This offers patronage opportunities to politicians who provide health centres or pay for medical treatment. A survey of households combined with qualitative interviews by Chen and Cammett found that party activists enjoy easier access to health care than those Lebanese who do not partake in political activism such as electioneering, because political parties 'act as gatekeepers to benefits that are supposed to be social rights available to all citizens with demonstrated need'.[38] Again, these insecurities reach deep into the middle class, although the poor are more likely to be affected.

A large number of Lebanese continue to rely on resources controlled by the political and economic elites. Access to jobs, health care and education can be used as patronage instruments. The anthropologist Aseel Sawalha quotes one displaced Lebanese about the difference between patronage during and after the war:

> During the war, I used to ask the [militia] leader to find me an apartment, or find me a job. After the war, the politicians sensed that we are not completely dependent upon them as before. But they are trying to keep us under their control. They want us to be like sheep that they own. They want us to realise that we cannot get anything without their intervention.[39]

Hariri hemmed in

By the mid-1990s Hariri was realising the constraints of his position. The Lebanese economy was not growing as fast as he had hoped, and the problem of government debt was becoming obvious. Rival political elites—such as speaker of parliament Nabih Birri—were trying to curtail Hariri's influence. The popular Lebanese perception of Hariri was starting to turn, not seeing him as a selfless benefactor so much as a self-serving entrepreneur. This sentiment was best expressed in 1998 in a wildly popular book by Najah Wakim, a Nasserite parliamentarian who made detailed but ill-documented allegations of corruption among Lebanon's political elite, particularly concerning Hariri.[40] Hariri had so far relied on Syrian support—or at least toleration—for his economic project, but from this side too he was facing increasing opposition by a regime that resented the billionaire's independence in a political system they otherwise tightly controlled. This culminated in the election of army chief of staff Émile Lahoud as president in November 1998. Hariri and Lahoud had a fraught relationship in the 1990s. Hariri opposed Lahoud's election but had to accept him eventually, given his strong Syrian backing. Hariri decided to step down as prime minister.[41]

At around the same time, a shift within the Syrian regime was undermining Hariri's relations with Damascus. In 1994 Hafiz al-Assad's son and anointed successor Bassil died in a car crash. Assad's other son,

Bashar, was subsequently groomed for succession, increasingly sidelining Hariri's allies within the Syrian regime. In late 1998 Bashar al-Assad appears to have assumed responsibility for the 'Lebanon file' from vice-president 'Abd al-Halim Khaddam.[42] Hariri had built up close relations with Khaddam in 1985 when they had both rallied Lebanese support for the ill-fated 'militia agreement'. Another blow to Hariri's influence was the demotion of Hikmat Shihabi from the position of chief of staff in 1998. He was considered another ally of Hariri within the Syrian regime. In June 2000 Shihabi briefly sought refuge from the reach of the Syrian regime, fearing to be targeted in an 'anti-corruption' drive.[43] Shihabi fled via Beirut airport, having spent time at Hariri's mansion while recovering from medical treatment. Shihabi and Khaddam may have been considered threats by the younger generation around Bashar. There was also a sectarian dimension, because Khaddam and Shihabi were both Sunni Muslims in an 'Alawi-dominated regime.

In the first half of the 1990s relative harmony among Lebanon's political elite was maintained through a Saudi–Syrian accord on the international level and rent-creation and rent-sharing in the economic field. The pillars of this stability, however, were shaky. The Saudi–Syrian accord was undermined by lack of progress in the Israeli–Syrian peace negotiations and the uneasy coexistence between Hariri's 'reconstruction' and Hizballah's 'resistance' agendas. Bashar al-Assad's rise from 1994 onwards upset this balance further. Hariri's reconstruction came under increasing pressure as government debt increased. It was in this latter arena that Lahoud targeted Hariri's interests from 1998 onwards. Lahoud entertained a neo-Shihabist vision of Lebanon. He had rebuilt the post-war armed forces to overcome sectarian divisions. Just as Shihab had sought to rein in the power of the *zu'ama*, so Lahoud was seeking to rein in what he regarded as the corruption of Lebanon's post-war elite, particularly Hariri. In his inaugural speech in November 1998 he asserted the 'rule of law' and several of Hariri's protégés were subjected to corruption investigations.[44] Shihabist technocrat Salim al-Huss succeeded Hariri as prime minister. His new 'technocratic' cabinet excluded most Hariri loyalists, but also the former militia leaders. However, the close Syrian ally Michel al-Murr remained interior minister and became a key power centre in the al-Huss cabinet.

The new government replaced Hariri's protégés at the head of reconstruction agencies. Nabil al-Jisr lost his post as head of the CDR and faced a corruption investigation.[45] Yaqub Saraf replaced Hariri loyalist Nicolas Saba as governor of Beirut. Solidere, Hariri's most important reconstruction project, ground to a halt. The company started complaining about delays in construction permits, which unnerved investors.[46] In 1999 Solidere reported that its profits had fallen by 30 per cent and in 2000 the company recorded losses.[47] Hariri needed to return to office in order to regain control over the institutions that regulated reconstruction. George Corm, an implacable critic of Hariri and his technocrats, became the finance minister in the al-Huss government. He toned down government borrowing, the maturity of the Lebanese-pound-denominated bonds on offer was extended, and the government started marketing Eurobonds denominated in foreign currencies instead.[48] These instruments carried lower interest rates because of the lower currency risk.[49] Corm's actions antagonised Lebanon's commercial banks, which started diversifying their operations to reduce overreliance on government debt.[50] Corm faced opposition to his policy from the central bank, still dominated by Hariri technocrat Riyadh Salameh, as well as from the minister of economy, trade and industry, Nasir al-Sa'idi.[51] The latter had never become as closely associated with Hariri as Fu'ad Siniura or later Bassil Fulayhan had but he was a dyed-in-the-wool neoliberal who subscribed wholeheartedly to Hariri's economic project. Winner of the Milton Friedman post-doctoral scholarship at the University of Chicago, Sa'idi was vice-governor at the central bank from 1993 to 2003 and lead negotiator of the EU–Lebanese Association Agreement, a free-trade pact with the EU.[52] Between 1998 and 2000 Sa'idi curtailed Corm's ability to fundamentally change the mode of government debt management.

Lahoud had excluded Rafiq Hariri from some important levers of economic power. Hariri reacted by building up a popular base to win elections. In the early 1990s Hariri had sought to control economic policy but paid little attention to electoral politics. In the 1992 election he did not put together a separate electoral list, but was one of the major forces ensuring the successful conduct of the elections. The vote was meant to legitimise the *pax Syriana* and the political order agreed at Ta'if. However, the Syrians and their Lebanese allies were faced with a boycott from predominantly Christian forces, who felt that they were the losers from the Ta'if accords. One Muslim politician who supported the boycott was Tammam Salam, thus drawing the ire of the Syrian regime. Hariri tried to convince Salam to participate but failed, leading to friction between the two politicians.[53] By 1996 Hariri realised he had to become more openly active in elections to bolster his stand vis-à-vis his political rivals.[54] His most important battleground was Beirut, where he faced two established Sunni politicians: Salim al-Huss and Tammam Salam. Lebanese electoral politics revolves around compiling 'lists' in alliances that often cut across political rivalries. In Beirut Salam and al-Huss refused to join a list largely determined by Hariri. Al-Huss formed a rival list, while Salam ran as an independent. A third list was headed by the leftist parliamentarian Najah Wakim, who was a fierce critic of Hariri. Al-Huss, Salam and Wakim all made it to parliament, but Hariri's list won fourteen of nineteen seats in the capital. Hariri had started engaging in an electoral contest with the established representatives of 'Sunni Beirut' but had not yet vanquished them completely. In the rest of the country Hariri picked up seats for political allies by getting them on the electoral lists of local power brokers. Particularly important were Hariri's deals with Walid Junblat and Nabih Birri, who were benefiting from electoral rules tailored to their needs by the Syrian regime.[55] Hariri also became active in the 1998 municipal elections, sponsoring thousands of candidates who then owed their allegiance to him. He was particularly successful in Sidon and Beirut.[56]

Maqasid as a 'bank of political resources'

The way in which Hariri built up a popular support base and the sectarian aspect of this strategy are best illustrated by looking at his rivalry with Tammam Salam. Salam was the son of a leading Beirut *za'im*, representing the city's Sunni bourgeoisie. Hariri was a leading member of the new contractor bourgeoisie. Both were allied to Saudi Arabia. In their electoral competition in 2000 the provision of philanthropy to Beirut's Sunni community became a central issue. While Salam headed the Maqasid association, Hariri revived the Hariri Foundation and opened health centres and schools, while exploiting the financial weaknesses of Maqasid.

Maqasid's pre-war financing had been based on the privileged position of Beirut's Sunni bourgeoisie. It rested on two pillars, grounded in the political economy of pre-war Lebanon: returns on real-estate investment and school fees. In 1967/8 Maqasid derived 39.3 per cent of its income from property rents.[57] Maqasid's real-estate investment reflected the privileged access to bank credit and land of Beirut's Sunni bourgeoisie. Land was donated by private individuals or obtained from the government. Maqasid owned an estimated 17 per cent of Beirut's commercial centre before the war.[58] It owned warehouses and office buildings that were catering to the expanding service sector; 47.2 percent of its income came from school fees, reflecting the ability of Beirut's expanding Sunni middle class to pay for education. Maqasid itself was an engine for the creation of this class through its provision of education, which was unavailable from the state sector.

Maqasid played a central role in constructing a specific 'Sunni Beiruti' identity. It was founded by Beirut's Sunni notables in 1878 in response to the expansion of Christian missionary schools and to provide access to a 'modern' education for Beirut's Muslim children. Maqasid was thus very much a Sunni association: Maqasid schools did not cater for Christians; religious education played a big role in the curriculum; and the Sunni mufti had great influence.[59] Maqasid was also strongly 'Beiruti':[60] its philanthropic practices and its celebrations, publications, speeches and rituals made constant reference to a Sunni Muslim and Beiruti identity. Maqasid 'represented' Sunni Beirut, but also established a social hierarchy, with the Sunni notables at the top. Between its foundation in 1878 and the 1960s, Maqasid was transformed into a 'modern bureaucracy' run by Beirut's Sunni bourgeoisie, consisting of professionals, businessmen, politicians, etc. drawn from the small pool of Beirut notable families.[61]

Maqasid was thus an expression of the power of Beirut's Sunni bourgeoisie—both in terms of financing, which was linked to the political economy that underpinned the power of this class, and of the vision of community it promoted: Sunni, Beiruti, and ordered by a strict hierarchy, with the city's notables-turned-bourgeoisie on top. The presidency of the Maqasid therefore provided control of 'a bank of political resources'—both economic and symbolic—by which Beirut's Sunni bourgeoisie maintained its power.[62] The position was fought over by Beirut's leading or aspiring Sunni leaders.[63] However, the politician Sa'ib Salam managed to stay in the post of Maqasid president from

1958 to 1982, when he handed over to his son Tammam. Sa'ib Salam gained firm control of the association by increasing the constitutional power of the Maqasid presidency, attaining extensive powers of patronage, which could be reconverted into votes at election time:[64] selective access to free or subsidised education and employment for a thousand people. Salam's status of 'representing' Sunni Beirut was the basis on which he could stake a claim to the post of the prime minister, the highest position reserved for a Sunni Muslim in the confessional state. As Bourdieu has noted, 'representing' a group as a leader is a central building block in the construction of group identity.[65] The logic of confessional power sharing dictates that politicians who seek office need to 'represent' their community. This was a central mechanism in the reproduction of the culture of sectarianism. The confessional state shaped leaders' sectarian strategies, rather than a sectarian society overwhelming a 'weak' state.

Rising social tension within Lebanon, the alliance of the PLO with Lebanese leftist forces and the arming of Christian militias led to the outbreak of civil war in 1975. The militias challenged the traditional *zu'ama*. In the predominantly Sunni Muslim quarters of Beirut the Murabitun militia—financed by the Palestinian Fatah and by Libya[66]—challenged Salam's claim to be the legitimate representative of Sunni Beirut. Murabitun's 'progressive' Nasserite ideology contrasted with the conservatism of the Saudi king, with whom Sa'ib Salam had allied himself. The struggle between Salam and Murabitun thus reflected wider social and regional faultlines. During the civil war Lebanon lost its position as financial intermediary between the Arab East and Western financial markets. This undermined the economic power of Lebanon's pre-war bourgeoisie and necessarily affected Maqasid. Rent income from real estate plummeted. Beirut's commercial centre became a no-go area, and many of the association's buildings were destroyed. As Beirut's middle class became increasingly impoverished, Maqasid had to reduce school fees.[67] The association came to depend on Saudi financial aid. In 1975 it received $2.6 million from Saudi Arabia; in 1980 Crown Prince Fahd promised to finance a technical school in Beirut to the tune of $9 million; and from 1981 to 1993 Maqasid received an annual subsidy of LL100 million.[68] As the access of Beirut's Sunni bourgeoisie to economic capital fell during the civil war, Salam's international alliance with Saudi Arabia became decisive for maintaining his position as the leader of 'Sunni Beirut', based as it was on the ability to finance Maqasid's operations.

Hariri and electoral politics in Beirut, 1998–2000

In 1982 Sa'ib Salam handed the presidency of Maqasid to his son, and in 1985 he went into exile in Switzerland. Murabitun was defeated in 1982 by Israeli forces, and again in 1984 and 1985 by the Shia Amal and Druze PSP. Islamist groups such as Jama'at Islamiyya and al-Ahbash appeared on the Sunni political scene. By the end of the civil war Lebanon's Sunni politics was fragmented among the remnants of popular Nasserite movements, Islamist groups, *zu'ama* such as Salam in Beirut and 'Umar Karami in Tripoli, and members of the new contractor bourgeoisie such as Rafiq Hariri. Beirut's Sunni bourgeoisie resented Hariri for appropriating their properties in central Beirut. Many in this class saw Hariri, the farmer's son from Sidon, as an outsider in their circles. The remnants of popular Nasserite movements and Sunni Islamist groups resented Hariri as someone who did not do enough for his Sunni community.[69] The Islamist al-Ahbash engaged in a campaign against both Hariri and Tammam Salam in 1996 over the sale of cemeteries by Maqasid to Solidere.[70] Al-Ahbash was thought to enjoy the support of the Syrian regime and had one MP.

At the same time, religious authority in the community was highly fragmented. The position of mufti had remained vacant since Shaykh Hassan Khalid had been assassinated in 1989. His deputy, Muhammad Rashid al-Qabbani, was the most obvious choice as his successor. However, Syria was said to have prevented the election, happy to maintain the power vacuum at the head of the Sunni community. Islamic groups such as al-Ahbash opposed Qabbani and sought to promote one of their own to the position. The Sunni community thus had a prime minister who was more concerned with the economy than communal politics, *zu'ama* who had been weakened by the civil war, remnants of the popular Nasserite movement, and an array of Islamist movements, who were also unable to impose hegemony on the community. It was these forces that Hariri had to contend with when he was trying to impose his authority on the Sunni community, a process which started in around 1996.

An important step in gaining control in the Sunni camp was the election of Qabbani to the position of mufti in December 1996. Syria had finally signalled its approval when Qabbani was received in Damascus by Syrian president Hafiz al-Assad two days prior to the election. The electoral process was tightly managed by advisers to Rafiq Hariri in order to produce the desired outcome.[71] One was Muhammad Samak, who had started liaising with Dar al-Fatwa, Lebanon's Sunni authority, on Hariri's behalf as early as the 1980s, and was a member of its advisory council.[72] The other was Ridwan al-Sayyid, a Lebanese University professor who advised Hariri on Islamic politics.[73] They composed a new electoral law which was passed on the morning before the election. The new rules reduced the number of those eligible to vote for a new mufti from over one thousand to ninety-six, consisting only of politicians and members of the Sunni religious establishment. Members of Islamist organisations such as al-Ahbash and Jama'at Islamiyya were excluded to ensure Qabbani's election. One cleric lambasted 'Rafiq al-Hariri, who wants to impose total control over all public and private institutions', saying that Dar al-Fatwa had 'become an annex of the Lebanese government.'[74] By elevating Qabbani to the position of mufti, Hariri won an ally who could help him impose at least a semblance of discipline on Lebanon's unruly Sunni religious scene.

Hariri took up some of the pet causes of the new mufti, but not all of them. In 1998 President Elias Hrawi allied with parliamentary speaker Nabih Birri to pass a law that would have introduced civil marriage. Lebanese personal-status law is a matter for the different communities, making cross-confessional marriages impossible unless one party converts. As Sunni mufti, Qabbani led a forceful campaign against the law, allying with Sunni Islamists and gaining support from Shia, Druze and Christian religious leaders. Hariri took Qabbani's side and refused to sign the law. This had two advantages for Hariri. Firstly, he could present himself as the advocate of a 'Sunni' cause, one that was spearheaded by the mufti and by Sunni Islamist groups. Equally important—if not more so—were power struggles within the troika of president, prime minister and speaker of parliament. Hariri was opposing a policy introduced by Hrawi in alliance with Birri. Of course, these two leaders were representing 'their' confessional communities too, thus giving such power struggles a sectarian dimension.[75]

In 1996 Hariri started to move against Maqasid. It had become completely dependent on Saudi financing during the civil war and, since it had been catering for an increasingly impoverished population in Beirut, school fees brought in less than during the pre-war era. More importantly, income from property rent never reached pre-war levels: its share of total income fell from 42 per cent in 1967/8 to 2 per cent in 1997/8.[76] Maqasid's properties in Beirut's commercial centre were expropriated in exchange for shares, while some land was sold to Solidere.[77] Although it received compensation and a seat on the Solidere board, this was not enough to make up for the loss of pre-war property rent.[78] Property rights had effectively passed from the old Beiruti bourgeoisie to the new contracting bourgeoisie, a fact deeply resented by some representatives of the old order. In an ironic twist, Hariri pledged that the profits he was to derive from $125 million worth of Solidere shares he bought in January 1994 would go directly towards financing the Hariri Foundation, as well as other charities chosen at his own discretion.[79] While the Hariri Foundation thus gained Solidere as a source of financing, Maqasid could not recover the city centre as a source of income. The association's financial situation was severe, with debts of $15 million in 1996.[80] Only Saudi support was keeping Maqasid afloat, but from 1996 onwards this financial support ceased. The current Maqasid president, Amin al-Da'uq, pointed to the cost of the Gulf war and the falling oil price as reasons why the kingdom stopped payments.[81] What is important for our analysis is that the Saudi action helped Hariri in his political struggle against Tammam Salam.

In previous chapters we have seen how Hariri had recruited experts in their fields to fulfil various tasks: the Oger engineers around Fadl Shalaq who cleaned up Beirut in 1982 and then ran the CDR after 1991, and the bankers Riyadh Salameh and Fu'ad Siniura, who came to run the central bank and the finance ministry respectively. Similarly, he would use his allies to liaise with confessional leaders. For instance, Dawud Sayigh managed Hariri's relations with the Maronite Patriarch and Hariri's adviser Muhammad Samak was tending relations with the mufti.[82] When Hariri decided to style himself as a 'Sunni leader' by providing social services, he also procured the relevant 'experts' by poaching them from Maqasid. Even before the 1996 election Hariri had won over Salim Diab, a Maqasid board member who had previously been a Salam loyalist. Diab was the chairman of the board of Ansar sports club and had the ability to mobilise Beirut's youth during election time. Ansar had received financial support from Hariri as early as 1986,[83] and Ansar played a significant role in mobilising support for Hariri during the 1996 elections.[84] In 1998 Diab founded another charity, the Beirut Association for Social Development, which played a role in the election campaign in 2000. There is an economic element to the relationship between Hariri and Diab, who owns 49 per cent of the engineering consultancy LACECO International, which benefited from several contracts from Saudi Oger.[85] Former Oger employee Bilal Alaily is the company's executive director.

Hariri also won over several Maqasid board members, such as Muhammad Ghaziri and Sami Nahas, who were both also on the Solidere board. The alliances of Maqasid board members were not determined by ideological issues. The fact that Hariri was simply a more powerful politician than Salam was likely to have been decisive. When Hariri and Salam fell out, Beirut's Sunni notables had to decide where their loyalties lay, and many gravitated towards the billionaire contractor rather than the son of the *za'im*. Diab left the Maqasid board, but many members associated with Hariri stayed on after 1996. Hariri also poached health and education professionals from Maqasid. For instance, the general manager of the health and social services directorate, Dr Nur al-Din al-Kush, had previously been a doctor with Maqasid before setting up a network of Hariri Foundation health centres.[86] Beyond Maqasid, Hariri attracted other figures from popular and Nasserite Sunni movements. Walid 'Idu had been a magistrate but had also been a supporter of Murabitun during the civil war.[87] He was elected to parliament on Hariri's list in 2000 and vociferously attacked Tammam Salam's presidency of Maqasid.[88]

Hariri did not just poach personnel and board members from Maqasid, but also expanded the grassroots provision of services to the urban poor in predominantly Sunni neighbourhoods. In 1999 he built a school in Tariq al-Jadida, a predominantly Sunni neighbourhood of Beirut, which had been a stronghold of the Murabitun during the civil war. In the first eight months of 2000—before the parliamentary elections in September that year—the Hariri Foundation opened no less than six health centres in Beirut. The main centre was situated in Tariq

al-Jadida.[89] Five 'satellite centres' were opened in areas of the capital
that also tended to be predominantly Sunni or have large Sunni populations.[90] Unlike Maqasid, Hariri could count on financial support from
the Gulf to shoulder the high set-up cost of his health centres.[91] Hariri
used the opening of these health centres in his campaign, bringing
together the members of his Beirut electoral list.[92] Another initiative
founded in 1998 was the Beirut Association for Social Development,
set up by Salim Diab.[93] Its social centres are again mainly—but not
exclusively—located in predominantly Sunni areas.[94] Hariri also
worked to organise the student loan recipients of 1983–96 more formally: in 1994 an alumni association was founded, and a year later it
had about 450 members.[95] The alumni association even started playing
a political role, for instance sending delegations to liaise with other
troika members on Hariri's behalf.[96]

Maqasid found it increasingly difficult to compete with the Hariri
Foundation. Financial difficulties forced the association to close down
some schools, while teachers and other staff were made redundant.[97]
The Hariri Foundation provided superior facilities in its schools and
health centres, and attracted teaching and medical staff previously
employed at Maqasid. Hariri allies such as Walid 'Idu accused Salam of
'politicising' the association and being responsible for the parlous state
of its finances,[98] suggesting that Hariri and his foundation were better
able to work for the betterment of the Sunni community than Salam
and the Maqasid. Hariri thus superseded Salam as the prime representative of Sunni Beirut. As a result of Maqasid's decline, Salam lost his
seat in the 2000 parliamentary elections, while all the candidates on
Hariri's list were elected to parliament. Salim al-Huss also lost his seat,
and later complained that Hariri's victory was simply due to the billionaire's spending power.[99] Salam decided to step down as Maqasid
president in order to, as he said, avert any damage to the association.[100]
Amin al-Da'uq, a long-time ally of Salam, assumed the presidency and
proceeded to 'depoliticise' the association. In 2003 several new faces
on the Maqasid board illustrated Hariri's rising, but not absolute, influence there.[101] Once Hariri stopped perceiving Maqasid as a political
threat, he started supporting it again: in 2003 he forgave Maqasid $35
million in debt, held by his Banque Méditerranée.[102]

Two points are crucial to make here. The first is that Hariri's ability
to assume the mantle of 'Sunni' leadership in Beirut was due to his

superior ability to finance education and health services. This reflected the decline of the pre-war bourgeoisie and the rise of Gulf contractors, especially Rafiq Hariri. Beirut's pre-war bourgeois Sunni families did not completely disappear, but in the 1990s their political representation shifted from a *za'im* (Salam) to a Gulf contractor (Hariri). Yet the relationship of Beirut's notables with the two leaders was different. Sa'ib Salam had been *primus inter pares* among Beirut's Sunni notables in the pre-war period, having to fight off challenges for the Maqasid presidency and for the post of prime minister. Hariri was immune to such challenges. The pre-war Maqasid had relied on financing grounded in economic resources controlled by the Sunni bourgeois families as a whole. In contrast, Hariri's philanthropy relied solely on his own wealth, originally accumulated as a contractor in Saudi Arabia but increasingly linked to rent appropriation in Lebanon's post-war economy. As such, Hariri as a representative of Lebanon's new contractor bourgeoisie had not only subdued the Salams but Beirut's Sunni bourgeois families as a whole. This difference in financing between Salam's Maqasid and the Hariri Foundation finds expression in the conspicuousness of Salam and Hariri in their respective philanthropic endeavours. The Salam name does crop up occasionally in the different institutions associated with Maqasid, but on the whole the association presents itself as an initiative by Beirut's Sunni notables rather than springing from the 'vision' of a particular individual.[103] In contrast, the Hariri Foundation bears the founder's name and his image is conspicuous in the health centres and schools from posters and banners outside the centres to the employees' PC desktop background.[104]

The expansion of health centres did not stop in 2000, but continued thereafter. The comparison of clientelist methods by the Hariri Foundation and Maqasid offers revealing insights into the ways in which the outsider Rafiq Hariri, who initially tried to appear as a 'national' and cross-sectarian figure, was nonetheless 'disciplined' into behaving like a Sunni leader. The foundation stresses that the aim of its health and social services directorate is the provision of primary health care to all Lebanese communities without discrimination as to race, gender or religion and that Hariri Foundation medical centres do not turn anyone away.[105] In that sense, the Hariri Foundation health and social services mirrored the claims about non-sectarian recruitment of its student loan programme, 1983–96. The student loan programme did not actively dissuade non-Sunni Muslims from applying but, since recruitment worked through religious and social organisations of the Sunni community, access was simply much easier for Hariri's own confessional group. Similarly, the health centres were more accessible to Sunni Muslims due to their location. The main health centre in Beirut was opened in 2000 in Tariq al-Jadida, in the heart of Sunni Beirut. Smaller 'satellite centres' also tended to be located in predominantly Sunni areas. In 2001 two centres were opened in Sidon, followed by the main centre for the north in Tripoli in 2002 and a satellite centre in 'Akkar.[106]

The centres were thus located primarily in regions where Lebanon's Sunni population is concentrated.[107] The Hariri Foundation health centre in the predominantly Christian neighbourhood of Karm al-Zaytun represents an exception. Cammett takes this as a sign that Hariri's main concern was electoral rather than sectarian. It was a signal that Hariri was courting some non-Sunnis to win the parliamentary elections in Beirut.[108] Melani Cammett and Sukriti Issar argue convincingly that electoral considerations shaped the strategy of the Hariri Foundation.[109] They conducted their research after Rafiq Hariri's death in 2005, when his son Sa'd was in charge, but their findings are a reasonable approximation of the elder Hariri's strategy too. Compared to Hizballah, the Hariri Foundation provides more services in areas with a large population of non-sect members. The authors explain this variation with reference to the differing aims of the two organisations: while the Hariri Foundation is mainly seeking electoral support, Hizballah are also mobilising the Shia population behind a military campaign. However, the fact remains that most centres were located in predominantly Sunni neighbourhoods, suggesting that Hariri's electoral strategy was based on courting Beirut's Sunni community first and foremost.

Representatives of the Hariri Foundation maintain that Hariri wanted to expand the activities of the foundation much further but was hemmed in by rival political forces. They cited several mechanisms: first, the health ministry had to accredit new health centres.[110] Secondly, the Hariri Foundation seeks acceptance by local politicians, such as the leader of the local council, the *ra'is baladiyya*.[111] Finally, there was always the potential that health centres would become the target for anti-

Hariri protests, a possibility realised during the time of great political tension after Hariri's death.[112] Cammett and Issar show that Hariri was by no means exclusively a sectarian leader. However, the logic of Lebanese politics dictated that Sunnis remained his core constituency.

My evidence from Hariri's electoral campaign in Beirut in 2000 demonstrates that his philanthropy in Beirut confirmed rather than challenged the image of 'Sunni Beirut', which Maqasid had fostered in the previous decades. Beirut was a city with a large Sunni population, if not a majority. An electoral strategy in the capital therefore necessarily had to include winning the votes of Sunnis. This required Hariri to show that he was best able to provide for the community. Hariri's efforts do not negate his strategy to win votes beyond his own community, or his other persona as a 'national' figure above the sectarian fray, but they complement it. In a different context, Vloeberghs had written about Hariri's 'double-sided position as a Lebanese and as a Sunni politician': 'Hariri took great pains to carefully cultivate both profiles, a dynamic that allowed him to mobilise whichever portrait would serve his interests best.'[113]

The health centres provided ample patronage resources for Hariri.[114] The Hariri Foundation created an unknown number of jobs. The foundation stresses that it advertises its positions and that all staff are tested for their skills. Some physicians are permanently employed by the Hariri Foundation, others are from outside. Another patronage resource is health-care provision itself. Circumstantial evidence suggests that the Hariri Foundation's patients are predominantly Sunni Muslims with low incomes. Almost all Hariri Foundation health centres are located in predominantly Sunni areas. According to figures of early 2008, 74.3 per cent of patients had no medical insurance.[115] The medical centres provide a high level of care at low cost to the patient. Medication, for instance, is imported from France, packaged with the Hariri Foundation logo, and given out at between 20 and 30 per cent of the normal market price. The Hariri Foundation caters for Sunni Muslims left behind by the failings of the Lebanese health system: those without medical insurance who have difficulties paying for the high cost of medicine.[116] The Hariri Foundation health centres alleviate the social effects of post-war economic policies: poverty and deprivation and the insufficient provision of health services by the state.

SOCIAL CRISIS AND HARIRI'S SECTARIAN TURN: 1998–2000

The political economy of sectarianism

Authors who consider sectarianism the primordial force determining Lebanese politics interpret the country's history since the fifteenth century as a succession of sectarian struggles for primacy, and the civil war as simply the latest round of this ongoing conflict.[117] Yet sects have not been fully formed, coherent and unitary actors since the Middle Ages. Their political relevance is rooted in modern capitalism, colonialism and state-building. The colonial encounter was central in instituting the 'culture of sectarianism', especially European trusteeship of various confessional power-sharing schemes which started in 1840.[118] Another element was the differentiation of economic roles among different sects, with Christians more likely to be in charge of the dynamic sectors of the economy which were being integrated into circuits of European capital.[119] If sectarianism is constructed, it can also be transformed or overcome. The puzzle that constructivists then need to address is how sectarianism is being reproduced.[120] There are three ways in which the political economy of clientelism plays a central role in this reproduction. The *za'im* provides jobs, education or health care to followers on an exclusive basis. These are given as 'private goods': only followers receive these benefits due to their personal relationship with the leader. This relationship is usually mediated by local intermediaries who distribute benefits but also make sure that the beneficiaries reciprocate by giving political support, especially votes at election time. This material exchange is framed in symbolic exchanges, validating the patron's social status and ruled by a 'moral economy' of clients' expectations.

Secondly, confessional schools, health centres and workplaces may practise a 'banal' sectarianism.[121] Everyday practices such as the presence of religious or confessionally charged symbols, or commemorations and rituals, reinforce sectarian identity. While these sectarian practices often go unnoticed in times when sectarian conflict is dormant, they reproduce group identities which can be called upon when a conflict turns 'hot'. Finally, the *za'im* provides 'public goods' which cannot be restricted to followers alone. Examples include the restoration of urban patrimony. Similarly, not all public services are necessarily delivered exclusively to supporters. For instance, many hospitals and health centres are open to all—although there may still be gradations in costs which non-supporters have to bear. These public goods can still reproduce sectarianism. After all, what 'public' is being addressed? Health centres, schools or restored urban patrimony may acquire confessional connotations simply through their location. A school or health centre in a predominantly Christian area will be considered a means of bettering the particular community it serves, even without restricting access specifically to a politician's clients—what Cammett had called 'bricks and mortar clientelism'.[122] There is thus an expectation that leaders work for the betterment of the community by providing services to the 'confessional public'. The discourse of the patron providing for the confessional community is a way of 'imagining' the community.[123]

Hariri's policies concentrated wealth, resulting in high unemployment and continued poverty, while most Lebanese remained dependent on politicians for the provision of jobs, education or health care. This was the economic basis of clientelism. Inequality and a lack of public services were a direct result of Rafiq Hariri's neoliberal economic policies. Neoliberalism thus reproduces the political economy of sectarianism. A more equal economy and non-sectarian public services would have transformed sectarian practices. The post-war economy was, of course, not the first one to concentrate wealth and deny services to the population. In the pre-war period the zu'ama built a 'merchant republic', in which a few merchant and banking houses monopolised trade and finance. Tax rates were kept low and the state provision of services remained at a minimum. Confessional charities linked to zu'ama were the main avenues of sectarian clientelism. This only changed under the more developmentalist President Shihab, who expanded public schooling in particular, without however fundamentally transforming the system. During the civil war militia leaders sidelined zu'ama as the main confessional leaders. They used resources such as their control of local markets in foodstuffs, fuel or electricity to control populations. These militia leaders then sought service ministries in the post-war period to perpetuate the provision of patronage. Gulf contractors such as Hariri were using their personal wealth for patronage. The neoliberal post-war economy was not the first one where wealth was concentrated at the top and redistributed downwards along largely confessional lines. However, my account of the post-war economy shows how this pattern of inequality was being reproduced over time.

Accusing a politician of sectarianism is a serious charge in Lebanon because it is associated with the extreme violence meted out during the civil war. At the same time, it would be absurd to claim that there is any politician in Lebanon who stands above the sectarian fray. What is required is a clear definition of the nature and dimensions of sectarianism, as these differ among the various leaders. Sectarian leadership has several dimensions, and not all Lebanese politicians are sectarian in the same way. It can be broken down into four component parts. First, overtly religious agitation; secondly, defence of the community in military terms and in the political game; thirdly, the provision of services such as jobs, health or education to the community; and finally, the international alliances a politician cultivates. A comparison between Hariri and other Lebanese politicians reveals the nature of Hariri's sectarianism. The religious component of sectarianism is strongest among Sunni and Shia Islamists. They seek a specifically Islamic political order. Hariri stayed away from religious agitation, but he did make an effort at neutralising any Islamist challenges to his position as the dominant Sunni politician. To this end, he built a close alliance with the Sunni mufti of Lebanon, Muhammad Rashid al-Qabbani, by supporting his election in 1996.

The military defence of the community is a theme that was particularly prevalent among leading Christian politicians in the 1970s and 1980s. As leftist and Arabist Lebanese movements were allying themselves with the PLO to challenge the Christian-dominated status quo in the 1970s, the Lebanese Forces under Bashir Gemayel were playing on Christian fears of annihilation by the Muslim majority in the Arab world. This anxiety fuelled a Lebanese particularist nationalism among Lebanon's Maronite Christians. The fear of being swamped by a Muslim majority in the Arab countries also facilitated Gemayel's alliance with Israel, another state fearful of annihilation by its Muslim-majority neighbours. Such existential fears have historically been uncommon among Lebanon's Sunni Muslims, who adopted political ideologies prevalent in other Arab countries. Furthermore, Hariri was a quintessentially civilian politician who came to his own in the post-war era. He posited his reconstruction project as the very antithesis to sectarian militia culture, and hence rejected any military defence of his community.

The Druze leader Walid Junblat is the most gifted Lebanese politician when it comes to defending his community's interest in the political game. His political manoeuvres and shifting alliances have given him political clout far beyond the demographic weight of the Druze. Rafiq Hariri was not as astute or as focused on defending Sunni communal interests in Lebanon's political game. However, from 1998 onwards he increasingly framed his political actions in such terms. As prime minister from 1992 to 1998 and 2000 to 2004, Hariri held the highest post a Sunni Muslim can obtain in Lebanon's sectarian power-sharing system. Policy debates with the Christian president and the Shia speaker of the house are necessarily framed in terms of the relative power of the respective sects. Any success of the Sunni prime minister is counted as a sign of strength for 'the Sunnis' per se. By this logic, Hariri's reconstruction project became a 'Sunni project', while resistance to Israel was the project of Hizballah. This does not mean that all Shia were opposed to reconstruction, or that Sunnis rejected resistance. The sectarian character rather arose from the fact that the main Shia group embraced resistance while the dominant Sunni politician was pushing reconstruction. Another important instance is Hariri's rhetoric against Salim al-Huss, who replaced him as prime minister from 1998 to 2000. Huss was a technocrat in the Shihabist tradition, rather than a traditional za'im. Huss was not steeped in clientelist politics, and his credentials of acting in defence of a specifically 'Sunni' interest were weak at best. From 1998 to 2000 Hariri attacked Huss on his economic record, but also charged that the technocrat was unable to effectively defend his community's interest. This specific reference to Sunni interest was a novel theme within Hariri's political rhetoric.

Hariri did not engage in religious agitation or militarised sectarianism. From the mid-1990s onwards he did, however, begin to pose as the main defender of his community's political interest, and his philanthropy allowed him to claim Sunni leadership in Beirut by neutralising the Maqasid association—thus politically damaging Tammam Salam—and expanding Hariri Foundation health centres. This change towards a more sectarian style of politics does not mean that Hariri approached Lebanese politics with a sectarian mindset: he simply sought to win the parliamentary elections in 2000. Popular sectarian mobilisation is highly contradictory: the billionaire architect of post-war neoliberalism was the representative of the poorest sections of the Sunni community. Hariri's sectarianism is thus highly populist, appealing to the population across class lines based on non-class identity. The contradictions do not stop here. As mentioned in chapter 3, the technocratic experts Hariri recruited came from across the whole confessional spectrum. Particularist populism ensures popular support, while technocratic leadership promotes the smooth running of capitalism.[124] Hariri's neoliberalism thus had various effects. His policies concentrated wealth and perpetuated poverty and unemployment, keeping the majority of the population dependent on political leaders. Secondly, Hariri increasingly embraced clientelism as a form of sectarian populism. He did so not out of sectarian conviction but to win elections. At the same time, he was hiring technocrats across the confessional spectrum to run state institutions or his own companies to ensure that they were well run. While post-war neoliberalism was crucial for understanding the reproduction of sectarianism, this form of capitalism does not impose a unified logic when it comes to particularist or universal identities. Hariri hired the 'cadres' of capitalist management according to largely universal principles of merit. At the same time, the billionaire pandered to confessional expectations of patronage to win votes from some of the poorest sections of society.[125]

5

RETURN TO POLITICAL CRISIS AND ASSASSINATION

2000–2005

The assassination of Rafiq Hariri on 14 February 2005 has been likened to a political earthquake that set off a crisis in Lebanon. The murder was followed by deep political polarisation unseen since the end of the civil war and flashes of at times intense violence. I argue that Lebanon's political crisis started long before 14 February 2005. In fact, the assassination is better understood as an effect of this wider crisis rather than as its cause. Once again, the effect that Rafiq Hariri as an individual had on Lebanese history can only be understood in its wider structural framework. The course of reconstruction was not simply determined by Hariri's vision, but expressed the interests of a powerful capitalist who reproduced neoliberal economic practices to shape post-war accumulation and who had to contend with populist local militia leaders. Similarly, Hariri's assassination was part of wider developments in regional politics. International factors were the cause of the deterioration of the political situation. Hariri returned as prime minister in 2000 after two years out of office. The Syrian–Israeli peace process had broken down; the Palestinian–Israeli process was to follow; the 11 September 2001 attacks prompted the Bush administration to engage in a 'war on terror', and in 2003 to invade Iraq. The international consensus on which Lebanon's peace settlement had rested broke down: the

US acceptance of Syrian predominance over Lebanon; the Saudi role in guaranteeing Syria's position through its ally Rafiq Hariri; and the de facto toleration by both the USA and Israel of Hizballah's military role. Hariri became caught up in these power struggles.

When he returned as prime minister, Hariri intensified his drive to 'neoliberalise' the Lebanese economy. Distributive struggle over economic resources again played an important role in terms of domestic intra-elite struggles between Hariri and the former militia leaders. Not only did Hariri restore the Solidere project to profitability, he also attacked rent-creation mechanisms that primarily benefited his opponents. Former militia leaders relied on these state resources to maintain their patronage networks, and Hariri's attack on these mechanisms hit their ability to maintain their leadership position. Neoliberal economic orthodoxy became Hariri's weapon against rival elites.

The US–Syrian rift and its effect on Lebanese politics

Lebanon's political economy is the focus of this book, but we need to understand the regional and global political context to explain the causes of the rift that resulted in Rafiq Hariri's assassination in 2005. Ta'if had represented a US–Syrian accord brokered by Saudi Arabia. Damascus was allowed to marginalise all opposition to its dominance in Lebanon. In return, Syria reoriented its policy towards the USA: it joined the anti-Saddam coalition of 1991 and engaged in a peace process with Israel. The Clinton administration from 1993 to 2000 tolerated Syria's support for Hizballah in Lebanon, assuming that a successful conclusion of the peace process would 'domesticate' the Shia militia. However, in March 2000 the Syrian–Israeli track collapsed, and blame has variously been heaped on Syria, Israel and the US mediators. The strategic importance of the Golan Heights and fundamentally different visions of peace were the underlying causes of the failure. The US–Syrian relationship deteriorated over the next five years. In May 2000 Israel unilaterally withdrew its troops from South Lebanon, bolstering the standing of Hizballah as the only Arab force to have brought about an Israeli withdrawal from occupied land by force of arms. The failure of the Israeli–Palestinian track in July resulted in the outbreak of the second Palestinian Intifada in September.

Hafiz al-Assad had died in June, and was succeeded by his son Bashar, who left Syrian foreign-policy orientation essentially unchanged. Yet Assad also tolerated the intensification of conflict between Hizballah and Israel, which entered a particularly intensive phase between April 2001 and April 2002. While the Jewish state had withdrawn all its troops from South Lebanon, it held on to a small strip of land referred to as the Shib'a Farms, which it considered to be originally Syrian rather than Lebanese. Hizballah used the continued occupation of that small area to legitimise rocket attacks there. The increasing violence of the Intifada moved the Shia militia to escalate its attacks. Assad thus combined a posture of conflict with the readiness for compromise towards the USA and Israel.

US global strategy turned more aggressively military after 11 September 2001. The invasion of Afghanistan and later Iraq signalled a return to military intervention on a scale not seen since the Vietnam War. America's neoconservatives used the attacks to promote their project of remaking the Middle East, which revolved around 'preventive war' and 'regime change' in Iraq. The 11 September attacks were decisive for the realisation of the plans of neoconservative strategists, but these ideas had been developed over many years, if not decades. The Iraq war of 2003 represented a decisive shift of emphasis towards a more aggressive US strategy. The Middle East stood at the centre of this shift, and its political systems were to be remade to foster liberal democracies willing to make peace with Israel. The parallels to the onset of what Fred Halliday had called the 'second Cold War' in 1979 are striking: a perceived decline in US military superiority, a 'right-wing offensive' of nationalist forces, capitalist crisis, and—importantly—a sense of threat emanating from the Third World in general and the Middle East in particular.[1]

In both 1983 and 2003 US administrations were seeking confrontation with Syria, where grudging accommodation had previously been the norm. While Reagan considered Syria a client of the 'evil empire', the Bush administration implicitly included it in the 'axis of evil'. The neoconservative design to remake the Middle East put the Ba'th regime under increasing pressure. Threatened by American actions after 2000, the Syrian regime sought to tighten its grip on Lebanon by strengthening its closest allies, mainly former militia leaders and the military and intelligence establishment. The regime therefore attempted to curtail Hariri's power and influence. The businessman–politician was increasingly perceived to be a threat because of his wealth, his alliance with Saudi Arabia, and his strong relations with an increasingly hostile France, as well as the USA, which had long been pressurising Damascus.

After 11 September 2001 Syria initially cooperated with American requests for intelligence sharing on al-Qa'ida, and was not included in George W. Bush's original 'axis of evil' speech in January 2002. However, Syria's continued support for rejectionist organisations such as Hizballah and Hamas created tension. In June 2002 Bush warned that Syria 'must choose the right side in the war on terrorism by closing terrorist camps and expelling terrorist organisations'.[2] The Syrian regime opposed the US invasion of Iraq and backed Saddam Hussain.[3] They did so for economic reasons,[4] and in rejection of the principle of US-imposed 'regime change' in Arab countries. After the start of the invasion of Iraq in March 2003, tension rose further: while Bashar al-Assad expressed his confidence in popular resistance to the US occupation, the Bush administration started accusing Syria of channelling fighters into Iraq.[5] The most tangible effort at pressuring Syria came from Congress. In spring 2002 US legislators passed the Syria Accountability and Lebanese Sovereignty Act (SALSA), strongly supported by the pro-Israeli American Israel Public Affairs Committee (AIPAC). It threatened sanctions against Syria if it did not withdraw from Lebanon, give up its programme of weapons of mass destruction, and stop supporting terrorism. The Bush administration was opposed to the legislation because it did not want to jeopardise intelligence cooperation with Syria and wanted to keep the spotlight on Iraq.[6] The bill was eventually passed in October 2003 and signed in December.

The shift in US policy also affected intra-Arab relations. The US-led invasion of Iraq caused fear in Damascus and suspicion of the intentions of other Arab states. Saudi Arabia's reaction to the invasion was 'confused':[7] outward opposition was coupled with tacit approval and support, which could not have gone unnoticed in Damascus. Jordan's King 'Abdallah similarly counselled the USA against war but ended up giving covert and tacit support.[8] Bashar al-Assad condemned Arab cooperation with the US agenda for regime change in no uncertain terms.[9] The issue of Lebanese 'sovereignty' played only a minor role in the gestation of the US–Syrian rift. Some neoconservatives had identified Lebanon early in the Bush presidency as a pressure point against Syria, but did not yet call for regime change.[10] Even as late as February 2004, US officials interviewed by the International Crisis Group gave the restoration of Lebanese sovereignty a low priority in a list of demands from Syria, with Iraq and the Arab–Israeli conflict much higher up the list.[11] Calls for Lebanese sovereignty had a purely instrumental character for the Bush administration. Regarding the Syrian side of the rift, US pressure led Damascus to tighten its control over Lebanon, rather than loosen it. This curtailed the powers of Saudi ally Rafiq Hariri and threatened his grip on the Lebanese economy.

Lebanese politics, 2000–2004: rising opposition and Syrian reassertion

The Israeli withdrawal in 2000 revived the opposition to Syrian dominance in Lebanon, a trend which occurred along sectarian lines. Opposition was strongest among Christian political forces. In the 1990s the most prominent Christian leaders had been excluded from post-war politics because of their opposition to Syrian dominance, especially Michel Aoun, Amin Gemayel and Samir Geagea. Within his community, President Lahoud was seen as a Syrian client rather than an effective defender of Christian interests. This exclusion resulted in a sense of 'Christian frustration', which translated into an increasingly vocal opposition to the Syrian presence after the Israeli withdrawal. From September 2000 onwards the Maronite Patriarch Nasrallah Butrus Sfair called on Syrian troops to leave Lebanon.[12] A coalition of Christian politicians came together in the Qurnat Shahwan meeting in April 2001.[13] While they asserted that Israel was the biggest threat to Lebanon, they called for a Syrian withdrawal and a return of the army to South Lebanon, a move that would have curtailed Hizballah's room for manoeuvre.[14] The Patriarch supported their demands. Opposition to Syrian dominance broadened beyond the Christian community when Druze leader Walid Junblat also spoke out in favour of a 'reassessment' of relations with Syria in the autumn of 2000 and 'minimal parity in Lebanese–Syrian relations' in March 2001.[15] Junblat only returned to the Syrian fold in May 2002, after a reconciliatory meeting with vice president 'Abd al-Halim Khaddam.[16]

Non-sectarian voices such as the leftist journalist and academic Samir Qassir also started criticising Syrian meddling, but this did not change the fact that the fault-line of opposition or support for the Syrian position ran largely along sectarian lines. The biggest Shia movements continued to support Syria's presence in Lebanon: Hizballah benefited from Syria's support for its resistance strategy, while Amal's Nabih Birri relied on Damascus to ensure his influence in the troika and to contain his intra-communal rivals. Leading Sunni political and religious figures also remained loyal to Syria. Rafiq Hariri maintained that Syria's presence was vital to maintaining peace among Lebanon's confessional groups, while some Sunni religious figures attacked the Maronite Patriarch's critical stance vis-à-vis Damascus.[17] The likely success of anti-Syrian opposition should not be exaggerated. In June 2000 Lebanon's leading politicians flocked to Damascus to pledge allegiance to Bashar al-Assad at the funeral of Hafiz al-Assad.[18]

The Syrian regime responded to the opposition challenge with a mixture of repression and symbolic concessions. The Lebanese security apparatus was strengthened to confront Syria's opponents. This was directed by two individuals in particular: Lahoud ally Jamil al-Sayyid was promoted to become the head of the general security directorate, while Syria's military intelligence in Lebanon was headed by Rustum Ghazala from October 2002 onwards. Opposition activists were arrested or intimidated, especially journalists and student activists.[19] In August 2001 the period of legal detention before charge was extended from twenty-four to forty-eight hours.[20] In September 2002 Murr TV was closed down for being too critical of Syrian dominance in Lebanon.[21] Pressure was also exerted to keep LBC in line, the TV station previously associated with the Lebanese Forces.[22] Symbolic concessions included the occasional release of Lebanese detainees, a partial withdrawal of 6,000 Syrian troops from Beirut in June 2001, and in March 2002 the first state visit to Lebanon by a Syrian president since 1975 as a token of respect for Lebanese sovereignty.[23]

Hariri sat on the fence regarding Syria and the Lebanese opposition. On the one hand, he opposed Émile Lahoud's beefing up of the security services. Both Birri and Hariri repeatedly complained that the security services were tapping their phone-calls.[24] On the other hand, he was unable or unwilling to openly oppose Syrian-inspired authoritarian measures. Hariri continued to justify the Syrian military and intelligence presence, telling *Le Monde* in February 2001:

> The Syrians are here to help us. And when we no longer need their presence in Lebanon we will ask them to leave. But since the regional situation is what it is today, I think it is more important to think of the means to ensure security, stability and development in our country instead of having trouble with our brothers, friends and the Arab countries.[25]

Hariri also expressed hope for an opening in Syria itself, brought about by Bashar al-Assad's accession: 'The Syrian President clearly stated in the swearing in speech that he would modernize Syria, that he wanted to open the economy and make it competitive. He said that the Syrian relations with Lebanon were getting stronger. I think he is implementing what he has declared.'[26]

Hariri's reaction reveals a lot about his pragmatic attitude to authoritarianism. He accepted authoritarian practices as long as they furthered his political or economic agenda, for instance when he called on the army to confront trade union protests in 1996.[27] His allegiance was to the kingdom of Saudi Arabia, one of the most repressive regimes of the Middle East. Nor was he fundamentally opposed to Syrian authoritarian practices in Lebanon; he had condoned the post-war marginalisation of all anti-Syrian forces. He was criticised by international human rights organisations for his silence on the fate of Lebanese and Palestinians who had 'disappeared' during the civil war and were thought to be detained in Syrian jails.[28] After 2000 Hariri expressed unease with the authoritarian crackdown. He was unable to prevent the detention of journalists critical of the security establishment.[29] He failed to condemn a wave of arrests of anti-Syrian activists of Aoun's Free Patriotic Movement and Samir Geagea's Lebanese Forces in August 2001, while on a visit to Pakistan.[30] Hariri's comments in parliament are revealing: 'No one in the country wants to be prime minister in this climate. Legislation rules prohibit this amendment. But failure to vote [in favour of these measures] will create political problems the country can do without. So we will agree to the amendment even against my conviction.'[31] Another example is Hariri's silence on the closing down of Murr TV, a television channel critical of the Syrian presence.[32] Hariri's stance on the invasion of Iraq betrayed his awkward position vis-à-vis Syria. He mirrored the Saudi tactic of public condemnation coupled with tacit support. In September 2002 Hariri opposed military action: 'We and the rest of the Arab countries are all opposed to an American attack of Iraq ... because problems are not solved by using force. If Saddam Hussein does not respect UN resolutions, there are many ways to make him to do so—but not by an attack.'[33] In March 2003 Hariri was reported to have urged Sunni clerics from 'Akkar and Dinniya to distance themselves from violent anti-American protests against the Iraq invasion.[34]

The issue that determined Hariri's relations with Damascus most of all was his stance towards Hizballah. The prime minister was coming under increasing pressure from Washington to move against the Shia movement. Congress had blocked the disbursement of a $50 million financial aid package to Lebanon in May 2001 because of the Lebanese government's continued support for Hizballah.[35] Hariri rejected a list of US demands to the Lebanese government, put out after the 11 September attacks: disarming Hizballah, extraditing individuals wanted in the USA for their role in attacks on US interests in Lebanon in the 1980s—including Hizballah operative 'Imad Mughniyya—and freezing Hizballah assets in Lebanese banks.[36] Hariri asserted the continued legitimacy of Hizballah efforts to recover the Shib'a Farms, referring to Hizballah as 'the resistance'.[37] He also rejected the deployment of Lebanese troops in southern Lebanon prior to an Israeli withdrawal from the Shib'a Farms.[38] Hariri maintained that the terror suspects were not in Lebanon.[39] He also used his influence with French president Jacques Chirac to keep Hizballah off an official EU list of terrorist organisations.[40] Furthermore, finance minister Fu'ad Siniura refused to accede to US demands to freeze Hizballah's financial assets.[41]

Despite Hariri's continued support for Hizballah, he began to display public frustration with the militia. The tension between 'reconstruction' and 'resistance' became particularly intense after the Israeli withdrawal, when the Jewish state and the Shia militia were testing each other's limits. On 16 February 2001 Hizballah attacked an Israeli patrol on the Shib'a Farms—a day after Hariri had promised Jacques Chirac that there would be no 'provocation' of Israel from the Lebanese side.[42] Hariri met Lahoud and Assad and, in an unprecedented step, issued a statement criticising Hizballah and claiming sole authority for the government to regain occupied land.[43] He withdrew the statement after an emergency meeting with Hizballah leader Shaykh Hassan Nasrallah, but his frustration was now plain to see. In the meeting Hariri reportedly sought to persuade Nasrallah to coordinate his actions with those of the state. A similar incident occurred in April 2001, when Hariri's *Mustaqbal* newspaper criticised a Hizballah attack in a front-page editorial, asking: 'Can Lebanon bear an operation of this kind, with all its political, economic and social consequences? Was it wise to carry out this operation and does its timing suit the overall interest of Lebanon?'[44] Hariri faced Syrian anger, and Assad cancelled a meeting with the Lebanese premier. Over the following months Hariri urged Assad and Iranian president Muhammad Khatami to accord economic policy greater importance than resistance.[45] Relations between Hariri and Hizballah improved after April 2002, once the Shia movement reduced its attacks, but the fundamental tension between 'resistance' and 'reconstruction' persisted.

Hariri failed to win over either Damascus or its Lebanese opponents. The opposition complained about his continued horse-trading with the other troika members, Birri and Lahoud.[46] The Damascus regime, mean-while, was becoming increasingly suspicious of Hariri. Bashar al-Assad's rise to the presidency in the late 1990s had coincided with a curtailment of Hariri's room for manoeuvre, epitomised by the election of Émile Lahoud in 1998. For a regime that is highly sensitive to any challenge from Lebanon, Hariri's criticism of Hizballah must have represented a significant provocation. Another irritation was Hariri's invitation to Michel Aoun to return to Lebanon in 2001.[47] The general was in exile in France, and his followers represented the most vocal opposition to Damascus's policies in Lebanon. Hariri's alliance with Saudi Arabia and its lukewarm opposition to and tacit acceptance of the invasion of Iraq also marked the prime minister out as a possible threat.

Bashar al-Assad's policy was to curtail Hariri's power in Lebanon by supporting rival leaders, particularly President Lahoud and speaker Nabih Birri. In one newspaper interview Bashar al-Assad subtly suggested that he saw President Lahoud at the top of the pyramid within the troika, while taking a swipe at Hariri's claim to manage the economy:

> We, in Syria, like everyone else in the world, believe in the hierarchy of the state and it is only natural that the President of the republic is the head of this hierarchy. The head of the hierarchy does not represent only the

political or the economic aspects but all aspects. As a result all aspects of the Lebanese society culminate with the President of the republic.[48]

Syrian support for Lahoud resulted in the strengthening of the security agencies, controlled by Lahoud ally Jamil al-Sayyid. Nabih Birri was also bolstered vis-à-vis Hariri, most notably in a cabinet reshuffle of April 2003. Hariri was forced to drop key allies, while Birri and other close Syrian supporters were given extra posts.[49] By the latter half of 2003 Lahoud was indicating his desire for an extension of his presidential term, while Hariri was betting on an alternative president more open to his economic agenda. It was this dispute about presidential succession that was to dominate 2004.[50]

Hariri was also affected by internal Syrian politics. Rising US pressure affected dynamics within the regime. The reshuffling of regime personnel had started even before Hafiz al-Assad's death and in preparation for Bashar's accession. As a result, regime figures allied to Hariri were weakened. Three in particular lost the ability to influence Lebanese affairs, curtailing Hariri's ability for sympathetic Syrian policies: 'Abd al-Halim Khaddam, Hikmat Shihabi and Ghazi Kan'an. Both Shihabi and Khaddam were extremely close to, and trusted by, Hafiz al-Assad, and were members of the six-man committee charged with running affairs of state after Assad's heart attack in 1983. A third individual with ties to Hariri was the 'Alawi officer Ghazi Kan'an. He had been chief of Syrian military intelligence in Lebanon since 1982 and behaved like Assad's viceroy in the country, receiving Lebanese politicians in his base at the border town of 'Anjar in the Biqa' valley. Khaddam, Shihabi and Kan'an played important roles in policy-making in Damascus and were therefore attractive allies for Hariri. Hafiz al-Assad had tended to set the broad strategic outlines of policy, leaving his lieutenants to formulate the details. This had given Khaddam, Shihabi and Kan'an great scope for influencing Syria's Lebanon policy. Cultivating the goodwill of these three individuals was crucial for Hariri in maintaining good relations with Damascus in the 1980s and 1990s.

All three men were marginalised, either in preparation of Bashar al-Assad's succession or afterwards. The 'Lebanon file' was transferred from Khaddam to Bashar in 1998. Khaddam was often rumoured to harbour ambitions to succeed Hafiz al-Assad, but he did help to ensure a smooth takeover by Bashar. In 1998 Shihabi was removed from the post of chief of staff, in all likelihood because he opposed Bashar al-Assad's accession.[51] In June 2000, when Shihabi was staying in Hariri's mansion in Beirut to recover from medical treatment, news reached him that charges of embezzlement had been brought against him in Syria.[52] He left the country via Beirut airport, with Khaddam and Junblat seeing him off. Although he was allowed to return in July 2000, he remained marginalised. In October 2002 Ghazi Kan'an was promoted to the head of the political security directorate to oversee the crackdown on internal Syrian opposition. In October 2004 he was promoted to the post of minister of interior. While this gave him greater influence within Syria, it ended his role in shaping Syria's Lebanon policy. His position in Lebanon was taken up by Rustum Ghazala, previously the head of Syrian military intelligence in Beirut. Kan'an's departure weakened Hariri, while Ghazala's arrival strengthened Lahoud and his security apparatus, which enjoyed good relations with the Syrian official.[53]

'A very political economy':[54] Hariri attacks the militia leaders

To reiterate one of the underlying insights of this study, relations within Lebanon's confessional elite cartel are not just determined by sect or international politics, but also by economic interest. Lebanon's post-war economy was based on a bargain between Hariri and rival elites who had emerged from the civil war. First, he had to share neoliberal rents with his rivals, and secondly, 'service ministries', which could be used for patronage, were run by former militia leaders. The military and intelligence establishment around army commander and later president Émile Lahoud also took its share of government expenditure. This arrangement was unsustainable. Government overborrowing in particular pushed public finances ever deeper into debt. When Hariri returned as prime minister in 2000, Lebanon was facing financial crisis. Hariri resurrected rent-creation mechanisms he had originally created—reconstruction and government debt management. Meanwhile, Hariri and his technocrats were assaulting rent-creation mechanisms benefiting the former militia leaders and the military and intelligence establishment. All this occurred against a backdrop of rising tension between Syria and Lebanon's opposition, with Hariri in between. Hariri's liberalisation drive from 2000 to 2004 was motivated both by the desire to 'rescue' the Lebanese economy and to undercut the economic power of his political rivals.

Avoiding financial crisis

When Rafiq Hariri returned to the post of prime minister in October 2000, Lebanon was facing financial crisis. Although the Hariri team blamed the previous al-Huss government for the explosion of debt, the rent-creation mechanisms put in place during Hariri's first term in office from 1992 to 1998 actually contributed a greater share of the burden. The most important cause was government overborrowing, which stabilised the Lebanese currency but also pushed up debt-servicing cost.[55] Hariri allies at the head of the central bank and the finance ministry had been responsible for this policy. High government expenditure on reconstruction, 'service ministries' and military expenditure further contributed to recurrent deficits. Debt was held by domestic commercial banks and their depositors. The high concentration of deposits suggests that key investors, which had accumulated their wealth outside Lebanon, were controlling the bulk of government debt—including Hariri and his Banque Mediterranée. This elite effectively acted as a buffer between the Lebanese government and international financial markets. Much of Hariri's energy over the next few years was consumed by efforts to maintain the confidence of key investors. The fact that investors and policy-makers were closely networked with each other made this task easier, but Hariri had to keep guaranteeing government debt service and the convertibility of the Lebanese pound to US dollars. Hariri was trying to achieve this in a period when other countries were experiencing deep financial crises and trust in 'emerging markets' was low. In 2001 and 2002 banks were becoming increasingly reluctant to buy Lebanese-pound-denominated treasury bills, leaving the central bank to finance the government deficit. By June 2002 the central bank held a quarter of total treasury bills.[56] Similarly, dollarisation as measured by the value of deposits in US dollar as a percentage of the value of total deposits rose from a low of 61.0 per cent in March 2000 to a peak of 74.2 per cent in May 2002.[57] The roll-over of treasury bills denominated in Lebanese pounds depended on maintaining a high level of Lebanese pound deposits, with which banks could finance these purchases.

The central bank also faced increasing difficulties selling Eurobonds. The share of such debt denominated in foreign currency rose from 24.3 per cent of total government debt in May 2000 to 40.7 per cent in October 2002, just before the Paris II meeting.[58] Eurobonds tend to carry lower interest rates than treasury bills because investors do not face 'currency risk', the risk of devaluation. Yet, should such devaluation happen, the Lebanese government would be saddled with relatively higher debt in Lebanese pound terms. The IMF and central bank label Eurobonds as 'foreign debt' and 'external debt' respectively, although these bonds remain very much domestic because they are held by Lebanese commercial banks and investors. For instance, 75–80 per cent of a Lebanese Eurobond offering in July 2001 was said to have been bought by Lebanese investors, the rest by 'sympathetic Gulf investors'.[59] Eurobonds show up in the annual report of the Association of Lebanese Banks (ABL) as 'other government bills'. This category also includes 'certificates of deposit' from the central bank, of which more below. The value of 'other government bills' held by Lebanese commercial banks rose from LL903 billion in 1997 to LL7,894 billion in 2001.[60] Lebanese commercial banks and their depositors thus remained the main beneficiaries of the high interest payments that Lebanese government had to make. However, by the first half of 2002 the central bank had to buy Eurobonds worth $1.85 billion which investors did not want to take. It only managed to offload the bonds to unspecified Gulf and South East Asian investors after Hariri had personally lobbied 'leading figures' in these regions.[61]

The indicators for dollarisation, the central bank's difficulties in marketing Eurobonds and falling net foreign-exchange reserves show that by early 2002 creditors were considering abandoning the Lebanese pound. As one unnamed Lebanese financier put it in July 2001:

> Wealthy Lebanese already keep some money, their safety savings, in foreign banks. … As long as the perceived risk of government default is low they'll keep the bulk here. You'll know that has changed if and when you see capital flows out of the country. Then the merry-go-round will suddenly stop.[62]

Hariri's task was to keep the merry-go-round going. He did so by winning financial and political support from his foreign allies France and Saudi Arabia.

Lebanon was by no means unique in facing financial collapse. A wave of financial crises had enveloped developing countries from 1982 onwards, when Mexico indicated its inability to repay its debtors. The mainstream view of financial globalisation—capital account liberalisation—holds that it emerged spontaneously because it is more efficient.[63] An alternative view identifies financial globalisation itself as the cause of the crisis because 'hot money' injected into an economy can easily be withdrawn.[64] This increases volatility and the incidence of crises. Financial crises can have three possible outcomes. First, a country may manage to obtain unconditional funding and to restore 'confidence', in which case financial crisis is avoided. Secondly, if the country fails to restore confidence it may obtain a conditional bail-out, usually from the IMF. Thirdly, it can default and refuse to repay all or part of its debt. The first scenario is extremely rare, but it is what happened in the Lebanese case. The second scenario is the most common one. Creditors then benefit from IMF pressure on debtors to repay all or most of their debt, even at the cost of economic growth or social development. The third case is very rare, although Argentina in 2001 is a significant exception.

The relationship of the Lebanese government with four actors determined the outcome: with creditors; the IMF; the USA; and 'white knights'—a third party that may come to the rescue.[65] Debtors find it easier to maintain confidence if they face fewer creditors, and if the creditors are domestic rather than foreign. The IMF is more likely to lend support to restore confidence if a country's policy conforms to a neoliberal economic logic, especially if the country has a history of long engagement with the IMF, which therefore has a 'stake' in the success of a country's policy and stands to lose credibility if the country defaults. More importantly, the USA can exert pressure on IMF decisions, either for geostrategic reasons or to protect the interests of US investors. Finally, lenders other than the IMF can provide funds, acting as white knights. However, the IMF and the USA seek to fend off any challenges of the IMF's status as the lender of last resort for troubled economies.[66]

The Lebanese government faced a small number of predominantly domestic creditors: key depositors and the six largest commercial banks. This made it easier for Hariri to maintain investor confidence. However, indicators such as dollarisation, difficulties in marketing

Eurobonds and falling net foreign-exchange reserves suggested that investors were losing confidence. In September 2001 Hariri blamed pressures on the currency on malicious rumours spread by his political opponents:

> The national currency is stable. But its stability is shaken by political tensions. The current exchange rate of the Lebanese pound reflects reality, but during disputes in the past few days we heard from some media outlets that money is being transferred to outside Lebanon. … The report is untrue. … Politicians must also be attentive to the fact that differences of opinion can occur but the economy should not be used in discord, for example someone who is in conflict with Rafiq Hariri [should not] say the pound is going to collapse.[67]

In early 2001 Hariri set out his plans to bolster the currency and tackle the public debt, based on financing through Eurobonds rather than T-bills, raising new taxes such as VAT, privatisation, and encouraging economic growth by reducing red tape and lowering direct taxes.[68] The most important project, however, was to organise an international conference at which foreign donors would provide concessionary loans and thus cut the cost of debt-servicing. A first conference in Paris in February 2001 had brought together French president Jacques Chirac, European Commission president Romano Prodi and World Bank president James Wolfensohn, but only resulted in soft loans and grants worth $458 million.[69] Hariri suggested that the value of the new loans he was seeking at a second such conference was in the order of $5 billion.[70] Much of his energy was taken up by this project of organising Paris II, as the conference in November 2002 came to be known.

Hariri unsuccessfully sought to obtain IMF endorsement for the Paris II meeting. The Fund sent a representative but did not pledge any money, and thus signalled its disapproval for the government's plan. The IMF had no 'stake' in the success of Lebanon's currency peg. In other countries, such as Turkey and Argentina, the IMF had invested much of its credibility into the currency pegs in the 1990s and had therefore been prepared to prop up the fixed exchange rate regimes even when they were no longer salvageable.[71] The relationship with Lebanon had been much more hands-off, not least because the government had been borrowing primarily from domestic banks rather than international lenders. Mazin Hanna, an official in the prime minister's office who was closely involved in the IMF negotiations, describes Hariri's relationship with the IMF in these terms:

> Hariri was never interested in the IMF, except when he felt that he needed the IMF in order to solicit help for Lebanon and funding. When he found that he could not convince them of his argument, he simply decided, 'Okay, I'm going to pull a macro-assistance programme without the IMF'.[72]

The IMF's lukewarm reaction to Paris II was due in part to its recent experience in Argentina.[73] The Fund had unsuccessfully propped up the Argentinian dollar peg until late 2001, when the country was finally forced to devalue. The thinking of the IMF directors is expressed in its annual report on Lebanon in October 2001.[74] The report criticised Lebanon's 'stubbornly high fiscal deficit' and the US dollar peg, which made the economy less competitive. It also took a negative view of central bank purchases of T-bills. Significantly, however, the IMF directors were split on the merits of exchange rate devaluation.[75] Devaluation would have led to skyrocketing inflation, especially because a large proportion of goods consumed in Lebanon are imported. Furthermore, it would have meant a major loss of wealth by depositors and by banks. The IMF could be much bolder in suggesting that local Lebanese creditors take a 'haircut'—as the burden-sharing by creditors is called in IMF-speak—than if creditors had been from Wall Street, which exerts great influence on the IMF via its close relations with the US Treasury.

Hariri sought to convince the IMF that his economic policy programme conformed to the logic of neoliberal restructuring. Paris II was thus a major spur for the formal development of a coherent economic policy programme. Prior to his accession to the prime ministership Hariri had remained vague on his economic policy plans. He only said he would replace the 'contractionary' policy of the al-Huss government with a 'growth-oriented' programme.[76] In late 2000 the Hariri government published a first ten-point plan, which included privatisation, reducing customs barriers, joining the WTO, and an association agreement with the EU.[77] The actual list of policies with which Hariri sought to convince the IMF—and other international donors—to supply funds at Paris II was drawn up at the 'Paris I' conference in February 2001. As Hanna describes it:

And while no serious pledges were done at the time [of Paris I], at least there was an outline being provided at the time by the countries and institutions that will end up putting money into Lebanon. By drawing a … roadmap for us, saying that: 'If you want this money, this is what you should do.' And this is when, going back, Rafiq Hariri decided: 'Okay, we're going to put in a value added tax, we're going to go into the Euromed agreement, we're going to lower customs rates, we're going to prepare for privatisation, etc. etc.' And by the time Paris II occurred, all those prior actions, if you want, were already fulfilled.[78]

'Landmark' policies included the following: the 'Open Skies' policy liberalising air traffic at Beirut airport as well as a cut in customs duties in November 2000; the initialising of an association agreement with the EU in January 2002; launching VAT the following month; and restructuring the state-owned Middle East Airlines (MEA) for privatisation.[79]

In order to sell these policies to the IMF as suitable to 'outgrow' government debt, Hariri relied on a new set of technocrats. This second generation of Hariri technocrats was younger than the first generation (such as Fu'ad Siniura or Fadl Shalaq). While the first generation had previously worked for the Hariri companies, the second generation were recruited from international financial institutions such as the IMF to work in UNDP or World Bank-financed 'capacity-building' schemes in the Lebanese administration. Hariri's economic adviser Nadim Munla hired most of them, most importantly Bassil Fulayhan. The dynamics of network-building shaped Hariri's policies because the various elites attracted to his network brought their specific expertise and worldview to bear on the 'solutions' Hariri required. Bassil Fulayhan was the main Lebanese negotiator with the IMF, assisted by Mazin Hanna.[80] At times, the two men used Hariri's private jet to travel to important meetings.[81] In April 2002 Hariri himself travelled to Washington to meet representatives of the IMF, the World Bank and the US administration.[82] Hariri and his technocrats failed to sway key directors, including managing director Horst Köhler, the director of the Middle East department, Paul Chabrier, and deputy managing director Eduardo Aninat, who was responsible for the Lebanon file.[83]

As the most influential shareholder in the IMF, the USA could have pressed it to grant aid despite its economic assessment, as it had done in the case of Russia in 1998.[84] However, no such support from the USA was forthcoming; it sent a delegate to Paris II but did not pledge any aid. To the disappointment of the Lebanese, this US delegate was not a high-profile representative such as Secretary of State Colin Powell, but the much more junior Middle East peace envoy William Burns. Reportedly, the US stance discouraged Japan from pledging any financial aid, while other Western states such as Germany, the UK and Spain also abstained.[85] This stands in marked contrast with the 'Friends of Lebanon' meeting in 1996. It had been organised by the Clinton administration and resulted in pledges of $3 billion in direct financial aid by thirty donors.[86] In 1996 Hariri had just helped to negotiate an agreement which established formal rules of engagement between Hizballah and the Israeli forces, rules which helped keep any conflagration between the two parties to a minimum until the war of 2006. The Clinton administration was then still hopeful of negotiating a peace agreement between Syria and Israel, followed by a similar accord involving Lebanon. Taming Hizballah seemed merely a function of a deal with Damascus. The situation in 2002 was very different: the US outlook was now determined by hawkish neoconservatives.

Since Wall Street banks had no direct stake in Lebanon, the US government had little incentive to override the IMF's negative assessment. Furthermore, the status of Hizballah remained at the forefront of American thinking on Lebanon. Hariri denied that his refusal to cooperate with US demands to pressure Hizballah affected the American stance.[87] Despite Hariri's denials, there was a widespread assumption that the US would make the provision of financial aid at Paris II conditional on the Lebanese government taking concrete steps to rein in Hizballah.[88] In the end the IMF and the USA both declined to support Paris II beyond sending delegates to the conference.

The IMF and the USA were marginal to resolving Lebanon's financial crisis. In most critiques of neoliberalism and the management of financial crises the USA plays a central role as the driving force of financial globalisation, shaping the rules of global finance.[89] Secondly, a 'Wall Street–IMF–Treasury complex' is seen as manipulating developing-country debt crises to benefit US finance.[90] However, these insights are less relevant for cases of financial crisis where Wall Street has no direct stake—such as Lebanon. Criticism of global neoliberal finance must therefore go beyond the 'core' of global capitalism and pay more attention to how capitalism works at the periphery. The success of the

Paris II conference therefore depended on the support of two countries, France and Saudi Arabia, acting as white knights, who came to the rescue. They were the biggest donors, followed by other Gulf states and Malaysia. Lebanon received a total of $3 billion in concessionary loans and an additional $1.2 billion in project financing.[91] French support was crucial for organising the conference. As a major IMF shareholder, an EU member and a member of the G7 biggest industrialised economies, France had the clout to call such an international donor conference. Saudi Arabia's role was primarily financial: it provided the highest pledge at Paris II at $665 million, followed by France ($475 million) and the Gulf states Kuwait and the UAE as well as Malaysia ($285 million each), followed by Bahrain and Qatar ($190 million each).[92] French support for Paris II was due to Hariri's close relations with President Chirac. The French leader pursued an activist Middle East policy, and relied on local allies to formulate and realise this strategy. Among these local allies was Rafiq Hariri. The Lebanese billionaire had already started cultivating his relations with the French political class in the 1980s.[93] In 1979 he had acquired a large French contracting company when he bought Oger. Ever conscious of the symbolic value of real estate, Hariri also bought the former residence of Gustave Eiffel. Reflecting his status as a close ally of Saudi Arabia, he received diplomatic status as 'third councillor' at the Saudi embassy. Politically, Hariri proved 'helpful' to the French government. He was said to have contributed to freeing French hostages in Lebanon during Chirac's government from 1986 to 1988, gave $15 million to the Institut du Monde Arabe in Paris, and lent a strong hand to French investors in a collapsed Saudi bank.[94] Hariri built up a close relationship with Jacques Chirac.[95] Chirac supported Hariri's post-war policies, and in the 1990s repeatedly called on Christians to participate in public affairs to legitimise the post-war order while cold-shouldering the Christian leaders in exile in France, Michel Aoun and Amin Gemayel.[96] The greatest proof of close cooperation between the Chirac and Hariri administrations came in April 1996 during Israel's bombing of Lebanon, dubbed Grapes of Wrath, when French shuttle diplomacy helped end the crisis and established a set of rules between Israel and Hizballah. Hariri presented French involvement as a result of his international network of contacts.[97] Hariri and Chirac helped to further each other's agendas in the Middle East, and Chirac's view of Lebanon and the region was strongly influenced by Hariri.[98] The close relationship between Hariri and Chirac explains French support for Paris II. Even the timing of the conference was determined by France: Hariri had to await Chirac's re-election in April 2002.

The second white knight was Saudi Arabia. The reason for the kingdom's involvement was its long-standing support for Hariri's policies in Lebanon. In order to understand the importance of this Saudi action, we must turn to an IMF working paper published in 2008.[99] The authors were trying to understand how Lebanon had avoided financial crisis despite extremely high government debt. The reasons they identify are a 'dedicated' investor base consisting of Lebanese depositors and the perception by both commercial banks and depositors of an 'implicit guarantee' from donors or international financial institutions.[100] While not explicitly linking this guarantee to Saudi Arabia, the report repeatedly mentions the Saudi and Kuwaiti deposits to the central bank during the 2006 war, thus suggesting that Saudi Arabia is the source of the guarantee.[101] Paris II in November 2002 was of course important in creating the perception of such an 'implicit guarantee' from the Gulf countries. Other important episodes were a Saudi deposit of $600 million with the Lebanese central bank at a lenient interest rate in 1998.[102] Even more crucial was Saudi involvement in buying up $1 billion worth of Eurobonds that Lebanese banks had refused to purchase in April 2002.[103] This was the turning point, after which dollarisation receded. The share of US dollar deposits in total deposits declined steadily from a peak of 74.2 per cent in May 2002 to 66.1 per cent in February 2004, when the dispute over the presidential succession affected investor confidence.[104] The Eurobond purchase of April 2002 and the 'implicit guarantee' that came with it represented the end of a journey for Lebanon's political economy—a journey into financial dependency on Saudi Arabia: only the kingdom's 'implicit guarantee' kept the merry-go-round of government borrowing going. Lebanon is therefore a particularly stark example of the position of non-oil Arab states as 'second-order rentiers' in a state of dependency on the rentier oil monarchies of the Gulf.[105] The implications for Lebanese domestic politics are enormous: Saudi Arabia stood between Lebanon and financial crisis, and thus gained a say in Lebanese politics.

From 2002 onwards—at a time when Syria and Iran were emerging as Saudi Arabia's main opponents both in the region and in the Lebanese arena—Lebanon's economic dependence provided the kingdom with leverage over the very heart of the country's economy.

As soon as Paris II had been concluded, all the relevant measures of financial stress improved. Interest rates on two-year treasury bonds fell from 14.6 per cent in October 2002 to 9.4 per cent in December 2002, and further to 8.0 per cent in November 2003.[106] Dollarisation had been receding since April 2002, when Saudi Arabia had signalled its 'implicit guarantee' by buying Eurobonds. After Paris II the share of dollar deposits continued to fall further. Paris II had a salutary effect on interest rates for private-sector borrowers. Interest rates on Lebanese-pound-denominated loans from Lebanese commercial banks fell from 16.3 per cent in October 2002 to 10.4 per cent in January 2005.[107] Interest rates on US dollar loans continued their decline, which had started in early 2000. Yet despite the decline in interest rates, provision of credit to the private sector actually stagnated after November 2002, while public-sector debt continued to rise and Lebanese banks started lending abroad.[108] The central bank continued buying treasury bills and, in November 2003, a year after Paris II, it held exactly a third of those in circulation.[109] The central bank continued financing these purchases by selling certificates of deposit (CDs) to commercial banks.[110] The banks and their depositors did have to accept a reduction in profits after Paris II. The government reached a deal with Lebanon's commercial banks to reschedule government debt. The banks agreed to exchange the equivalent of the value of 10 per cent of their deposit base into non-interest-bearing bonds of a maturity of two years. The combined interest received from treasury bills and other government bills (which includes Eurobonds and treasury bills), and bonds and financial instruments with fixed income (which include CDs) fell from $2.2 billion in 2002 to $1.8 billion in 2005, with the share of bonds and financial instruments with fixed income rising.[111] The prize for keeping the merry-go-round going was to slow it down.

Lebanon managed to avoid financial crisis for two reasons: first, because of the small creditor base of key Lebanese investors, who acted as a buffer between the Lebanese government and global financial markets; secondly, because France and Saudi Arabia were willing to act as white knights who provided financing at concessionary rates. The USA did not support Paris II beyond a token presence because Wall Street banks had little stake in Lebanese debt and because the Lebanese government was unwilling to move against Hizballah. Similarly, the IMF disagreed with the Hariri government over the feasibility of sustaining the currency peg, which appeared dangerously similar to the failed Argentinian and Turkish pegs. The IMF had no stake in Lebanon because relations had previously been at arm's length. The Fund did not provide any funding at Paris II. The 'implicit guarantee' provided by Saudi Arabia gave the kingdom great leverage over Lebanon's 'very political economy'.

Saving Solidere

Hariri worked hard to salvage rent-creation from government debt. He also revived reconstruction. After Salim al-Huss had succeeded Hariri as prime minister, Hariri ally Nabil al-Jisr was removed as head of the CDR.[112] Hariri loyalist Nicolas Saba was replaced as governor (*muhafiz*) of Beirut. Solidere began complaining about delays in construction permits, which unnerved investors.[113] In 1999 the company reported that profits had fallen by 30 per cent, and in 2000 it recorded losses.[114] All this changed when Hariri returned to the post of prime minister. In December 2001 Hariri protégé Jamal 'Itani became CDR president.[115] Birri's brother left the CDR board of directors, reducing the speaker's ability to influence the agency's policy. Solidere's net profits climbed sharply from $1.9 million in 2001 to $42 million in 2002.[116] Major projects, such as a giant shopping centre, were finally approved.[117] Regulation was liberalised: a new property-ownership law was passed in 2001, removing restrictions on non-nationals owning property.[118] Solidere could market properties directly to Gulf Arabs, an opportunity which Hariri enthusiastically advertised in the Gulf media.[119] The powers of the CDR were bolstered. It became the exclusive conduit of foreign-financed reconstruction projects and its funding was increased.[120] This was particularly important because foreign funding became Hariri's preferred means for financing major infrastructure projects, with $1.2 billion in project financing pledged at Paris II.[121]

Attacking 'service ministries'

Hariri salvaged the rent-creation mechanisms that he controlled and from which he benefited most: reconstruction and government debt. However, he attacked those mechanisms that primarily benefited his opponents. This led to struggles within the troika of president, prime minister and speaker: first, with Nabih Birri, the speaker, who was a former militia leader and derived patronage resources from his control of 'service ministries' as well as several state-controlled enterprises; and secondly, President Emile Lahoud, who sought to appropriate state resources on behalf of the military and intelligence establishment and to deny investment opportunities to Hariri. Both Birri and Lahoud were close allies of the Syrian leadership. The conditions attached to Paris II became a weapon in Hariri's arsenal: privatisation, the introduction of VAT, reducing government expenditure, removing trade restrictions and liberalising markets. Hariri tried to cut expenditure on 'service ministries' and on security and defence. Such cuts to spending ministries—particularly welfare—are a hallmark of neoliberal fiscal policy. The 'three presidents' struggled over spending by the Council of the South, which was Birri's fief, and expenditure of military and security agencies, which was Lahoud's main concern.

Privatisation was particularly controversial because it revealed very different visions about the role of the state. These alternative visions were linked to the means by which Hariri, Lahoud and Birri accessed rents in the post-war economy. Hariri's privatisation programme was designed to create investment opportunities for members of the new contractor bourgeoisie such as himself, who had access to the necessary funding and the expertise to buy up state enterprises. Lahoud was concerned with maintaining state control over strategic industries such as telecommunications because he associated his power with the state machinery. As a former militia leader serving a popular base, Birri regarded state-owned companies as means to extend patronage to his followers. Hariri clashed with Lahoud over telecommunications and with Birri over Middle East Airlines (MEA). In the case of MEA, Hariri's privatisation plans undermined his rivals' access to rent, while opening new opportunities for rent-creation and rent-appropriation for private investors such as himself. In the case of mobile telecommunications, Lahoud was keen to curtail Hariri's ability to privatise rent previously appropriated by the state. Hariri's privatisation drive was therefore deeply political.

The biggest bone of contention was the fate of mobile telecommunications. While Hariri advocated their full privatisation, Lahoud wanted the state to retain control of mobile-phone revenues. In the end, Lahoud's position prevailed. Two companies—Libancell and Cellis—had received ten year build–operate–transfer (BOT) contracts to run the mobile-phone network from 1994 to 2004. France Telecom owned two-thirds of Cellis while the brothers Taha and Najib Miqati owned the rest.[122] The brothers belonged to the 'new contractor bourgeoisie', having acquired wealth in Gulf contracting and a wartime analogue mobile-phone network in Lebanon.[123] Najib Miqati used his position to enter politics, and from 1998 to 2004 he was minister of transport and public works. Lebanon's other mobile-phone operator, Libancell, was majority-owned by the Dalloul Group, controlled by 'Ali and Nizar Dallul.[124] They are the sons of Muhsin Dallul, defence minister from 1992 to 1998 and a prominent member of the Lebanese National Movement during the civil war and a close ally of Syria.[125] 'Ali Dallul is married to a stepdaughter of Rafiq Hariri.[126] The original BOT contracts of 1994 were symptomatic of the way in which the new contractor bourgeoisie, and those linked to civil-war movements, were appropriating rents created in Lebanon's post-war economy. Despite the close network between political elite and mobile-phone operators, the relationship between government and companies tended towards conflict. Both the Hariri and al-Huss governments imposed various charges on the mobile-phone companies and turned down offers to convert the ten-year BOT contracts into twenty-year operating licences.[127] The Hariri government unilaterally cancelled the original BOT in June 2001 hoping it could raise more money from other bidders.[128] These hopes were not fulfilled. The global IT bubble had just burst and the government failed to attract a bidder for the licences. It had to reinstate Cellis and Libancell and resume negotiations with them.[129]

Lahoud and Hariri disagreed over the fate of the mobile-phone licences. The president argued that the state should 'recover' the operations of the mobile-phone companies, thus effectively nationalising them.[130] In contrast, Hariri sought complete privatisation. What was at stake were the large profits of the duopoly. In 1998 revenue from mobile-phone operations reached $440 million.[131] The government also took a cut from the mobile-phone operators. World Bank calculations suggest that government income from telecommunications amounted to LL650 million, or 13.9 per cent of total government revenue, in 2001.[132] Lahoud's proposal won out despite a deal between Hariri and Lahoud brokered in April 2002.[133] The telecommunications ministry was controlled by Jean-Louis Qurdahi, an ally of the president. He was in a position to veto any of Hariri's privatisation plans. The existing operators left the sector: Najib Miqati sold his stake in Cellis to France Telecom, while 'Ali Dallul said he would not seek a new licence. In December 2002 the mobile-phone companies formally transferred their assets to the state, opening the way for tenders to be put up for auction in January 2003.[134] A turning point was reached in the cabinet reshuffle of April 2003, when Hariri was forced to retain Qurdahi as telecommunications minister. In September 2003 the cabinet approved the telecommunication minister's proposal to let two private companies run formally state-owned mobile-phone networks, rather than privatising them by granting them operating licences.[135] Lahoud's design to reassert state control over the mobile-phone networks had defeated Hariri's privatisation plans. Hariri had hoped to open up new opportunities for investment and capturing rent. Lahoud's aim was to channel the rents from the mobile-phone operators to the state. This betrayed fundamentally different visions of the state and the division of economic power: while Hariri's plans would have strengthened the new contractor bourgeoisie or foreign investors, Lahoud sought to beef up the machinery of the state, the executive of which he headed. Not only was Hariri's neoliberalisation drive checked by the failure to privatise the mobile-phone networks, Lahoud even managed to roll the process back and to extend state control over the industry. Subsequently, state income from telecommunications rose to LL1,310 billion in 2004, equivalent of 17.4 per cent of government revenue.[136]

While Hariri faced opposition from Lahoud in the field of telecommunications, he was also in dispute with Birri, over the privatisation of national carrier MEA. The company was potentially highly profitable because of Lebanon's expanding tourism sector. Hariri wanted to sell the company to a private investor which would restore profitability by

cutting staff. Birri had used control of MEA to provide jobs for his followers, and was keen to defend their interests. This basic difference in
outlook coloured the conflict over MEA's future. Few companies have
mirrored the fortunes of Lebanon's bourgeoisie like MEA. It was
founded in 1945 by members of Beirut's pre-war bourgeoisie, including
Sa'ib Salam and a relative of Salim al-Huss. The owners used their political and business contacts in the Gulf and the USA to establish MEA as a
major regional airline.[137] However, in 1961 Yussuf Baydas gained majority ownership of MEA. The Palestinian–Lebanese owner of Intrabank
belonged to a new bourgeoisie that was challenging Lebanon's established business families during the Shihabist era (1958–70). MEA was a
symbol of Baydas's arrival at the centre of Lebanon's business life. The
bank collapsed in 1966 because key depositors had turned against
Baydas, and the Lebanese government and central bank were unwilling
to prop up the arriviste businessman. The bank became a state-owned
holding company, Intra Invest. In the 1980s Roger Tamraz ran Intra and
unsuccessfully sought to gain control of MEA on behalf of businessmen
networked around Kata'ib and the Lebanese Forces.[138]

In 1996 the chairman of Intra Investment Company was Mahmud
Skayni, an ally of Nabih Birri.[139] A former militia leader had thus gained
control of the holding company, including its 62.5 per cent stake in
MEA. However, MEA was in financial difficulties and required fresh
capital.[140] The central bank eventually provided $179 million and
received 90 per cent of the share capital in return, leaving Intra with 9
per cent and Air France with 1 per cent.[141] Intra's shareholding in MEA
and hence its influence had been diluted. In political terms this was a
defeat for Birri and a victory for Hariri: while Intra was headed by
Birri's ally Skayni, central bank governor Riyadh Salameh was close to
Hariri.[142] The prime minister also gained greater operational influence
on the company in 1997, when MEA chairman Khalid Salam was found
to have accepted commissions for an extremely unfavourable aircraft-
leasing deal with Singapore.[143] Salam was replaced with Muhammad
al-Hut, a former central bank employee who would later be close to
Sa'd Hariri's Future Movement.[144] The struggle over MEA reveals fundamentally different conceptions of the Lebanese economy held by
Nabih Birri and Rafiq Hariri. The former militia leader needed it as a
patronage instrument to provide jobs to his clientele. As a result MEA

suffered a huge wage bill. In 2001 it employed 4,500 people, including 160 pilots, to operate nine aircraft.[145] In 1996 the company lost $50 million because of Israel's attacks during Grapes of Wrath but also because of mismanagement.[146] Many employees had received their jobs as a favour from Birri.[147] The logic of Lebanese politics required that the speaker defend the workers' interests. In contrast, Hariri had an eye on MEA's potential as a profit-making concern, which meant that the company had to shed workers to prepare it for privatisation.

After Hariri returned to the post of prime minister in 2000, he tackled MEA. In March 2001 Birri reportedly agreed to its privatisation in return for increased funding for the Council of the South, his main patronage vehicle.[148] The patronage resources taken away from him at MEA would be given back through the Council. Plans were drawn up to make 1,300 of the company's 4,500 staff redundant, using a $60 million loan from the World Bank to compensate them.[149] Birri's acquiescence to MEA restructuring allowed rival movements to court Amal supporters among the airline's staff. Hizballah organised strikes and protests in defence of MEA's predominantly Shia workforce.[150] 'Ali Qansu from the Syrian Socialist Nationalist Party (SSNP) used his position as labour minister to protect the workers, hinting that the choice of redundancies could be decided along sectarian lines.[151] Worse, Birri felt that Hariri had broken the promises made in March 2001: in late 2001 Hariri proposed cutting funds for the Council of the South rather than increasing them.[152] In the end, 1,280 employees were sacked, while 740 were shifted to affiliate companies. In 2002 MEA recorded a slim profit of $3 million, its first in twenty-five years.[153] While Hariri protégé al-Hut managed to cut the MEA workforce and rationalise the route network, actual privatisation was thwarted by Hariri's opponents.

Birri and Hariri were engaging in a similar tussle over Electricité du Liban (EDL), where Hariri sought to privatise profits while Birri defended the interests of his clientele. The company had managed to maintain operations throughout the war, but by the end it had insufficient generating capacity, and no up-to-date customer records. Hariri's reconstruction drive raised generating capacity from 700 MW in 1990 to 2,315 in 2002, but the company never recovered the ability to collect payment for electricity provided.[154] Only 55 per cent of electricity produced was actually paid for, according to a parliamentary report from 2001.[155] Estimates of EDL's debt ranged from $1 billion to $2 billion.[156] The beneficiaries of free electricity included a wide range of groups, prompting George Corm, finance minister from 1998 to 2000, to call EDL 'the cave of Ali Baba and the 40 thieves'.[157] Birri was one of the politicians whose clientele had an interest in preventing the privatisation of EDL. Hariri had promised privatisation of the power sector at Paris II, but EDL was never actually privatised and remained in financial crisis, resulting in frequent power cuts.[158] The saga of EDL illustrates the conflicting agendas of Hariri and Birri: to privatise state enterprises to encourage profit, or to retain them for patronage.

Persistent poverty

Hariri's second neoliberalisation drive, from 2000 to 2004, left the mechanisms intact by which poverty, deprivation and inequality were reproduced: regressive taxation and 'crowding out' of credit, and reduced access to health and education services. The tax system became even more regressive than it already was. Indirect taxation is considered highly regressive because lower-income households tend to spend a greater share of their incomes on consumption and are hit disproportionally hard by VAT. Direct taxation was extremely low in Lebanon. The Hariri government introduced VAT in February 2002.[159] In neoliberal economic theory it is regarded as an easy way to raise revenue while not 'distorting' incentives by taxing those who aspire to high incomes. VAT was meant to compensate for cuts in customs tariffs linked to the signing of an EU association agreement.[160] By 2004 VAT accounted for 23.5 per cent of total government revenue, including grants.[161]

Commercial bank lending to the government 'crowded out' investment for private businesses, especially in agriculture, industry and among small and medium-sized enterprises (SMEs). This trend continued after Paris II, despite a drop in interest rates. The rate on two-year treasury bills fell from 14.6 per cent in October 2002 to 8.0 per cent in November 2003; the rate on Lebanese-pound-denominated loans fell from 16.3 per cent to 11.7 per cent over the same period.[162] The problem of insufficient lending to private-sector businesses remained. Claims on the private sector actually fell from 87.7 per cent of GDP in

December 2000 to 74.2 per cent in December 2004.[163] Lebanon's commercial banks diversified away from lending to the public sector, but did not necessarily lend to private businesses. Banks preferred to expand by providing loans to consumers: credit to individuals increased from 11.9 per cent to 16.1 per cent of total credit between 2000 and 2004.[164] Another strategy was to expand abroad. The value of foreign assets of Lebanese commercial banks increased from 50.8 per cent of GDP in December 2002 to 63.1 per cent in December 2004.[165] The underdeveloped banking sectors in Arab economies such as Egypt, Jordan and Syria provided attractive arenas for expansion. In short, industry and agriculture—and particularly SMEs—continued to suffer from a shortage of credit.[166]

The lack of credit for those businesses and sectors that create employment perpetuated poverty and inequality in income and access to education and health services. A follow-up to the 1998 study of living conditions did find that the percentage of households suffering from deprivation had fallen from 30.9 per cent to 24.6 per cent between 1995 and 2004, with severe deprivation reduced from 6.8 per cent to 5.2 per cent.[167] However, a closer look at the results revealed the failure to tackle poverty in post-war Lebanon. Measures of educational deprivation improved by default: an older generation of Lebanese, among whom illiteracy was more common, had passed away.[168] Great inequalities in educational provision and intense competition for more prestigious private education persisted. The report revealed failings in areas that had been a priority of post-war reconstruction: the increased usage of bottled water as the main source of drinking water from 5.1 per cent to 32.0 per cent suggested that the provision of drinking water was insufficient, even after massive investment in the sector.[169] Income-related indicators actually show a rise in deprivation: the dependency ratio—the number of persons employed in proportion to the number of household members—increased from 25.0 per cent to 31.6 per cent, reflecting the limited availability of employment opportunities.[170] The first report that used reliable measures of household income to measure poverty in Lebanon found that 28 per cent of the Lebanese population lived in poverty in 2004, while nearly 8 per cent lived in extreme poverty.[171] This confirmed the impression of earlier estimates in the 1990s. Persistent poverty and inequality in income and opportunities provided the continued basis for clientelist practices. Hariri continued expanding his foundation, opening new health centres.

The political sociology of neoliberalism, 2000–2004

Rafiq Hariri's second neoliberalisation drive saw Hariri and his technocrats engage in a struggle with former militia leaders and the military and intelligence establishment. The different types of elites followed different economic logics: creating rents for the new contractor bourgeoisie; and appropriating rents as patronage resources respectively. The struggle over the restructuring of the state also continued. Hariri and his technocrats sought privatisation of state-controlled enterprises, trade liberalisation, continued control of debt management and an intensification of the Solidere project. Former militia leaders—especially Nabih Birri—fought against privatisation. President Lahoud opposed the privatisation of the mobile-phone network because state control over this cash cow conformed to his neo-Shihabist vision of a 'strong' state. Hariri managed to preserve two rent-creation mechanisms, which he had put in place and from which he benefited through his investment in finance and construction: government debt and reconstruction. The Paris II conference, at which Saudi Arabia and France came to the rescue of an ailing Lebanese economy, was the greatest success during these years. The rent-creation mechanisms that Hariri attacked were controlled by his political opponents: the spending of service ministries and state-controlled enterprises. He was only moderately successful in his campaign. He did maintain control of government debt management, rescued the Solidere project, and managed to restructure some state-owned enterprises, such as MEA. However, widespread privatisation eluded him. Similarly, he never managed to cut spending to the extent he would have liked.

In designing the policies of his first premiership, between 1992 and 1998, Hariri had relied on a 'first generation' of technocrats drawn from employees of his construction company Oger and from his banks. They included key figures such as Fadl Shalaq and Fu'ad Siniura. The policies of the second neoliberalisation drive of 2000 to 2004 were developed by a 'second generation' of Hariri technocrats, most importantly Bassil Fulayhan, who was minister of economy, trade and industry between 2000 and 2003. A comparison of these two generations of technocrats reveals different ways in which neoliberal technocratic expertise can be 'political' and the different ways in which such technocratic elites are 'politicised'. The first-generation technocrats were more obviously 'political' because they had been Hariri's employees, and some of them had even had close personal relationships with him. The best example is Fu'ad Siniura's joint political activism with Hariri in the Arab Nationalist Movement. The second generation was drawn from the IMF and World Bank. They considered themselves more purely 'technocratic' and 'non-political'. Initially, they tended to be interested in neoliberalism as an economic rather than a political project. Few of them actually joined Lebanese politics as part of the 'Hariri camp', in the way the first-generation technocrats had. However, because they were pushing neoliberalism as an economic project, they inevitably became associated with Hariri's political project. This meant that, eventually, they came to openly associate themselves with the billionaire politician.

After becoming prime minister for the first time in 1992, Hariri had tried to reform the government bureaucracy by removing 5,600 civil servants, a move which was considered by some politicians as an attack on their personal power-base;[172] 3,000 government employees were indeed removed, but further 'retrenchment' proved impossible.[173] Hariri therefore drove forward the hiring of Lebanese finance experts who had experience in international financial institutions. They were to bolster the institutions that Hariri relied on to develop and implement neoliberal rent-creation mechanisms: the central bank and the Ministry of Finance. One of the new technocrats was Muhammad Shatah. He left the IMF in 1993 to become deptuty governor of the central bank, and he describes Hariri's thinking thus:

> Of course Hariri was a product of the Lebanese diaspora, he had worked in Saudi Arabia. … There were two Lebanons, there were two countries: there were Lebanese abroad, in New York, in London, IMF, Riyadh and Dubai. And there was the Lebanon that stagnated for fifteen years. Professionals had left the country, and the bureaucracy had hardly any skills. So it was natural for him to look for those types. And he … in '92, '93 … every time there was a vacancy—again, the central bank is important … he reached out and hired people basically from abroad, ready to come back or who had just come back.[174]

Just as the Gulf city had been the 'benchmark' for Hariri's vision of neoliberal urbanism, the finance expert from the IMF or the World Bank was his benchmark for a successful bureaucracy. Initially, the main function of the second-generation technocrats in the 1990s was not overtly 'political' in the sense of occupying cabinet posts, it was 'technical' in that they strengthened the ministries and agencies of the 'right hand' of the state. They improved the functioning of the Ministry of Finance, the prime minister's office and the central bank, institutions which were the instruments for implementing neoliberal rent-creation mechanisms.

Since Hariri had failed to reform the civil service by sacking employees, he encouraged the creation of parallel structures with the help of the World Bank and the United Nations Development Programme (UNDP). The initiative for implanting young Lebanese technocrats from international financial institutions in the Lebanese state machinery came from Hariri ally Fu'ad Siniura.[175] Hariri's economic adviser, Nadim Munla, helped recruit several Lebanese who were working at the IMF. Munla provided a link between the two generations: he had worked as a senior manager at the Hariri-owned Mediterranée Investors Group in the 1980s before joining the IMF.[176] In the early 1990s Munla returned to Lebanon as an adviser to Hariri and Fu'ad Siniura. At that time he started recruiting other Lebanese finance experts. For instance, he persuaded Bassil Fulayhan to return to Lebanon to assist the reform of the finance ministry. Fulayhan had been educated at AUB and Yale and obtained a Ph.D. from Columbia University before becoming an adviser to the Saudi executive director at the IMF in 1988.[177] In 1993 Munla invited him to head a UNDP-financed project at the finance ministry, which was concerned with improving customs administration and tax collection, managing the public finances and debt.[178] Fulayhan then designed a project financed by the UNDP and the World Bank, the aim of which was to reform customs administration, the cadastre and land registration, and tax administration.[179]

While Munla was overtly 'political', most other technocrats who returned to Lebanon sought to avoid politicisation. Mazin Hanna—himself a second-generation technocrat who assisted Fulayhan in relations with the IMF—stresses that Fulayhan regarded his role as non-political and sought to distance himself from any factions:

A person like Bassil Fulayhan would not have worked in Lebanon at the time had he not had a UN umbrella to work under. So you had people who were careful to come into the administration but work under a project. ... I mean, obviously [the Lebanese] administration could not afford them. Second, they were not political people, so they did not want to be politically labelled as this group or that group. Working for the World Bank or the UNDP, was ... you know, you become a kind of consultant, international consultant, without the stigma of being [with] this or that person. Because these projects would continue regardless of who's prime minister and who is minister, etc.[180]

Hanna argues that Fulayhan 'admired Rafiq Hariri but he admired him at a distance' and that 'in '92, '93, '94, '95, Bassil was not perceived as a Hariri person'.[181] Despite this desire for 'insulation', Fulayhan's work at the finance ministry was deeply political: the civil service reforms that he implemented were so closely linked to Hariri that he became associated with the billionaire's camp by default. Fulayhan caught Hariri's attention in 1994, and the prime minister started consulting him on policy issues.[182]

When Hariri stepped down as prime minister in 1998 technocrats such as Fulayhan came under pressure to leave due to their association with the businessman.[183] According to Hanna, the new finance minister, George Corm, did not trust Fulayhan because of his association with Hariri. Hanna maintains that Fulayhan was made to feel 'uncomfortable' and was urged to resign. Other second-generation technocrats also resigned, such as Hanna himself. The distrust of the al-Huss administration is a sign that the second-generation technocrats had become associated with Hariri, even if they flaunted their technocratic and non-political credentials and operated under the 'umbrella' of the UNDP or World Bank. They came to be associated with the 'Hariri camp' not because of an explicit alliance with the businessman-prime minister but because they were pushing the neoliberal restructuring of the state, a project that strengthened Hariri. Ironically, the rejection by Corm and al-Huss pushed Fulayhan to ally himself politically to Hariri. After resigning from the finance ministry he started working directly for Hariri. As Hanna puts it: 'Bassil took a leap at the time, of moving from this, if you want, international consultant profile that he had, into a more political, close collaborative to Hariri.'[184]

This politicisation of 'apolitical' neoliberal technocrats through politicians is not unique to Lebanon. The economist Dani Rodrik has described the politicisation of supposedly non-political and technocratic economists:

> When I wrote my monograph 'Has Globalization Gone Too Far?' I had been surprised at some of the reaction. ... I expected of course that many policy advocates would be hostile. But my arguments were, or so I thought, based solidly on economic theory and reasoning. A distinguished economist wrote back saying 'you are giving ammunition to the barbarians.' In other words, I had to exercise self-censorship lest my arguments were used by protectionists! The immediate question I had was why this economist thought barbarians were only on one side of the debate. Was he unaware of how, for example, multinational firms hijacked pro-free trade arguments to lobby for agreements—such as intellectual property—that had nothing to do with free trade? Why was it that the 'barbarians' on one side of the issue were inherently more dangerous than the 'barbarians' on the other side?[185]

Rodrik's comment points to a tendency among mainstream economists, inclined as they are towards free markets, to ignore the rent-seeking and market distortions of corporations or politicians who support neoliberalism. The Hariri technocrats saw Hariri as an ally against anti-market 'barbarians' such as former militia leaders and the Syrian regime. In the process, they turned a blind eye to his monopolistic tendencies. The apolitical neoliberal technocrats of Lebanon regarded Hariri as a vehicle for realising their economic ideas, based on orthodox neoclassical economics. The relationship between politician and technocrat thus embodies the relationship of neoliberalism as an economic orthodoxy with a political project of asserting class power.

Fulayhan and other second-generation technocrats were crucial in developing and implementing the second neoliberalisation drive. While Hariri was out of office from 1998 to 2000, he did not put forward concrete economic policy proposals. Instead, he simply promised to present a plan developed by 'a coherent, unified, and enlightened economic team that does not yearn for the obsolete policies of the 1950s and 1960s, and is capable of confidently and vigorously interacting with the rest of the world'.[186] This describes the second-generation technocrats well, especially Fulayhan, who stood on Hariri's Beirut list in the 2000 parliamentary elections and was minister of economy and trade from 2000 to 2003. In this capacity he managed relations with the IMF, the EU and the WTO.[187] Fulayhan was also the main architect of the policy proposals presented to the Paris I and Paris II meetings in 2001 and 2002, which provided the framework for Hariri's second neoliberalisation drive of 2000–4.[188] Fulayhan was the main source of ideas for this, and he was the technocrat mediating between the Lebanese and the international scene.

Sectarian identity seems to have been less important for the second generation of Hariri technocrats than it had been for the first. Bassil Fulayhan was a member of Lebanon's small Protestant community. He sustained heavy burns from the bomb that killed Rafiq Hariri in February 2005. While he was fighting for his life in a French hospital, the business magazine *Lebanon Opportunities* published a plea for his recovery, which contrasts Fulayhan's rise due to expertise with the personal ties of the first generation:

> Praying for Basil Fulayhan: Professor, economist, consultant, politician, technocrat, friend, and now warrior. He never worked for Saudi Oger, not a Sunni, not from Saida, didn't go to school with Rafik Hariri, but was an academic and consultant of an international organisation. Still, he was the right hand man of Hariri, and his economic confidant. Basil defied much of the mythical conventional wisdom and climbed to the top. His political career was almost a miracle, breaking the confessional taboo, to become one of the top ministers in the country.[189]

Assassination

Rafiq Hariri's time as prime minister after 2000 was highly frustrating for the businessman-politician. While he managed to avoid financial crisis and revived reconstruction, his opponents in the troika were blocking privatisation and expenditure cuts. More ominously, the rising tension between the USA and Syria was undermining Hariri's relationship with the Damascus regime. The Syrian regime was increasingly suspicious of Arab governments allied to the USA—including Saudi Arabia. Hariri was being drawn into the confrontation between Syria and the USA on the international level, and between Syria and the opposition on the Lebanese. He remained uncommitted to either side, preferring to keep his options open. However, the Syrian regime associated him with the Franco-US-sponsored UN Security Council resolution 1559 of 2 September 2004, which opposed the extension of Émile Lahoud's term, called for a withdrawal of Syrian forces, and for the disarming of Hizballah. In the eyes of the Syrian regime Hariri had crossed the line and become an enemy. Hizballah, too, found cause to be suspicious of Hariri.

The source of Syrian insecurity was increasing US pressure. Neoconservative plans to remake the Middle East by bringing about 'regime change' threatened Ba'thist rulers in Damascus. US policy presented its Arab allies Saudi Arabia, Egypt and Jordan with a dilemma: while they were opposed to regime change in principle, they had to support Washington's policy in the region because of their economic and military dependence on the USA. The Syrian regime grew increasingly suspicious of America's Arab allies. The consolidation within the Syrian regime led to a reliance on tight networks of the most trustworthy allies and an increased reliance on regional and confessional ties. The politics of military coups in the 1950s and 1960s displayed similar patterns of relying on kin, clans and regional and confessional proximity to build trust. This was the basis for the 'Alawi-dominated regime of Hafiz al-Assad.[190] The ruling network arguably became more 'Alawi as a result: Sunni stalwarts of the regime such as 'Abd al-Halim Khaddam, Hikmat Shihabi and Mustafa Tlass were sidelined. 'Alawi networks surrounding the Assad family were gaining greater influence, including Bashar's siblings Maher and Bushra, as well as the latter's husband, Assaf Shawkat.[191] The reliance on family, regional or sectarian networks in times of pressure is not necessarily a sign of a sectarian ideology, and there was still an important Sunni component in the regime, including Mustafa Tlass's son Manaf.

In Lebanon, the Damascus regime worked to strengthen its closest allies and to defeat the opposition. The announcement that Lahoud's term would be extended beyond the constitutional end of his presidential term in September 2004 was only made in August.[192] Syria's closest allies supported the move, including interior minister Elias Murr and his father Michel. The predominantly Christian opposition opposed the extension. Ever careful to position himself favourably, Walid Junblat stated that he 'does not favour' another term for Lahoud but would accept it if it were 'dictated by regional and political conditions'.[193] The Syrian regime appears to have been fairly confident that it could control the Lebanese arena by keeping Lahoud in the presidential palace. In late August Birri and Hariri were individually summoned to Damascus. As has been widely reported since, Bashar al-Assad told Hariri in no uncertain terms that the alternative to extending Lahoud's term would be chaos in Lebanon, allegedly threatening to 'break Lebanon' over the heads of Hariri and Junblat.[194] The Lebanese parliament passed the constitutional amendment on 3 September 2004. Only 29 of 125 deputies voted against the extension. Hariri's bloc voted for Lahoud, but most MPs subsequently refused to congratulate the president.[195] Syria had flexed its muscles.

One day before the constitutional amendment was voted through in the Lebanese parliament, the UN Security Council had adopted resolution 1559. The resolution had been introduced by the USA and France. The Security Council declared its support for 'a free and fair presidential election in Lebanon conducted according to Lebanese constitutional rules devised without foreign interference or influence'.[196] In a clear reference to Syria, it also 'called upon all remaining foreign forces to withdraw from Lebanon'. It also called for the 'disbanding and disarmament of all Lebanese and non-Lebanese militias', a reference to Hizballah and Palestinian armed factions. The resolution represented a clear rejection of Syrian dominance in Lebanon and of the principle of armed resistance to the Israeli occupation of the Shib'a Farms. After the UN had been used to legitimise the US-led invasion of Iraq in 2003, Damascus must have felt that the international body was now being used to target Ba'thism in Syria. What was worse for Assad, while France had opposed intervention in Iraq, Chirac was now the main source of pressure. It is easy to see why the Syrian regime saw Hariri's hand behind this. Chirac and Hariri had maintained close relations since the 1980s, and Hariri was one of the French president's Middle Eastern confidants. Chirac had organised the Paris II meeting on Hariri's behalf. So when Chirac turned against Syria, the regime blamed Hariri.

Chirac had been the driving force behind resolution 1559. American neoconservatives had tried to push for action against Syria, but even as late as spring 2004 the Bush administration was frustrating hardliners in Congress by only applying the Syria Accountability and Lebanese Sovereignty Act (SALSA) in a piecemeal fashion.[197] It was Chirac who persuaded the USA to use the Lebanese issue to act against Syria.

According to interviews with French diplomats conducted by the International Crisis Group (ICG), Chirac used a meeting with Bush at the G8 summit in June 2004 to push for joint action against Syrian meddling in Lebanon.[198] The policy was being questioned within the French diplomatic corps, but the diplomats interviewed by the ICG pointed to the close relations between Chirac and Hariri as the source of the initiative. Interviewed by journalist Nicholas Blanford, former army military intelligence chief and Hariri adviser Johnny 'Abdu admitted that Hariri had used his influence with Chirac to 'put pressure on Syria not to extend Lahoud's mandate'.[199] However, 'Abdu maintained that Hariri was only interested in a single element of resolution 1559, namely to prevent the extension of Lahoud's mandate. How the demand for Syrian withdrawal entered the resolution is unclear. The call to disarm Hizballah was included by the USA, for whom the Shia militia was the main concern.[200] 'Abdu would later claim that Syrian withdrawal and disarming Hizballah were not Hariri's 'priorities' at the time.[201]

Hariri took a careful stance on resolution 1559. He did not condemn its content, arguing that the resolution's 'implementation should await the proper timing' and 'it should be implemented after peace [with Israel]'.[202] Regarding the reasons for the French stance vis-à-vis Syria and Lebanon, Hariri hinted at the importance of Franco-US relations in determining France's policy: 'With regard to both the Lebanese–French and Syrian–French issues, some elements were inexistent a year ago. The change was dictated by some factors related to France's situation and its international relations.'[203] Hariri in effect claimed that Chirac was targeting the Syrian regime and Hizballah more aggressively than Hariri had intended. Hariri allies and aides interviewed by Blanford claim that Hariri had warned Bashar al-Assad of the resolution and offered his help to tone it down, and that he urged Chirac at the end of September 2004 not to push for its implementation to ease pressure on Syria.[204] Bashar al-Assad was not convinced. The Syrian regime would later claim that Hariri had drafted the resolution on board his yacht in Sardinia, together with Junblat ally Marwan Hamada and Lebanon's former minister of culture Ghassan Salameh, a claim denied by Hariri's aides and allies interviewed by journalist Nicholas Blanford.[205]

Hariri had become the focal point of Syrian fear, the hinge that connected the domestic Lebanese scene with US and French pressure on

Syria and Hizballah. His prodding was not the only reason for Chirac's desire to pressure Syria over Lebanon. Resolution 1559 provided an opportunity to mend relations with the USA after the acrimonious fall-out over Iraq. Chirac was angry with Bashar al-Assad because French companies had lost out on a gas deal in Syria and Damascus's allies in Lebanon were blocking Hariri's neoliberal privatisation policy, which France had made a condition for dispensing Paris II aid.[206] Neoliberal economics was not the cause of Lebanese political tension, but it was deeply implicated in the foreign-power tussle over Lebanon. Political leaders' powers of wealth and patronage depended on the economic structure. Neoliberal reforms benefited Rafiq Hariri, a Saudi ally, while Lahoud's statism and Birri's clientelist welfarism strengthened Syria's allies. The debate over economic policy thus mixed economic ideologies, sectarian power-sharing and foreign-power meddling.

The political tension was not felt only on the level of elite politics, but also led to popular mobilisation. Protests organised by the GCWL labour confederation in May 2004 turned into a violent confrontation with the army in Hay al-Sullum in Beirut's southern suburbs.[207] The deaths of five protesters led to mutual recriminations among Lebanon's politicians, who accused each other alternately of mobilising the protesters and seeking to discredit the army. Despite this violent incident, relations between Hariri and Hizballah appeared to improve at this time. According to Nicholas Blanford, Hariri and Nasrallah started holding regular secret meetings and established a relationship of trust at this time.[208] In November 2004 a demonstration by 3,000 protesters demanding an end to Syrian control was followed by a much larger gathering of 100,000 people demonstrating against UN Security Council resolution 1559.[209] This popular mobilisation sharpened tension between the two camps.

The municipal elections of May 2004 provided an interesting gauge of Hariri's popularity and the reception of his ambiguous strategy vis-à-vis Syria among Lebanese voters.[210] Hariri managed to organise a joint electoral list with Salim al-Huss and Tammam Salam in Beirut. The Beirut Unity List duly won all twenty-four seats in the capital, but a low turnout of only 23 per cent undermined the image of victory. In Hariri's home town, Sidon, a list backed by Nasserite MP Mustafa Sa'd won all twenty-one seats on the council, defeating Hariri's list. This defeat and the lacklustre victory in Beirut show that Hariri's ambiguous stance towards Syria did not pay off at the ballot box, and that voters appeared disappointed with the prime minister's record. This stands in sharp contrast to the lionisation of Hariri just eight months later, when his assassination was followed by popular protests against Syrian domination.

Hariri refused to remain in office after the extension, and was replaced by the ageing Tripoli za'im 'Umar Karami. Security and defence portfolios were taken by politicians strongly associated with Syria. The North Lebanese Christian za'im and Assad ally Sulaiman Franjiyya became interior minister. Karami installed his ally Elias Saba in the finance ministry. The mood in the country grew much darker when Marwan Hamada was targeted in a bomb attack in October. This was linked to his outspoken opposition to the extension of Lahoud's term and his vote against this measure. Hariri still maintained an ambiguous position vis-à-vis Syria and the opposition. In December 2004 the 'Bristol Gathering' brought the opposition together, including the Lebanese Forces, Aoun's movement, Qurnat Shihwan, and Walid Junblat.[211] In a joint declaration they demanded an end to Syrian interference in Lebanese domestic affairs and the replacement of the Karami administration with a wholly neutral government before the elections of May 2005. The meeting was the most significant expression of a unified opposition thus far. Junblat's leading role was particularly important because he gave the movement depth beyond the Christian community. He had been infuriated by the assassination attempt on his ally Marwan Hamada. Hariri did not participate in the meeting, although some members of his parliamentary bloc did. They included Bassil Fulayhan, whose attendance signalled the complete politicisation of this initially 'apolitical' technocrat.[212] Possibly, Hariri hoped to act as a 'bridge' between the Syrian regime and the opposition. He sought to gain a position of strength by once again sweeping the field in parliamentary elections, scheduled for May 2005. Again he provided benefits to supporters, as exposed in the 'olive-oil scandal', which saw Hariri's charities distributing olive oil in the run-up to the election.[213] However, the electoral law presented by interior minister Sulaiman Franjiyya on 27 January 2005 was designed to curtail Hariri's chances by splitting Beirut into three districts and incorporating the surrounding villages into the Sidon constituency.[214] These measures diluted

Hariri's predominantly Sunni vote in the two cities. The electoral law is said to have moved Hariri to finally throw in his lot with the opposition. But he never had the chance to do so: on 14 February 2005, he was assassinated in a massive bomb blast near Beirut's Corniche.

Both the Syrian regime and Hizballah had a motive for the assassination: Hariri's alleged contribution to UN Security Council resolution 1559. Both have demonstrated their ruthlessness vis-à-vis political opponents. The Syrian regime has been blamed for political assassinations in Lebanon including its allies Kamal Junblat in 1977, whose alliance between leftist Lebanese movements and the PLO had threatened to slip out of Damascus's grip in 1977, and René Mouawad, president-elect of Lebanon in 1989. By 2004 Rafiq Hariri had also become an ally who was in danger of leaving Damascus's control. Hizballah has cultivated an image as a mighty military force which, however, turns its guns only at the external enemy rather than internal Lebanese opponents in order not to exacerbate sectarian tension or foster Lebanese opposition to its status as an armed force. However, in 2008 Hizballah would turn its weapons against internal enemies in March 14, and in 2013 the movement acknowledged its intervention in the Syrian civil war. The intervention in 2008 was in response to the Siniura government unearthing the movement's fixed-line telephone network, which was of great military importance. The challenge to the Syrian regime due to the uprising in Syria, meanwhile, threatened its ability to receive supplies from Iran. In both cases, Hizballah felt that it was facing grave strategic threats to its ability to confront Israel.[215] The international investigation into the Hariri assassination first made very public accusations against the Syrian regime.[216] However, in March 2008 the independent commission charged with investigating the crime started blaming an unidentified 'criminal network'.[217] In May 2009 leaks to German news magazine *Der Spiegel* suggested that the investigation had turned its attention to Hizballah.[218] In June 2011 the tribunal charged with trying Hariri's assassination sent indictments against four alleged Hizballah members to the Lebanese authorities.[219] Hizballah, meanwhile, rejected the accusations and implied that Israel had doctored the telecommunications data that provided the evidence for the indictments.

*The Lebanese political crisis, regional tension and Hariri's
neoliberalism*

The return to political crisis in Lebanon was driven by rising regional
tension. A US–Syrian rift developed due to the shift in US global strategy. This shift mirrored the 'second Cold War' in that it reflected US
fears of threats from the Third World, especially the Middle East. The
neoconservative project to remake the Middle East culminated in the
invasion of Iraq. The resulting US confrontation with Syria also strained
relations between Damascus and Riyadh. This breakdown in Saudi–
Syrian concord led to rising tension between Hariri and the Bashar
al-Assad regime. The rise in regional tension coincided with a revival
of anti-Syrian opposition in Lebanon due to the Israeli withdrawal in
2000. This opposition was primarily, although not exclusively,
Christian, reflecting the exclusion of Christian anti-Syrian leaders from
Lebanese politics in the wake of the civil war. Damascus became
increasingly fearful of Hariri's position: as a Saudi ally he could potentially be able to turn his own Sunni community against Syria and could
connect the Lebanese opposition and the wider US project of remaking
the Middle East.

This was the context in which Hariri launched his second neoliberalisation drive when he returned as prime minister in 2000. He revived
rent-creation mechanisms that benefited him and other new contractors: government debt management and reconstruction. He also
sought to open up new investment opportunities for foreign and
Lebanese capital through privatisation, to cut government spending on
welfare and the military. Privatisation and the cuts in spending on service ministries undermined patronage instruments of former militia
leaders, especially parliament speaker Nabih Birri. Cuts in military
expenditure represented an attack on the military and intelligence
establishment, headed by President Émile Lahoud. Since these leaders
were among Syria's closest allies in Lebanon, the neoliberalisation
drive was regarded as an attack on Damascus's position in Lebanon. It
was developed and implemented by the second generation of Hariri
technocrats, who had been recruited from the IMF in the 1990s and
considered themselves 'insulated' from Lebanon's political factions.
However, their advocacy of neoliberalism as an economic project nec-

essarily 'politicised' them because neoliberal restructuring of state and society strengthened Hariri, for whom neoliberal restructuring was a political project. The second generation technocrats thus drifted into, and were attracted to, the Hariri camp.

'Actually existing neoliberalism' involves the adoption of global policy templates in specific local political contexts. After 2000 Rafiq Hariri adopted a new set of neoliberal templates: the privatisation of the mobile-phone networks and MEA, as well as Paris II 'conditionality' that was akin to the conditionality of World Bank and IMF structural adjustment programmes. However, these policies were adopted for local reasons. Hariri was pursuing the interests of Gulf capital in profitable investment opportunities in telecommunications and air transport. Secondly, privatisation was a means of cutting off access to patronage for Hariri's rival Nabih Birri. Lahoud's statism was designed to curtail Hariri's control over economic decision-making.

A particularly poignant episode was the Paris II conference in 2002. Thanks to donor support, Lebanon avoided financial crisis. The USA refused to endorse an international bail-out of Lebanon, most likely in order to press the Hariri government to move more forcefully against Hizballah. This was something Hariri was not willing to do, at least not then. Significantly, US capital had no direct stake in Lebanon because a class of wealthy Lebanese investors were in effect mediating between Lebanese and global finance. Lebanon avoided financial collapse through a bail-out arranged by France, and largely paid for by Saudi Arabia. This was due to long-standing personal alliances between Hariri and the leaders of France and Saudi Arabia. Rafiq Hariri used the 'conditionality' established at Paris II to pressure his domestic opponents into accepting neoliberal policies.

The rising tension between Damascus and Rafiq Hariri led to accusations that the Assad regime was behind his assassination. It is plausible to assume that Hariri pushed for resolution 1559, although he may only have supported the demand for Syria to cease meddling in the presidential elections, without necessarily supporting calls for Syrian withdrawal or disarming Hizballah. It is also plausible to assume that members of the Syrian regime felt that the businessman-politician had become too great a threat and sought to teach Lebanon's political class a lesson. Whoever assassinated Hariri and twenty-two other people exacerbated the political crisis in the country. The split between March 14 and March 8 polarised the country along sectarian lines, a division that deepened further after the 2006 war between Israel and Lebanon.

6

CONCLUSIONS

Rafiq Hariri was a larger-than-life figure: he was Mr Lebanon, a man with a vision to rebuild his country. His death therefore begs the questions of his 'legacy'. Did he realise his vision, or was it thwarted by his enemies? And was his vision any good for Lebanon to begin with? The term legacy implies a great deal of personal responsibility and a personal judgement of the man. When dealing with Rafiq Hariri's life, I was exercising the 'sociological imagination', using individual biography to explore the wider social process of neoliberalism coming to Lebanon. His posthumous legacy similarly needs to be put into a wider context. This chapter summarises what we have learned from looking at Rafiq Hariri's life, before extending the analysis to the period since 2005. As David Harvey has noted, neoliberalism is both an economic orthodoxy and a political project to extend the power of capital.[1] In Lebanon neoliberalism was driven by Rafiq Hariri and his technocrats, who embodied the two parts of the neoliberal equation. Hariri represented the interests of Gulf contractors, the class interest driving Lebanese neoliberalism. This is why his 'vision' revolved around putting luxury real estate into the centre of Beirut. Gulf contractors were set to benefit from the Solidere project, from the revival of Lebanon's banks through government borrowing, and from privatisation of state-owned entities. Writing about European capitalism, Karl Kautsky had written that capital 'rules' but does not 'govern'.[2] The state enjoys some autonomy from large corporate interests. Not so in Lebanon, where one of the wealthiest businesspeople headed the government and took over key sections of the state. Hariri's political biography is therefore the key to understanding the Lebanese post-war economy. He did not act on his vision by himself. His signature policies were developed and implemented by technocrats in key state positions. He placed former employees of his own companies, international banks, and of the IMF and World Bank at the helm of institutions such as the finance ministry, the central bank and the Council for Development and Reconstruction (CDR). While Hariri represented the class interests driving neoliberalism, these technocrats personified neoliberalism as an economic orthodoxy. Their access to political decision-making depended on Hariri's political sponsorship. Lebanese neoliberalism was the work of the Hariri network, which mobilised a variety of resources. To put it in terms of sociologist Pierre Bourdieu, Hariri was providing the financial capital and the technocrats were providing the cultural capital.[3] The tensions and contradictions of neoliberalism as an economic orthodoxy, and as a class project, find sociological expression in what Hourani had termed the 'Hariri network'.[4] Rafiq Hariri sought profits, but it was not his personal 'vision' that determined policy so much as his wider network of technocrats and business allies. Neoliberal technocrats attached themselves to the businessman-politician to fight anti-market 'barbarism'.[5]

Lebanese neoliberalism was hardly a carbon copy of the policies of Thatcher, Reagan or Pinochet, the cases that are most closely associated with this form of capitalism, but it did apply global templates in urban megaprojects and currency anchoring. The extent and scope of neoliberal restructuring, its very form, was determined by Lebanon's specific political field. We therefore need a historical sociology of classes, elites and state institutions to understand the opportunities and constraints under which the Hariri network was labouring, as well as the discourses of nation and religion, which are the language in which Lebanese politics is negotiated. Hariri and his technocrats were importing global templates of neoliberal urbanism, currency management and privatisation, but regional and domestic factors were setting the limits of Lebanese neoliberalism. Rafiq Hariri was not only a Saudi contractor but also the 'Saudi man in Lebanon', the 'voice of King

Fahd' in Lebanese civil war negotiations. Saudi foreign policy and the kingdom's relationship with Syria as the dominant foreign power in Lebanon, and with the USA as the global hegemon, shaped Hariri's room for manoeuvre. Rival elites were also curtailing Hariri's plans: former militia leaders, the military and intelligence establishment, remnants of the pre-war bourgeoisie and, of course, the Damascus regime. The latter was sidelining all opponents in Lebanon and using a divide-and-rule strategy among its allies, with occasional use of violence 'pour encourager les autres'.

Neoliberalism as a class project is more than just a set of policies, an ideology or a form of governmentality. We need more than intellectual history to grasp its spread, shape and scope. There were few, if any, members of what Mirowski had termed the 'neoliberal thought collective' in the Hariri network.[6] By itself, such intellectual connections tell us little about the travels of neoliberalism to Lebanon; Lebanese neoliberalism cannot be reduced to a set of policies. It is true that Hariri applied specific templates to Lebanon, but the choice of policies—urban megaprojects and a currency peg—was not determined by a universal shopping list. At one point some IMF directors criticised Hariri's policies in the early 2000s.[7] There can be policy disagreements within the universe of neoliberal policy possibilities. This is hardly surprising for an ideology. There is no single socialist policy either. Finally, neoliberal governmentality is an interesting lens, but not the most important one for our purpose, which is an account of Lebanon's political economy. The Hariri Foundation health directorate did embrace aspects of neoliberal government of populations, including data collection in large databases, which are a form of biopolitics. The more relevant point about the health directorate is its expansion due to electoral considerations in the late 1990s. Clientelism remained at the forefront of its work. This mode of operation could run counter to elements of neoliberal governmentality that the Hariri Foundation embraced. All these alternative perspectives are missing the essential element of neoliberalism. It is a form of intensified capitalism with its own forms of class conflict and state restructuring. Looking at Gulf contractor Rafiq Hariri as the driving force of Lebanese neoliberalism has allowed me to explain the main developments in its post-war political economy, including slow economic growth for much of his tenure, continued economic inequality and poverty, and a return to confessionalised patronage.

Hariri's birth put him squarely outside his country's political elite. The son of a smallholder from the southern city of Sidon rose to become prime minister not through leading a militia or belonging to a feudal family, but through the wealth he accumulated as a contractor in Saudi Arabia. The fact that it was possible to become so wealthy, and that Hariri managed to convert this wealth into political power back home, reveals profound economic and political changes. The civil war from 1975 to 1990 transformed Lebanon's role in the global and regional economy. Before the war Lebanon had been a conduit for Arab capital being invested in Europe or the USA, while European and American goods were entering the Middle East through Beirut port. Rents from trade and finance were accruing to a few families which had monopolised trade and finance. Capitalist agriculture precipitated a rural crisis and migration to the city, where new forms of popular politics were challenging the status quo. The rush to war was helped by the presence of armed Palestinian movements siding with the opposition forces. During the civil war Lebanon lost its role as intermediary between Arab and Western markets. The pre-war bourgeoisie did not disappear, but it lost its monopoly over the economy. Businessmen allied to the militias were gaining ground. Hariri and other Gulf contractors were entering the Lebanese economy and politics in the late 1970s after gaining great wealth in the oil boom. Hariri emerged as the most politically successful contractor because of his close alliance with Saudi Arabia, which saw him acting as the king's representative in Lebanese diplomacy. The struggles of the Gulf contractor with militia networks is one of the rarely told stories of civil war, a war fought not just over modalities of sectarian power sharing or foreign influence, but also the economic future of the country, the 'spoils of truce'.[8]

These 'spoils' came in the form of rent, the manipulation of markets and property rights to obtain 'excessive' profits. How rent is created and appropriated gives us a window into class politics in post-war Lebanon, and the economic logic of competing elites—especially Gulf contractor Hariri, former militia leaders such as Nabih Birri, and the military and intelligence establishment around President Émile Lahoud. The rent-creation mechanisms that the Hariri network was putting into place followed a neoliberal logic. The centrepiece of Hariri's vision was the Solidere project in central Beirut. It conforms to a neoliberal template: rent creation through reassigning property rights; place marketing through a mix of 'world-class' infrastructure, the privatisation of planning and disabling of municipal control; and the creation of an elite playground dissociated from the rest of the city.[9] It reproduced large-scale urban development projects in London, New York and the Gulf, and became a model to replicate in its own right. For instance, the Abdali project in Amman shares a similar business model, investors, and even planners. It is hardly surprising that a contractor such as Hariri would regard a real-estate project as his country's salvation.

Hariri had to win over key Beirut and national political elites to push the project through. The institutional vehicle he used was the Council for Development and Reconstruction (CDR), which had been founded in 1977 during a lull in the civil war as an autonomous and powerful public agency charged with reconstruction. A new law in 1991 extended these powers further, while a former Hariri employee was put in charge of the institution. The same law allowed the creation of Solidere and the transfer of property rights to the new developer, with shares as compensation for previous owners. Many on the Solidere board were close to Hariri, who was also a major shareholder, within the 10 per cent maximum limit for individual shareholdings. Solidere obtained extensive planning rights over the area. A large number of investors who developed the plots offered by Solidere came from the Gulf. The rationale of the project used the language of neoliberalism: making Beirut competitive in the global economy by providing world-class infrastructure. Solidere reproduced neoliberal urbanism, but it did so in a specific regional and local context: the driving force was Gulf capital, while local political elites had to be brought on board.

Hariri's other main policy initiative was the currency anchor. The Lebanese pound was managed so as to appreciate between 1992 and 1997, and has since remained stable. It had always previously been free floating. The desire for currency stability arose from both global and local concerns. The liberalisation of global finance since the 1970s has resulted in frequent financial crises, which usually involve currencies. An increasing number of countries have therefore pegged their currencies to a stronger one, usually the US dollar. Currency anchors are seen as a way of ensuring investor confidence in an economy, but currency defence can be costly, as it drives up interest rates. This is precisely what happened in Lebanon. Economist Toufic Gaspard has shown that the cost of debt servicing has been the biggest contributor to government deficits in Lebanon.[10] Most government debt instruments were snapped up by local Lebanese banks, including Hariri's Banque Méditerranée. The revival of Lebanon's banking sector in the 1990s thus depended not on channelling international investments into the wider Middle East—as had been the stated aim of Hariri's policy—but to earn high interest rates from lending to the government. The banking sector has become increasingly concentrated. Depositors also earn high interest rates and deposits are highly concentrated, suggesting that a small number of big players appropriate the bulk of the rent from government borrowing. Gulf investment features prominently. Hariri's Banque Méditerranée is a good example of a Lebanese bank founded by a Gulf contractor. Much of the deposits flowing into Lebanese banks originate from the Gulf, not least via the Lebanese diaspora there. The Hariri network was in charge of the institutions that were managing the currency: the finance ministry and the central bank. The currency peg was not just a policy imported from outside, it also spoke to the Lebanese wartime experience of repeated rounds of speculation against the currency, which enriched a group of speculators and impoverished ordinary Lebanese by wiping out the value of their savings and wages.

One feature that distinguishes neoliberalism from classical liberalism is the role of the state: while classical liberalism tended towards the laissez-faire state, and 'embedded liberalism' towards Keynesian demand management, the neoliberal state actively intervenes in the economy to create markets—without, however, managing demand.[11] This is what distinguished Rafiq Hariri's neoliberal state-building from the pre-war laissez-faire state. He sought control of strong agencies of economic management. The best examples are the CDR, the central bank and the finance ministry. These were the key state agencies concerned with central Beirut's reconstruction and with the currency anchor. Hariri and his technocrats were using the state to transfer property rights in central Beirut, to actively manage the value of the currency and the country's skyrocketing debt. All of these policies were entirely alien to the pre-war bourgeoisie, who had embraced a minimal state that would not interfere with their oligopolies in trade and finance. Hariri did not simply create new institutions out of thin air, but took over and retooled existing ones. Shihabist technocrats had founded the central bank and the CDR as autonomous entities beyond the reach of the *zu'ama* or militia leaders. Hariri used the powers of these agencies and bolstered them further. Hariri's state-building in Lebanon thus followed a global template of strengthening economic institutions, but it was also shaped by path dependency of existing institutions.

The neoliberal policy par excellence is privatisation. The Lebanese state does not own many enterprises but it controls several, such as Middle East Airlines (MEA). Hariri's rivals frustrated his attempts at privatising these entities. While Hariri wanted to create new investment opportunities for Gulf and other international investors, former militia leaders such as Nabih Birri saw them as a means of apportioning benefits to their clientele. This clientelist logic also underpinned the parts of the state not under Hariri's control. Hariri was in charge of agencies controlling the economy, but close Syrian allies such as President Lahoud had control of military and intelligence institutions and former militia leaders and *zu'ama* ran the service ministries. The latter were a means of channelling patronage resources to the politicians' clienteles. Pierre Bourdieu argued that neoliberal restructuring of the state strengthens its 'right hand', concerned with economic management.[12] This includes central banks, the finance ministry and, generally, those staff in state agencies concerned with 'balancing the books'. The 'left hand' of the state, meanwhile, is concerned with delivering services. The struggle over restructuring the Lebanese state was thus not just over sectarian power sharing but also over the 'right hand', which Hariri controlled and wanted to strengthen, and the 'left hand', which former militia leaders were perverting into patronage instruments. Lebanese state restructuring was thus comparable, but by no means identical, to similar processes observed elsewhere. Lebanese political elites were engaged in a genuine struggle over economic spoils. What matters, though, is that the nature of the spoils they were seeking depended on their economic agenda. Former militia leaders would seek patronage resources, while Hariri was seeking investment opportunities for himself and his class. Hariri's rivals were not necessarily 'anti-neoliberal'. They were happy to take a share of the profits

Hariri's schemes were generating; at times they even mimicked Hariri's schemes, such as real-estate development in Birri's fief of Verdun.[13] However, the state building projects they embraced did differ, echoing the debate over the 'left' and 'right' hands of the state.

In Rafiq Hariri's politics, neoliberalism met Lebanese sectarianism. A global shift in capitalism encountered what is considered the essence of local Lebanese political culture. Sectarianism is no primordial essence, but has been constructed since the nineteenth century. If it is a constructed category, then we need to understand how it is reproduced. Rafiq Hariri presents a fitting case study. While as a businessman he was initially not interested in playing the games of sectarian clientelism, the requirements of Lebanese electoral politics disciplined him into behaving more like a traditional Lebanese patron. His student loan programme from 1983 to 1996 assisted 32,000 students.[14] It benefited primarily, but by no means exclusively, Sunni Muslims from Lebanon's periphery. This is hardly surprising given that Hariri conducted the programme in the midst of a sectarian civil war. He was working through Sunni social and religious associations to recruit students. Evidence from one quantitative study of the association suggests that non-Sunni students were mainly recruited via militia leaders and politicians.[15] Paradoxically, the non-sectarian aspect of Hariri's student loan programme thus strengthened sectarian politicians.

Once the civil war ended, Hariri displayed a curious lack of interest in electoral politics. He did not directly participate in the first elections of 1992. He did not convert the enormous resources spent on the student loan programme into an electoral machine, only founding an alumni association in 1994. He even faced protests from Sunni associations in 1993 for neglecting the community. This changed in the late 1990s. Hariri built health centres and schools in predominantly Sunni neighbourhoods, and he politically neutralised the Maqasid association run by his main Sunni rival in Beirut, Tammam Salam. Hariri took advantage of the financial difficulties of Maqasid, which were themselves due to the decline of Beirut's Sunni bourgeoisie relative to the success of Hariri, a businessman and newcomer on the Beirut scene.

There is little evidence that the sectarian turn in Hariri's philanthropy sprang from an inherently 'sectarian mindset'. The necessities of electoral politics had forced him into Lebanese sectarianism.

Defenders of Rafiq Hariri point out that the technocrats he hired hailed from a variety of communities. His non-sectarian recruitment of experts and his sectarian populism chime with Wallerstein's observation of the role of universalist and particularist logics of capitalism: the managers of capitalism are hired according to universal principles to ensure its smooth running, while particularist populism is used to disable class-based resistance to a deepening of capitalism.[16]

In Arab states such as Egypt, Morocco, Tunisia and Jordan, the IMF and World Bank were crucial players pushing governments towards neoliberal restructuring. In Lebanon they played hardly any role. Hariri imported neoliberal models of urban redevelopment and governance, currency stabilisation and privatisation. A Gulf contractor, rather than the international financial institutions, was the driving force of neoliberalism in Lebanon. The country is not unique regarding the scale of direct political influence that Gulf capital wields; there are similarities in other Arab states. Jordan is a resource-poor economy which has come to rely heavily on investment from the Gulf, which has a strong political component. The 2013 coup that eventually brought President 'Abd al-Fatah al-Sisi to power in Egypt was followed by large-scale investment pledges by Gulf companies. Even in the Maghreb countries Morocco and Tunisia, Gulf investment has become a significant economic factor. Adam Hanieh first identified the phenomenon of Gulf capital and its internationalisation.[17] He was writing mainly about the Gulf Cooperation Council (GCC) itself, comprising Bahrain, Kuwait, Saudi Arabia, Oman, Qatar and the United Arab Emirates (UAE) and, to a lesser extent, about Lebanon and Palestine. It is time to extend the analysis of the political and economic effects of Gulf capital beyond the Gulf. A good example is the politics of large-scale urban-development projects which are proliferating across Arab capitals and which are almost exclusively financed by Gulf investors. Projects such as Abdali (Amman, Jordan), Rawabi (Bir Zayt, Palestine), Mediterranean Gate (Tunis, Tunisia), or Bu Raqraq (Rabat, Morocco) follow the Solidere model of a single agency taking charge of a large chunk of prime land to develop it for the high-end market. The same questions of property ownership and governance arise as in the case of Solidere. The case of Rafiq Hariri thus holds great comparative value for the study of Gulf capital in the Arab world.

Like father, like son? Lebanese neoliberalism under Sa'd Hariri

Lebanese neoliberalism stalled post-2005. However, we can still use the 'sociological imagination' to analyse Lebanese politics after Rafiq Hariri's death by charting the rise and decline of Sa'd Hariri's political fortunes. He is Rafiq Hariri's son and political heir, taking over the Hariri network after his father's assassination. While Rafiq had been an outsider struggling for a place in Lebanese politics, Sa'd was a political heir, and thus thrust into the position of *za'im*. He continued his father's economic policies, including a push for privatisation. These initiatives remained stuck in gridlock caused by Hizballah. The Shia movement gained political dominance after Syria was forced to withdraw its troops from Lebanon following the Hariri assassination. Popular demonstrations and international pressure made Syrian military presence untenable.

Rafiq Hariri had never built impersonal institutions insulated from outside interference, but relied on his network to develop and push through his economic policies. This had implications for succession. Due to the personalised nature of the Hariri network, only a family member was able to hold together the political and business interests that the elder Hariri had built. After Rafiq Hariri's death there was no social movement or political party that could have run without another Hariri at the helm. Before addressing economic policy, or lack of movement in this area, I will deal with the international politics of the post-Rafiq Hariri era. This was the period of the 'New Arab Cold War', between a coalition of so-called moderate Sunni states, which included Saudi Arabia, Egypt and Jordan, and the 'axis of resistance', including Iran, Syria, Hizballah and Hamas. The period saw a rise in regional sectarianism as Iraq descended into insurgency and civil war. Sa'd Hariri relied more heavily on leadership of the Sunni community than his father had done. The period is also characterised by the rising economic dependency of the Lebanese economy on the Gulf as a result of Rafiq Hariri's policies.

In international politics the US–Saudi–Syrian triangle remained important for Sa'd Hariri. From 2005 to 2008 the younger Hariri tried to break Syrian influence in Lebanon through popular mobilisation at home and an alliance with international powers. Hariri blamed the Syrian regime for the assassination of his father. Popular anguish at the impunity of the killing resulted in large-scale demonstrations, culminating in the 14 March 2005 protest by several hundred thousand Lebanese demanding Syrian withdrawal. Damascus pulled out its troops in April. From a more confessional perspective, the resulting March 14 coalition brought together Hariri as the main leader of the Sunni community, Walid Junblat as the main Druze leader, and several Christian forces who had formed the backbone of the pre-2005 anti-Syrian opposition, excluding Michel Aoun, who felt that his interests would be better served if he joined the rival March 8 coalition. The latter was led by Hizballah and comprised the other major Shia movement, Amal, as well as Aoun and several smaller political forces. March 8 remained allied to Syria and Iran. March 14 was supported by an array of international actors. The USA, Saudi Arabia and other allied European and Arab states supported Hariri's course against the Syrian regime.

This occurred in the context of a wider regional confrontation between a US-led coalition containing Israel and 'moderate Sunni' states such as Saudi Arabia, Egypt and Jordan, and a 'rejectionist' coalition comprising Iran, Syria, Hizballah and Hamas. Sa'd Hariri received strong support from Saudi Arabia and from a Bush administration which turned its attention from Iraq to Syria. There may have been hope that pressure on Assad could bring about regime change without having to roll tanks into Damascus, as the USA had done in Baghdad. France had been a driving force behind UN Security Council resolution 1559 and the assassination of President Jacques Chirac's personal friend Rafiq Hariri led to a decisive break with Damascus. Saudi Arabia's Crown Prince 'Abdallah—the real force in the kingdom by then—was incensed by the murder of Saudi ally Rafiq Hariri. Western powers chose international justice as the instrument to confront Assad. The UN International Independent Investigation Commission (UNIIIC) was established by the UN Security Council on 7 April 2005 to investigate the crime. The Special Tribunal for Lebanon (STL) was set up in May 2007.[18] It is mandated with prosecuting the perpetrators of the Hariri assassination as well as of later political assassinations of anti-Syrian figures. The mixed Lebanese–international court is a legal innovation because it represents the first time that an international tribunal tries a crime under national law. This is because the crime—a political assassination—does not fall under international jurisdiction, which usually deals with issues such as crimes against humanity. The rationale for establishing a hybrid court with international participation was that the assassination of 14 February 2005 constituted a threat to international peace and security.[19] The UNIIIC investigation and the STL have come in for tough criticism. Even commentators who support the goal of bringing the perpetrators to justice point out that the politicised nature of the investigation has damaged the tribunal.[20] The investigation and the tribunal were meant to pressure Syria and Hizballah. Defenders of the court have pointed out that it remains independent of any governments.[21] They argue further that, even if the intention was to corner Syria and Hizballah, the STL also establishes a new standard of accountability in a country where political assassinations have traditionally gone unpunished.

An initial report by chief investigator Detlev Mehlis in October 2005 pointed to the Syrian regime as the culprit.[22] Later reports under new investigators became more cautious, talking of a 'criminal network'.[23] In 2009 the Lebanese judiciary had to release four Lebanese security forces generals who had been detained in August 2005 on Mehlis's instigation. The climbdown was embarrassing but coincided with thawing relations between March 14 and its international backers, on one hand, and Syria with its Lebanese allies, on the other. The country had erupted in violence in May 2008 when Hizballah and allied militias overran strongholds of Hariri supporters in Beirut. This show of force led March 14 to back down over opposition demands to form a 'national unity government' that included them and the election of a new president. Importantly, the softening of attitudes was facilitated by a rapprochement between Syria and its international opponents. France under its new president, Nicolas Sarkozy, led the charge to improve relations. The USA acknowledged Assad's staying power and welcomed him back to the fold. Saudi Arabia was the most crucial actor effecting a rapprochement between Assad and Hariri. Personal negotiations between King Abdullah and Bashar al-Assad facilitated the formation of a Lebanese 'national unity government' under the premiership of Sa'd Hariri in November 2009.[24] Hariri travelled to Damascus in June 2010 to reconcile with the Assad regime. In September 2010 he withdrew his earlier accusation that the Syrian regime had assassinated his father. He apologised for what he said had been a 'political accusation'.[25] Syria's rapprochement with the USA and Saudi Arabia was not to survive the outbreak of the anti-Assad uprising in 2011. However, Sa'd Hariri's position in Lebanon remained circumscribed by the nature of US–Syrian and Saudi–Syrian relations between 2005 and 2011.

Rafiq Hariri had embraced 'sectarian populism' to win votes. Lebanese sectarianism spiked after 2005 due to Iraq's descent into sectarian strife in the wake of the 2003 invasion and the confrontation between the Sunni and Shia powers Saudi Arabia and Iran. It is therefore little surprise that Sa'd Hariri's leadership had a more sectarian character than his father's. Patronage to his confessional group remained crucial for Sa'd Hariri's position as a top politician. The assassination of the most powerful Sunni politician came as a major shock to Sunni Muslims, who interpreted Rafiq Hariri's killing as an attack on the community as a whole. Rafiq Hariri had not been universally loved within the community. His performance at the last electoral test during his lifetime, the municipal elections of 2004, had been lacklustre in cities with large Sunni communities such as Beirut and Sidon. However, his killing was interpreted as an attempt at reducing the community's influence in Lebanese politics. Lebanon's Sunnis therefore closed ranks behind Sa'd Hariri. The international tribunal and the quest for the truth—*al-haqiqa*, the slogan of the March 14 demonstration in 2005—became a major issue of communal defence. Personal leadership and communal interest had been merged. The post-2005 period saw intense electoral competition between March 8 and March 14. The 2009 elections led to an explosion of patronage among all political forces, fuelled by money from outside powers such as Iran and Saudi Arabia. The Saudi kingdom was said to have contributed 'hundreds of millions' of dollars to the election war-chests of Hizballah's opponents.[26] Sa'd Hariri expanded his clientelist network, upping the number of health centres offered by the Hariri Foundation. In January 2008 health centres advertised on the Hariri Foundation website numbered eleven; by January 2013 the number had reached thirty-six.[27] The new centres were concentrated in Sunni Muslim population centres such as Tripoli and 'Akkar. As Cammett and Issar have shown, the Hariri Foundation health centres targeted primarily but by no means exclusively areas with Sunni majorities.[28] An important novelty for Sa'd Hariri was the military defence of the community. His father had never armed his community. When March 8 called for a strike and protests in January 2007, tyres were burned, roads were blocked, and there were sporadic clashes between Sunni and Shia political movements. The presence of masked men, and possibly snipers, in the streets of Beirut—especially around Rafiq Hariri's alma mater, the Beirut Arab University—evoked the dark days of the civil war. According to a report by the International Crisis Group this was the point at which Hariri's supporters started asking their *za'im* for weapons.[29] Rather than founding a centralised militia, Hariri built up the capacities of a private security company called Secure Plus.[30] According to the ICG, Hariri armed local youths in the neighbourhoods dominated by his party in order to defend the largely Sunni population of these quarters.[31] These militias were no match for an onslaught by Hizballah and its allies, who overran areas dominated by Mustaqbal in May 2008. The cause of the Hizballah attack was a decision by the government of Fu'ad Siniura to dig up its separate fixed-line communications network, which had been of great strategic importance during Hizballah's confrontation with Israel in 2006.[32] Sa'd Hariri's experiment with arming his supporters had been a resounding failure.

Confessional identity had become more salient across the region in the wake of the Iraq invasion. The faultlines in the ensuing insurgency and civil war increasingly ran along sectarian lines. The regional contest between the Saudi monarchy, historically allied to Wahhabi clerics, and the Islamic Republic of Iran, with its revolutionary ideology based on a reinterpretation of Shia tradition, resulted in a strengthening of sectarian rhetoric. The intense sectarian violence in Iraq between 2006 and 2008 evoked strong sympathy from large sections of both Sunni and Shia populations in Lebanon. Hariri's close alliance to Saudi Arabia and Hizballah's link to Iran meant that the Lebanese conflict between March 8 and March 14, headed by Hizballah and Hariri respectively, became part of this wider regional struggle, framed as it was in sectarian terms. The regional context led to greater religious agitation in Lebanon. The mobilisation of Sunni Muslims was primarily political, but inevitably included a religious element, stoked by the political mobilisation of the Sunni mufti and religious shaykhs on behalf of the

Future Current.[33] The Hariri camp courted Islamists, especially in Tripoli and the 'Akkar region. It entered into an alliance with the Lebanese branch of the Muslim Brotherhood, pressed for an amnesty for militants arrested over Islamist violence in Dinniya in 2000, and recruited former Salafist Khalid Dahir as a parliamentary deputy.[34] Hariri himself did not engage in religious or sectarian agitation; but toleration for such discourses at the local level was part of maintaining broad Sunni support, including from Islamists. It would be a mistake, however, to read any ideological affinity into the alliance between the Sunni leader Sa'd Hariri and the community's Islamists: relations were always utilitarian. As one Salafi militant interviewed by the International Crisis Group put it: 'In the past, whenever the Future Group needed us [the Salafis] in its fight against Hizballah, it would give us tremendous importance. But as soon as the confrontation was over, they would abandon us.'[35] Hariri was using a 'national' discourse at the national level while allowing his followers to use a more sectarian tone. A good example was the poster campaign of the Mustaqbal movement in Tariq al-Jadida prior to the 2009 elections.[36] One set of official Mustaqbal posters played on the slogan 'Lubnan awwalan' (Lebanon first), initially adopted at the second annual commemoration for Rafiq Hariri. The official poster campaign by the Future Movement replaced the word 'Lebanon' with concerns for all Lebanese such as economy, security or agriculture. However, a set of posters produced by local residents' associations in predominantly Sunni Tariq al-Jadida proclaimed 'al-Sunna awwalan' (Sunna first). While the overarching political movement thus had a non-sectarian aura, grassroots supporters were free to agitate in sectarian terms.

Although international meddling and increasingly sectarian popular mobilisation were pushing economic concerns to the background, Sa'd Hariri tried to maintain control over the levers of economic management. He sought to keep Solidere going, to manage government debt and prevent financial crisis, and privatise state-controlled entities. Solidere and the currency anchor were limping on, but the split between March 8 and March 14 created governmental gridlock which made privatisation impossible. Lebanon's economic fortunes remained dependent on the influx of Gulf funds from investors and tourists, while donors' 'implicit guarantee' prevented financial collapse. Sa'd

Hariri made sure that key institutions concerned with managing neo-liberal rent-creation remained within his purview. The finance ministry stayed in the hands of technocrats close to Hariri and Fu'ad Siniura. Jihad Az'ur (July 2005–July 2008), Muhammad Shatah (July 2008–November 2009) and Raya Haffar al-Hassan (November 2009–June 2011) were all technocrats. Az'ur and al-Hassan had worked under the umbrella of UNDP projects within the finance ministry. Such foreign-funded projects had been the recruiting ground for Hariri technocrats. Similarly, Shatah had been recruited from the IMF and had worked in the central bank. All of them were close to Fu'ad Siniura, who was in charge of economic policy within the Hariri network. Central bank governor Riyadh Salama was reappointed in 2011. He was one of the architects of currency stability in the 1990s. An interesting development occurred in 2011, when Najib Miqati took over the post of prime minister from Sa'd Hariri. The wealth of the Miqati family had itself been founded on Gulf contracting before Najib Miqati branched out into telecommunications. Miqati appointed Muhammad Safadi as finance minister. He is another Gulf contractor with ties to the Saudi monarchy. Safadi was a safe pair of hands who could manage relations with Lebanon's creditors and the Saudi monarchy. As a result, central bank governor Salama and finance minister Safadi managed to maintain currency stability during a particularly politically turbulent phase of Lebanese history. Only the fall of the Miqati government in March 2013 brought about a major departure. The new cabinet under prime minister Tammam Salam included Amal man 'Ali Hassan al-Khalil as finance minister.

Privatisation remained at the top of Sa'd Hariri and Fu'ad Siniura's economic agenda. At the Paris III donor conference in 2007 the Siniura government pledged to sell the mobile-phone network, MEA and EDL. The involvement of international donors introduced an element of 'conditionality' which Siniura invoked to push privatisation against domestic opponents. However, while EDL and MEA saw some limited restructuring, neither was sold to private owners. Plans to sell the mobile-phone network were hotly contested within Sa'd Hariri's national unity government from 2009 to 2011, when the leftist tele-communications minister, Charbel Nahas, vigorously opposed any moves towards privatisation. This was not an issue of March 14 versus

March 8. Former militia leader Walid Junblat also opposed privatisation while he was part of Hariri's coalition.[37] Similarly, former militia leaders Birri and Junblat vigorously opposed any spending cuts to their patronage instruments, the Council for the South and the Ministry of the Displaced respectively.[38]

While privatisation and spending cuts at key welfare ministries were being blocked, Lebanon became ever more closely integrated into the circuits of Gulf capital. The country is now following the Gulf cycle of oil-induced boom and bust. Furthermore, any decline in stability carries the risk of Gulf capital withdrawing elsewhere. Lebanese migrants to the Gulf are an important source of household income for families at home.[39] Banking, tourism and construction were the drivers of strong economic growth in Lebanon, averaging 6.7 per cent annually from 2006 to 2010.[40] All three sectors are highly dependent on the Gulf. According to one estimate, tourism supports about a quarter of jobs.[41] In 2010 visitor numbers peaked at 2.2 million.[42] Lebanon's tourism sector remained highly dependent on the Gulf.[43] Gulf tourists often holiday in property they rent or buy rather than staying in hotels. Gulf tourism therefore also provides a boost to the Lebanese real-estate sector. Lebanon's banks were a popular destination for Gulf investors. Since about 2002 the Gulf has been experiencing a new oil boom. One source estimated oil windfalls between 2002 and 2006 to have reached $1.5 trillion, double those of the preceding five-year period.[44] Gulf capital was looking for outlets beyond the traditional investment in relatively safe industrialised country bonds and shares. The turn away from the USA as an investment destination was due to Gulf fears of a US crackdown on 'suspicious' Arab capital after 11 September 2001, the financial crisis of 2008, and increased investment opportunities in developing countries which were liberalising their economies. Social networks between the Gulf and other Arab countries played a role in directing these flows, for instance migrant workers. This is particularly relevant for Lebanon. Between 2004 and 2008 about $120 billion in capital outflows from the GCC states reached the Middle East or North Africa, with Lebanon and Egypt the prime recipients.[45] Interest in the mobile-phone companies to be privatised has come primarily from the Gulf.[46] Lebanese banks have become attractive destinations for Gulf depositors.[47] There was also some diversification in the business model of Lebanese banks, with increased lending abroad and consumer credit to Lebanese households.[48] Lending to the Lebanese government remains the backbone of the banks' business. In October 2015 claims on the public sector accounted for 20.6 per cent of total assets of Lebanese commercial banks, while 38.1 per cent were deposited with the central bank.[49] Gulf countries remain key to maintaining the stability of the Lebanese currency. During the 2006 war between Israel and Lebanon the central bank coordinated closely with the authorities in Kuwait and Saudi Arabia, which deposited a total of $1.5 billion with the Lebanese central bank.[50] In February 2008 Saudi Arabia agreed to deposit another $1 billion with the central bank.[51] Saudi Arabia thus continued to bolster investor confidence in the ability of the Lebanese central bank to maintain the currency peg.

Lebanon benefited from the latest oil boom in the Gulf, receiving remittances, tourism income and investment. However, this dependency on the Gulf also makes the economy highly vulnerable. In 2008, for instance, the profits of Solidere were dragged down by the bursting of the property bubble in Dubai.[52] The company had launched an international division in 2007, investing in Dubai at the height of the bubble. When the financial crisis reached the Gulf in 2008, Lebanese banks were fearful over their exposure to real-estate bubbles in these countries.[53] Lebanese fears subsided when the Gulf returned to oil-fuelled growth after 2008. However, the episode shows that Lebanon remains highly dependent on conditions in the GCC. Another example is tourism. Rising tension inside Lebanon and in neighbouring Syria resulted in lower tourism numbers in 2011. Following armed clashes in Tripoli, the UAE, Saudi Arabia, Kuwait and Bahrain issued travel warnings to their citizens in May and June 2012, telling them to avoid Lebanon.[54] The number of tourists plunged from a peak of 2.2 million in 2010 to 1.7 million in 2011, and has continued to decline since.[55] A large number of hotels, restaurants and nightclubs have had to close, cut staff or reduce wages. The real-estate sector is also affected, since Gulf tourists make up a large share of demand for new apartments.

Lebanon has become a vessel for Gulf investment, and is now almost completely dependent on the oil monarchies. Rafiq Hariri was the chief architect of this dependence. He was, of course, responding to wider structural incentives. This has had some positive effects in terms of investment, tourism and real estate. However, Lebanon is tied to cycles of boom and bust in the Gulf. Furthermore, political instability is undermining tourism to Lebanon. At a more structural level, the domestic recycling of petrodollars in real estate and finance represents a failure to transform the economy. Successful developing countries such as South Korea, Taiwan and Malaysia all produce products and services that they sell internationally. Lebanon still has little to offer beyond mountains, beaches, a pleasant climate and clever bankers. Rafiq Hariri took no steps to transform the Lebanese economy to a more sustainable model. His political rivals—mainly former militia leaders— have no workable model of economic development beyond predatory rent-seeking through state largesse. Technocrats of a neoliberal or a more statist persuasion are politicised. The alliance between Hariri and neoliberal technocrats has already been discussed. Leftist technocrats such as Charbel Nahas have had to ally themselves to March 8.[56]

The Syrian civil war is bringing about fundamental changes. The Assad regime has become preoccupied with its own survival at home, and is less able to shape events in Lebanon. Its local ally Hizballah therefore started playing a much more direct and dominant role in Lebanese politics. Moreover, Lebanese actors were for the first time interfering in Syrian affairs, rather than the other way round. Hizballah was the most active participant in this regard, but Hariri also tried to meddle. The influx of hundreds of thousands of Syrian refugees to Lebanon has also changed the country's politics. Since at least 1976 Syria had intervened in Lebanese affairs. At one level the Lebanese civil war of 1975–90 can be interpreted as Syria's successful struggle for mastery in Lebanon. This meant that Rafiq Hariri and his son Sa'd had to contend with Syria. The situation is rapidly changing now. Lebanese actors are intervening in the Syrian arena, something they had not been able to do while Assad's authoritarianism had held firm.[57] Hizballah openly acknowledged its military support for the regime when it joined Assad's forces in an assault on the Syrian city of Qusayr in April 2013. Mustaqbal parliamentarian 'Uqab Saqr was reportedly organising the supply of Saudi-sponsored weapons to the Syrian opposition via Turkey.[58] Wissam Hassan, a Lebanese security general close to Sa'd Hariri, was also reportedly involved in the gun-running. However, after accusations of ineffectiveness Saudi Arabia reportedly came to rely on alternative channels.[59] The rising tide of transnational Sunni militancy means that Hariri is losing the initiative on Syria. The Islamic State in Syria and the Levant—now known as the 'Islamic State'—claimed responsibility for a suicide bombing on 2 January 2014 which killed four people in the largely Shia neighbourhood of Harat Hurayk.[60] Such actors are beyond the control of established Sunni *zu'ama* such as Sa'd Hariri. Even domestic Islamist forces are increasingly moving out of the Hariri sphere of influence. In Sidon and Tripoli Salafi Islamists are defying Sa'd Hariri's leadership. In May 2012 the arrest of a Salafi militant in Tripoli led to a show of force by Tripoli Salafi militias and intensified fighting. In June 2013 followers of Salafi preacher Ahmad al-Assir clashed with the Lebanese army. Sa'd Hariri is thus losing the ability to control violence within his own community. Within the wider Sunni community, there is disappointment with Hariri's leadership.[61] A communal leader in Lebanon is expected to show strength and determination in defence of the community. The failure to protect predominantly Sunni neighbourhoods in confrontation with Hizballah in May 2008, his 2010 apology for accusing the Syrian regime of assassinating his father, and the winding down of some of his health centres have made Hariri look weak. His prolonged absence from Lebanon since 2011 has not helped matters. The self-imposed exile may be due to security reasons, but ordinary Lebanese who do not share the luxury of foreign abodes in France or Saudi Arabia may grumble about the privilege of their *za'im*—especially since other March 14 leaders such as Samir Geagea are still in the country. The weakening of the dominant Sunni *za'im* in the face of more anti-systemic forces mirrors the rise of militias challenging the pre-war *zu'ama* in the 1970s. Lebanon's confessional power-sharing system relies on the ability of sectarian leaders to strike bargains with their counterparts. This requires leaders to be able to 'deliver' their community—to obtain popular agreement for any deals that are being struck at the elite level. If *zu'ama* lose the initiative to popular and anti-systemic forces then they may lose the ability to strike a deal. Similarly, any political deal may become irrelevant if it does not contain violence by other forces within the community. Lebanon is entering another dangerous phase in its history.

NOTES

1. INTRODUCTION

1. Michael Young, 'Two Faces of Janus: Post-War Lebanon and its Recon-struction', *Middle East Report*, 209 (1998), p. 5.
2. George Corm, 'The War System: Militia Hegemony and Reestablishment of the State', in Deirdre Colling (ed.), *Peace for Lebanon? From War to Reconstruction*, Boulder: Lynne Rienner, 1994, pp. 215–30; René Naba, *Rafic Hariri: un homme d'affaires premier ministre*, Paris: Harmattan, 1999; Najah Wakim, *al-Ayadi al-sud*, Beirut: Sharika al-Matbu'at lil-Tawzir wal-Nashar, 2006.
3. The following authors are not themselves Hariri partisans, but they reflect these views, not least because the journalist Nicholas Blanford mostly interviewed supporters of Rafiq Hariri's son Sa'd for his book: Nicholas Blanford, *Killing Mr Lebanon: The Assassination of Rafik Hariri and its Impact on the Middle East*, London: I.B. Tauris, 2006; Talal Nizameddin, 'The Political Economy of Lebanon under Rafiq Hariri: An Interpreta-tion', *Middle East Journal*, 60, 1 (2006), pp. 95–114.
4. Nadim Shehadi and Elizabeth Wilmshurst, *The Special Tribunal for Lebanon: The UN on Trial?* London: Chatham House, 2007.
5. Blanford, *Killing Mr Lebanon*, p. 30.
6. Toufic Gaspard, *A Political Economy of Lebanon 1948–2002: The Limits of Laissez-Faire*, Leiden: Brill, 2004; Samir Makdisi, *Lessons of Lebanon: The Economics of War and Development*, London: I.B. Tauris, 2004.
7. Najib Hourani, 'Transnational Pathways and Politico-Economic Power: Globalisation and the Lebanese Civil War', *Geopolitics*, 15, 2 (2010), pp. 290–311; Reinoud Leenders, *The Spoils of Truce: Corruption and State-Building in Post-War Lebanon*, Ithaca: Cornell University Press, 2012; Fawwaz Traboulsi, *Social Classes and Political Power in Lebanon*, Beirut: Heinrich Böll Stiftung, 2014.

8. Traboulsi, *Social Classes*, pp. 23–9; Najib Hourani, 'Aid and redevelopment: international finance and the reconstruction of Beirut', in Daniel Bertrand Monk and Jacob Mundy (eds.), *The Post-Conflict Environment: Investigation and Critique*, Ann Arbor: University of Michigan Press, 2014, pp. 187–218.

9. Claude Dubar and Salim Nasr, *Les Classes sociales au Liban*, Paris: Presses de la Fondation Nationale des Sciences Politiques, 1976; Michael Johnson, *Class and Client in Beirut: The Sunni Muslim Community and the Lebanese State 1840–1985*, London: Ithaca Press, 1986.

10. Rafiq Hariri, *Statesmanship in Government: Emerging from War and Entering the Future*, Beirut: Arab United Press, 1999, pp. 16–17.

11. Hariri, *Statesmanship*, p. 25.

12. The idea of a more peaceful 'new' Middle East through economic integration goes back to Israeli politician Shimon Peres: Shimon Peres, *The New Middle East*, New York: Henry Holt, 1993.

13. Gaspard, *Political Economy*, p. xix; Nadim Shehadi, *The Idea of Lebanon: Economy and the State in the Cénacle Libanais 1946–54*, Oxford: Centre for Lebanese Studies, 1987, p. 5.

14. See for instance the report by the NGO Consumer Lebanon on the prevalence of monopolies: Consumer Lebanon, *The Consumers and the Exclusive Agencies in Lebanon*, Beirut: Consumer Lebanon, 2005.

15. A point made, among others, by Clement Moore Henry and Robert Springborg, *Globalisation and the Politics of Development in the Middle East*, Cambridge: Cambridge University Press, 2001.

16. Pakradouni's original article in *al-Sharq al-Awsat* newspaper was translated and presented in Karim Pakradouni, 'Arabising Lebanese Politics', *Middle East International*, 16 May 1997, pp. 21–2.

17. Hourani, 'Aid and redevelopment', p. 210.

18. Taylor Boas and Jordan Gans-Morse, 'Neoliberalism: From New Liberal Philosophy to Anti-Liberal Slogan', *Studies in Comparative International Development*, 44, 2 (2009), pp. 137–61; John Williamson, *A Short History of the Washington Consensus*, Barcelona: Fundación CIDOB, 2004, p. 2.

19. David Harvey, *A Brief History of Neoliberalism*, Oxford: Oxford University Press, 2005, p. 19.

20. This point is made repeatedly throughout the literature. See for instance Philip Mirowski, *Never Let a Serious Crisis go to Waste*, London: Verso, 2013, p. 40. Other examples include the following: Bob Jessop, 'Liberalism, Neoliberalism, and Urban Governance: A State-Theoretical Perspective', *Antipode*, 34, 3 (2002), p. 454.

21. Pierre Bourdieu, *Acts of Resistance: Against the Tyranny of the Market*, New York: New Press, 1998, p. 2.

22. Neil Brenner, 'Urban Governance and the Production of New State Spaces in Western Europe, 1960–2000', *Review of International Political Economy*, 11, 3 (2004), pp. 447–88.

23. Gérard Duménil and Dominique Lévy, *Capital Resurgent: Roots of the Neoliberal Revolution*, Cambridge, MA: Harvard University Press, 2004; Andrew Glyn, *Capitalism Unleashed: Finance, Globalization, and Welfare*, Oxford: Oxford University Press, 2006; Harvey, *Neoliberalism*; John Gerard Ruggie, 'International Regimes, Transactions, and Change: Embedded Liberalism in the Postwar Economic Order', *International Organisation*, 36, 2 (1982), pp. 379–415.

24. Harvey, *Neoliberalism*, p. 19.

25. Jamie Peck and Adam Tickell, 'Neoliberalising Space', *Antipode*, 34, 3 (2002), p. 384.

26. Mirowski, *Never Let a Serious Crisis go to Waste*, p. 43.

27. Timothy Mitchell, 'No Factories, no Problems: The Logic of Neoliberalism in Egypt', *Review of African Political Economy*, 26, 82 (1999), pp. 455–86; Robert Vitalis, 'The Democratization Industry and the Limits of the New Interventionism', *Middle East Report*, 187/8 (1994), pp. 45–60.

28. Aihwa Ong and Stephen J. Collier, 'Global assemblages and anthropological problems', in Aihwa Ong and Stephen J. Collier (eds.), *Global Assemblages: Technology, Politics, and Ethics as Anthropological Problems*, Oxford: Wiley-Blackwell, 2008, p. 13.

29. Wendy Larner, 'Neo-Liberalism, Policy, Ideology, Governmentality', *Studies in Political Economy*, 63 (2000), pp. 17–19.

30. *AUB Bulletin*, 31, 5 (March 1989).

31. Stephen Gill, *Power and Resistance in the New World Order*, Basingstoke: Palgrave Macmillan, 2003, p. 70.

32. Duménil and Lévy, *Capital Resurgent*.

33. Ong and Collier, 'Global assemblages', p. 11.

34. Peck and Tickell, 'Neoliberalising Space', pp. 381–2.

35. Charles Tripp, 'States, elites, and the "management of change"', in Hassan Hakimian and Ziba Moshaver (eds.), *The State and Global Change: The Political Economy of Transition in the Middle East and North Africa*, Richmond: Curzon, 2001; Leo Panitch and Sam Gindin, 'Global capitalism and American empire', in Leo Panitch and Colin Leys (eds.), *The New Imperial Challenge*, London: Merlin Press, 2003.

36. Sami Zubaida, *Islam, the People and the State: Political Ideas and Movements in the Middle East*, London: I.B. Tauris, 1993, p. 146.

37. Wendy Larner, 'Neoliberalism, Mike Moore, and the WTO', *Environment and Planning*, 41, 7 (2009), pp. 1576–93.

38. Roger Owen, *Lord Cromer: Victorian Imperialist, Edwardian Proconsul*, Oxford: Oxford University Press, 2004, p. ix.

39. Roger Owen, *Imperialism, Globalization and Internationalism: Some Reflections on their Twin Impacts on the Arab Middle East in the Beginning of the Twentieth and Twenty-First Centuries*, Washington: Center for Contemporary Arab Studies, 2004, p. 9.

40. Owen, *Imperialism*, p. 9.

41. Adam Hanieh, *Capitalism and Class in the Gulf Arab States*, London: Palgrave Macmillan, 2011.

42. Erik Ohlin Wright distinguishes between the stratification approach and the Marxist approach, which looks at the relationship of exploitation: Erik Ohlin Wright, 'Understanding Class', *New Left Review*, 60 (2009), pp. 101–16.

43. Hanieh, *Capitalism and Class*.

44. Koenraad Bogaerts, *Paradigms Lost in Morocco: How Neoliberal Urban Projects Challenge our Understanding of Politics in the Arab Region*, Minneapolis: University of Minnesota Press, forthcoming.

45. Mushtaq Khan and Jomo Kwame Sundaram, 'Introduction', in Mushtaq Khan and Jomo Kwame Sundaram (eds.), *Rent, Rent-Seeking and Economic Development*, Cambridge: Cambridge University Press, 2000, pp. 5–6.

46. Mushtaq Khan, 'Rents, Efficiency and Growth', in Khan and Sundaram (eds.), *Rent, Rent-Seeking and Economic Development*, p. 24.

47. Traboulsi, *Social Classes*, pp. 12–13.

48. Farid El Khazen, *The Breakdown of the State in Lebanon*, London: I.B. Tauris, 2000.

49. Brenner, 'Urban Governance'.

2. THE RISE OF RAFIQ HARIRI: 1976–1990

1. C. Wright Mills, *The Sociological Imagination*, Oxford: Oxford University Press, 2000.

2. C. Wright Mills, *The Power Elite*, New York: Oxford University Press, 1959, p. 98.

3. Balance of payment data compiled by the economist Toufic Gaspard illustrate these patterns: Gaspard, *Political Economy*, pp. 146–7.

4. Gaspard, *Political Economy*, p. 186.

5. The share of agriculture in GDP fell from 20.2 per cent in 1950 to 9.3 per cent in 1971–3. Growth in services outpaced growth in industry: commerce, transport, communication and finance grew from 36.1 per cent to 43.4 per cent of GDP while manufacturing only expanded from 12.1 per cent to 14.0 per cent: Gaspard, *Political Economy*, pp. 151–2.

6. They averaged about 20 per cent between 1950 and 1974, while

Singaporean rates rose from 18 per cent in 1960–6 to more than 40 per cent in 1970–9: Gaspard, *Political Economy*, p. 153.

7. Trade and services consistently captured over half of all commercial bank credit between 1964 and 1974, while the share of industry remained relatively lower: Marco Rettig, 'The Role of the Banking Sector in the Economic Process of Lebanon before and after the Civil War', M.Sc. thesis, SOAS, 2004, p. 32.

8. Johnson, *Class and Client*, pp. 25–6.

9. Carolyn Gates, *The Merchant Republic of Lebanon: Rise of an Open Economy*, London: I.B. Tauris, 1998, p. 7.

10. Salim Nasr, 'Backdrop to Civil War: The Crisis of Lebanese Capitalism', *MERIP Reports*, 73 (1978), p. 5.

11. Blanford, *Killing Mr Lebanon*, p. 14.

12. For the primordial argument see Edward Shils, 'The prospects for Lebanese civility', in Leonard Binder (ed.), *Politics in Lebanon*, New York: Wiley, 1966.

13. Gaspard, *Political Economy*, p. 84.

14. Nasr does not define what he means by 'banking activity': Nasr, 'Backdrop', p. 4.

15. Henry measures size by the value of the loan portfolio: Clement Moore Henry, 'Prisoners' Financial Dilemma: A Consociational Future for Lebanon?' *American Political Science Review*, 81, 1 (1987), p. 209.

16. For an account of the agreements between the two countries and how they bolstered US hegemony see David Spiro, *The Hidden Hand of American Hegemony: Petrodollar Recycling and International Markets*, Ithaca: Cornell University Press, 1999.

17. Hanieh, *Capitalism and Class*, p. 158.

18. Salim Nasr, 'The political economy of the Lebanese conflict', in Nadim Shehadi and Bridget Harney (eds.), *Politics and the Economy in Lebanon*, Oxford: Centre for Lebanese Studies, 1989, pp. 44.

19. *an-Nahar Arab Report and Memo* (*ANARAM*), 4 June 1984, p. 4.

20. Hannes Baumann, 'The "new contractor bourgeoisie" in Lebanese politics: Hariri, Miqati and Faris', in Are Knudsen and Michael Kerr (eds.), *Lebanon: After the Cedar Revolution*, London: Hurst, 2012/New York: Oxford University Press, 2014, pp. 125–44; Najib, 'Transnational Pathways', pp. 298–9.

21. Hanieh, *Capitalism and Class*, pp. 57–84.

22. *Middle East Economic Digest* (*MEED*), 21 November 2008, p. 74.

23. *ANARAM*, 4 June 1984, p. 6.

24. Unless otherwise indicated, the information on Faris is from *Middle East Intelligence Bulletin* (*MEIB*), November 2003, pp. 12–17.

25. *ANARAM*, 4 June 1984, p. 7.

26. Blanford, *Killing Mr Lebanon*, p. 14.
27. This is what Hariri related to his friend Robert Debbas: interview with Robert Debbas, Beirut, 27 February 2008.
28. Interview with Muhammad Mashnuq, Beirut, 6 November 2008.
29. According to Fu'ad Siniura, who was in the same ANM cell as Hariri: *al-Hayat*, 21 May 2007, available in English translation at: http://english.daralhayat.com/Spec/05–2007/Article-20070521-aeecdc4a-c0a8–10ed-01b2-ede88fe3e826/story.html, accessed 6 March 2008.
30. Blanford, *Killing Mr Lebanon*, p. 17.
31. Blanford, *Killing Mr Lebanon*, p. 17.
32. Unless indicated otherwise, this account of Hariri's business success is based on an interview with a business partner and friend to Rafiq Hariri: interview with Robert Debbas, Beirut, 27 February 2008.
33. Steffen Hertog, 'The Sociology of the Gulf Rentier Systems: Societies of Intermediaries', *Comparative Studies in Society and History*, 52, 2 (2010), p. 295.
34. Blanford, *Killing Mr Lebanon*, p. 18; interview with Robert Debbas, Beirut, 27 February 2008.
35. *Middle East Economic Survey* (*MEES*), 7 February 1977, p. 9.
36. Hazem Beblawi, 'The rentier state in the Arab world', in Giacomo Luciani (ed.), *The Arab State*, London: Routledge, 1990, p. 92.
37. Hariri Foundation, *A Promising Future*, Beirut: Hariri Foundation, 2004, p. 25.
38. Unless otherwise indicated, the following section is based on Emmanuel Bonne, *Vie publique: patronage et clientèle: Rafic Hariri à Saida*, Beirut: CERMOC, 1995.
39. Hariri paid for Mustafa Sa'd's medical treatment when he lost his eyesight in a bomb attack in 1985, but his son 'Ussama ran against Bahiya Hariri in several post-war elections: *al-Safir*, 23 January 1985, p. 8; *Middle East International* (*MEI*), 10 September 1996, p. 12.
40. Unless indicated otherwise, the following information is based on *ANARAM*, 7 February 1983, pp. 4–5.
41. According to the chairman and general manager of Saudi Lebanese Bank: interview with Sabah al-Haj, Beirut, 8 November 2008.
42. Hariri Foundation, *Hariri Foundation: The Origins and Prospects*, Beirut: Hariri Foundation, 1992, p. 45.
43. Fadl Shalaq, *Tajrabatyy ma'a al-Hariri*, Beirut: Arab Scientific Publishers, 2006, pp. 60–1.
44. Shalaq, *Tajrabatyy*, p. 78.
45. Importing forty heavy trucks from Saudi Arabia to expedite the clean-up cost $13 million alone: Shalaq, *Tajrabatyy*, p. 78; *al-Safir*, 6 September 1982, p. 4; *al-Safir*, 25 January 1985, p. 5.

46. *al-Safir*, 6 September 1982, p. 4.
47. Shalaq, *Tajrabatyy*, p. 52.
48. Shalaq, *Tajrabatyy*, p. 74.
49. Interview with Robert Debbas, Beirut, 27 February 2008.
50. Interview with Tammam Salam, Beirut, 23 January 2008.
51. Shalaq, *Tajrabatyy*, p. 60.
52. Interview with Charbel Nahas, Beirut, 2 June 2008.
53. Elie Salem, *Violence and Diplomacy in Lebanon: The Troubled Years, 1982–1988*, London: I.B. Tauris, 1995, p. 103.
54. Hanieh, *Capitalism and Class*.
55. *ANARAM*, 3 October 1983, p. 3.
56. According to al-Qusaibi's obituary in *The Guardian*, Rafiq Hariri had persuaded King Fahd to overrule his health minister. In April 1984 al-Qusaibi was dismissed. The *Middle East Economic Digest* wrote: 'Al-Gosaibi had incurred the displeasure of many in the past few months—health service companies and ministry officials alike—because of his aggressive style. "When he started in the job, everyone was 100 per cent behind him, but then things started to go wrong," one health company manager says.' Several hospital construction contracts were subsequently awarded without public tendering: *MEED*, 27 April 1984, p. 37; *MEED*, 18 May 1984, p. 67; *The Guardian*, 25 August 2010, p. 35.
57. Recounted in an obituary to al-Qusaibi, *The Guardian*, 25 August 2010, p. 35.
58. *Middle East Economic Survey* reported that Oger had secured a loan of over $72 million from Arab Bank to cover these contracts: *MEES*, 1 October 1984, p. B4.
59. Robert Vitalis, *America's Kingdom: Mythmaking on the Saudi Oil Frontier*, London: Verso, 2009.
60. Rachel Bronson, 'Understanding US–Saudi relations', in Paul Aarts and Gerd Nonneman (eds.), *Saudi Arabia in the Balance: Political Economy, Society, Foreign Affairs*, London: Hurst, 2005.
61. Fred Halliday, *The Making of the Second Cold War*, London: Verso, 1986.
62. Nazih Ayubi, *Over-Stating the Arab State: Politics and Society in the Middle East*, London: I.B. Tauris, 2001, pp. 197–214.
63. Sonoko Sunayama, *Syria and Saudi Arabia: Collaboration and Conflicts in the Oil Era*, London: I.B. Tauris, 2007.
64. David Pollock, 'Saudi Arabia's King Khaled and King Fahd', in Barbara Kellerman and Jeffrey Rubin (eds.), *Leadership and Negotiation in the Middle East*, New York: Praeger, 1988, pp. 147, 151.
65. William B. Quandt, quoted by Fawaz Gerges, 'Lebanon', in Yezid Sayigh and Avi Shlaim (eds.), *The Cold War and the Middle East*, Oxford: Oxford University Press, 1997, p. 96.

66. Deeb finds that Saudi Arabia maintained a deliberately ambiguous attitude; Sunayama maintains that the Saudis sought to dissuade Gemayel from signing it; Abu Khalil claims that Gemayel coordinated closely with the kingdom when he was negotiating with Israel: Marius Deeb, 'Saudi Arabian policy toward Lebanon since 1975', in Halim Barakat (ed.), *Toward a Viable Lebanon*, London: Croom Helm, 1988, p. 180; Sunayama, *Syria and Saudi Arabia*, p. 142; As'ad Abu Khalil, 'Determinants and characteristics of the Saudi role in Lebanon: the post-civil war years', in Madawi Al-Rasheed (ed.), *Kingdom without Borders: Saudi Political, Religious and Media Frontiers*, London: Hurst, 2008, p. 89.

67. *ANARAM*, 22 November 1982, p. 1.

68. Joe Stork, 'Report from Lebanon', *MERIP Reports*, 118 (1983), p. 6.

69. *ANARAM*, 22 August 1983, p. 4; Hourani, 'Transnational Pathways', p. 300.

70. *ANARAM*, 22 November 1982, p. 1.

71. *ANARAM*, 2 May 1983, p. 5.

72. For examples see *MEED*, 10 December 1976, p. 24; *MEED*, 4 March 1977, p. 24; *MEED*, 11 March 1977, p. 30; *MEED*, 7 October 1977, p. 29; *MEES*, 9 July 1979, p. I.

73. Salem, *Violence and Diplomacy*, p. 120; William Simpson, *The Prince: The Secret Story of the World's Most Intriguing Royal, Prince Bandar al-Sultan*. New York: Regan, 2006, p. 103.

74. There were still clear limits to Hariri's influence: it took a Damascus visit by the newly promoted information minister 'Ali al-Sha'ir as well as the intervention of King Fahd himself to produce a ceasefire agreement on 23 September 1983: Simpson, *The Prince*, pp. 105–8; Sunayama, *Syria and Saudi Arabia*, pp. 233, FN 21.

75. Blanford, *Killing Mr Lebanon*, pp. 25–6.

76. Salem, *Violence and Diplomacy*, p. 120.

77. Salem, *Violence and Diplomacy*, pp. 142–3.

78. *ANARAM*, 7 February 1983, pp. 4–5.

79. Interview with Charbel Nahas, Beirut, 2 June 2008.

80. Salem, *Violence and Diplomacy*, p. 103.

81. Rosemary Sayigh, *Too Many Enemies: The Palestinian Experience in Lebanon*, London: Zed Books, 1994, p. 135.

82. *ANARAM*, 27 June 1983, p. 7.

83. *ANARAM*, 18 July 1983, p. 4; *ANARAM*, 8 August 1983, pp. 7–8; Eric Verdeil, 'Reconstructions manquées à Beyrouth', *Les Annales de la recherche urbaine*, 91 (2001), p. 71.

84. Verdeil, 'Reconstructions', p. 72.

85. Sayigh mentions Uza'i, Burj al-Barajna and Shatila. It is not clear whether Oger's actions were coordinated with the army, but it did

coordinate with the Committee for the Development of the Southern Suburbs, an institution set up by Gemayel: Sayegh, *Too Many Enemies*, p. 134; Hariri Foundation, *Origins*, p. 68; Verdeil, 'Reconstructions', p. 61.

86. Hariri Foundation, *Origins*, p. 72.
87. Eric Verdeil, 'Une ville et ses urbanistes: Beyrouth en reconstruction', Ph.D. thesis, Université de Paris I Sorbonne, 2002, p. 539.
88. The information in this paragraph is derived from *ANARAM*, 22 August 1983, p. 4.
89. *al-Safir*, 25 January 1985, p. 5.
90. Verdeil, 'Reconstructions', p. 72.
91. *ANARAM*, 15 April 1985, p. 2.
92. Sayigh, *Too Many Enemies*, p. 187.
93. Salam ally Muhammad Mashnuq says that Salam left three reasons: first, security; secondly, because he wanted to care for his wife, who was in ill health; and thirdly, to allow his son Tammam greater leeway in developing as a politician in his own right: interview with Muhammad Mashnuq, Beirut, 11 June 2008. Sa'ib's son Tammam continued the family's political tradition, but never achieved his father's political weight.
94. Deeb, 'Saudi Arabian Policy', pp. 181–2.
95. Salem, *Violence and Diplomacy*, p. 180.
96. Blanford, *Killing Mr Lebanon*, p. 29.
97. Blanford, *Killing Mr Lebanon*, p. 29.
98. Shahram Chubin and Charles Tripp, *Iran–Saudi Arabia Relations and Regional Order: Iran and Saudi Arabia in the Balance of Power in the Gulf*, Oxford: Oxford University Press, 1996.
99. Bob Woodward, *Veil: The Secret Wars of the CIA 1981–1987*, New York: Simon & Schuster, 2005, pp. 396–8.
100. Deputy general secretary of Hizballah Na'im Qassim identified a CIA-trained special unit of the Lebanese army as the perpetrators, but does not mention any Saudi involvement: Naim Qassem, *Hizbullah: The Story from Within*, Beirut: Saqi, 2007, pp. 182–4.
101. Blanford, *Killing Mr Lebanon*, p. 65.
102. The attack was reported in the Lebanese press: *al-Safir*, 12 June 1985, p. 4.
103. *al-Nahar*, 30 May 1986, p. 5.
104. The condemnation of attacks is generally reported, rather than the attacks themselves: *al-Safir*, 15 February 1986, p. 5; *al-Safir*, 18 February 1986, p. 2.
105. 'Abdallah Bu Habib, *al-Daw' al-asfar: al-siyyasat al-Amirkiyya tijah Lubnan*, Beirut: Sharikat al-Matbu'at lil-Tawazi' wal-Nashar, 2007, pp. 175–7.

106. Blanford, *Killing Mr Lebanon*, p. 33.
107. Quoted by Blanford, *Killing Mr Lebanon*, p. 28.
108. Salem, *Violence and Diplomacy*, pp. 260, 262.
109. Michael Kerr, *Imposing Power-Sharing: Conflict and Coexistence in Northern Ireland and Lebanon*, Dublin: Irish Academic Press, 2005, p. 169.
110. Kerr, *Imposing Power-Sharing*, p. 160.
111. Blanford, *Killing Mr Lebanon*, p. 36.
112. This account of Ta'if relies on Theodor Hanf and Michael Kerr, who both interviewed participants of the conference: Theodor Hanf, *Coexistence in Wartime Lebanon: Decline of a State and Death of a Nation*, London: I.B. Tauris, 1993; Kerr, *Imposing Power-Sharing*.
113. The external aspect of the agreement, dealing with relations with Syria, had been agreed with Damascus and was non-negotiable. Hariri travelled to Damascus to run the new power-sharing formula past Assad. It was based on a paper agreed by Gemayel, Salem and Hariri in 1987 but had been rejected by Assad: Salem, *Violence and Diplomacy*, pp. 236–41; Kerr, *Imposing Power-Sharing*, p. 155; Hanf, *Coexistence*, pp. 589–90.
114. Hanf, *Coexistence*, p. 588.
115. Blanford, *Killing Mr Lebanon*, p. 37.
116. Hanf, *Coexistence*, pp. 594–5.
117. Hanf, *Coexistence*, p. 596.
118. Marwan Iskandar, *Rafiq Hariri and the Fate of Lebanon*, London: Saqi, 2006, p. 60.
119. Hrawi was clearly 'Syria's man as Lebanon's president': Hanf, *Coexistence* p. 595. Mouawad's status is somewhat more ambiguous. He was elected with Syrian approval and 'he was acceptable to the pro-Syrian forces because he had never left any doubt about his view that a settlement in Lebanon was only possible in agreement with Syria': Hanf, *Coexistence* p. 593. However, he alienated Syria by insisting on dialogue rather than violent confrontation with Michel Aoun, who still claimed the presidency for himself. There is therefore speculation that Syria had assassinated Mouawad: Hanf, *Coexistence*, pp. 590–5.
120. Blanford, *Killing Mr Lebanon*, p. 37.
121. The Israeli air force did not react to the Syrian air raid on Ba'abda, despite previous threats to do so. This was probably due to US pressure on the Israeli government: Hanf, *Coexistence* p. 611; Kerr, *Imposing Power-Sharing*, p. 158.
122. Blanford, *Killing Mr Lebanon*, p. 29.
123. Henry, 'Prisoners', p. 211; *ANARAM*, 8 November 1985, p. 10; Sibline company website, n.d 2009, available at http://www.scs.com.lb/

templates/controls/contenttemplates.aspx?MenuID=2548, accessed 10 July 2009.

124. *al Nahar*, 18 July 1987, p. 6.

125. *al-Nahar*, 5 December 1987, p. 5.

126. Henry, 'Prisoners', p. 214.

127. Representatives associated with traditional families also resigned from the board in May 1984. They were Fu'ad Buhsali, Robert Sursuq and Khaldun Subra: Kamal Dib, *Warlords and Merchants: The Lebanese Business and Political Establishment*, Reading: Ithaca, 2004, p. 231. Intra also lost its line of credit with Robert Sursuq's bank after he left the board in 1983: *ANARAM*, 23 July 1983, p. 2.

128. At the same time as Tamraz expanded Intra's influence he made it unaccountable to its shareholders: *ANARAM*, 12 September 1986, p. 11; *ANARAM*, 23 July 1983, p. 2; *ANARAM*, 29 April 1985, p. 5; *MEES*, 13 January 1986, p. B4–5.

129. *ANARAM*, 10 December 1984, pp. 4–5.

130. *al-Safir*, 25 January 1985, p. 5; *ANARAM*, 28 January 1985, p. 3.

131. *MEES*, 11 March 1985, p. B1; *ANARAM*, 4 March 1985, p. 6.

132. *ANARAM*, 10 October 1983, p. 8; *ANARAM*, 7 November 1983, p. 7.

133. The importance of these funds is illustrated by the brief resumption of PLO inflows in 1985, which pushed up the Lebanese currency. PLO financing for clashes with Amal were estimated at $300–350 million. This pushed up the value of the Lebanese pound from LL19 to the dollar to LL15.20 between April and July 1985: *ANARAM*, 19 December 1986, p. 6.

134. Nasr, 'Political Economy', p. 47.

135. The balance of payments account illustrates the large degree of speculation, with most of the capital account falling under the rubric of errors and omissions: Gaspard, *Political Economy*, pp. 146–7.

136. Christopher Towe, *Exchange Rate 'Fundamentals' versus Speculation: The Case of Lebanon*, Washington: IMF, 1988.

137. Gaspard, *Political Economy*, pp. 202–7.

138. *ANARAM*, 30 April 1984, pp. 2–6; *ANARAM*, 4 January 1986, p. 20.

139. Gaspard, *Political Economy* pp. 202–3.

140. *ANARAM*, 30 April 1984, pp. 2–6; *ANARAM*, 19 July 1985, pp. 2–3; *ANARAM*, 17 December 1984, p. 6. In March 1986 subscription to treasury bills became compulsory: Makdisi, *Lessons of Lebanon*, p. 72.

141. *MEES*, 24 August 1987, p. B1; *MEES*, 26 October 1987, p. B4; Makdisi, *Lessons of Lebanon*, p. 196.

142. Gaspard, *Political Economy*, pp. 203–4.

143. Dib, *Warlords and Merchants*, p. 224.

144. *ANARAM*, 23 July 1983, p. 2; Dib, *Warlords and Merchants*, p. 224.

145. Dib, *Warlords and Merchants*, p. 231.

146. *ANARAM*, 21 January 1985, p. 3; George Corm, *Le Liban contemporain: histoire et société*, Paris: Découverte, 2005, p. 208.

147. Bu Habib, *al-Daw'*, p. 178.

148. Bu Habib, *al Daw'*, p. 178.

149. Wakim, *al-Ayadi al-sud*, p. 51.

150. Several paragraphs in this section are based on parts of a chapter in a book published by Karthala. The author would like to thank Karthala for their permission to reproduce these here: Hannes Baumann, 'The ascent of Rafiq Hariri and philanthropic practices in Beirut', in Franck Mermier and Sabrina Mervin (eds.), *Leaders et partisans au Liban*, Paris: Karthala, 2012, pp. 81–106.

151. Hariri Foundation, *A Promising Future*, p. 12.

152. For instance in a TV interview with Marwan Iskandar: *al Safir*, 21 June 1983, p. 5.

153. Pierre Bourdieu, *Language and Symbolic Power*, Cambridge: Polity, 1991, p. 170.

154. Hariri Foundation, *Origins*, p. 23.

155. According to Salwa Ba'siri, leading employee: *al Safir*, 17 October 1985, p. 7. The original focus on 'Islamic society' was toned down in later publications of the Hariri Foundation, which stated: 'The work [of the Islamic Institute for Culture and Higher Education] was carried out regardless of political or sectarian affiliation': Hariri Foundation, *Origins*, p. 23.

156. It included a medical centre, vocational and nursing schools, a sports centre, and a studies centre for engineering: Hariri Foundation, *Origins*, pp. 25–33.

157. Interview with Mustafa Za'tari, Beirut, 31 January 2008.

158. *al-Safir*, 23 May 1985, p. 4.

159. *al-Safir*, 17 October 1985, p. 7.

160. *al-Safir*, 21 June 1983, p. 5.

161. After the Geneva Conference, Foreign Minister Elie Salem suggested that Hariri be made prime minister. Salem claims that President Gemayel was not opposed to the idea but did not want to go through the protracted bargaining associated with changing the prime minister: Salem, *Violence and Diplomacy*, p. 130.

162. For instance, in an interview with Marwan Iskandar, Hariri said he did not want to favour one group over the other: *al-Safir*, 26 June 1986, p. 5; Rafiq Hariri to *al-Safir*, 28 November 1984, p. 7; Fadl Shalaq to *al-Safir*, 18 January 1985, p. 7.

163. As set out in 'Supplemental Agreement IX (Renewal) Between The American University of Beirut And The Hariri Foundation For

Student's Evaluation Testing', 18 September 1986, American University of Beirut/Library Archives, AA:2.5.6.2, Career Guidance Center, 1991–7.

164. *al-Safir*, 16 April 1986, p. 7.
165. *al-Safir*, 17 October 1985, p. 7.
166. *al-Safir*, 17 October 1985, p. 7.
167. *al-Safir*, 28 November 1984, p. 7.
168. *al-Safir*, 21 September 1986, p. 7; Hariri Foundation, *Origins*, p. 212.
169. As set out in 'An Agreement between the Hariri Foundation (HF) and the American University of Beirut (AUB)', 21 January 1987, American University of Beirut/Library Archives, AA:2.5.6.2, Career Guidance Center 1991–7. See also *al-Safir*, 25 November 1986, p. 7.
170. Prior to announcing the continuation of support to staff salaries, Hariri met assistant secretary of state for Near East affairs Richard Murphy together with the head of the AUB management council, Christian Herter: *al-Safir*, 25 November 1986, p. 7.
171. The Americans also propped up the finances of the university. In April 1984 the US Senate Foreign Relations Committee endowed AUB with a trust fund of $50 million. The establishment of the trust fund coincided with the announcement that the USA would withdraw the 1,800 marines still lying offshore as part of the Multinational Force in Lebanon: *ANARAM*, 2 April 1984, p. 19. For a history of US government and philanthropic support for AUB, see Özlem Altan-Olcay, 'Defining "America" from a Distance: Local Strategies of the Global in the Middle East', *Middle Eastern Studies*, 44, 1 (2008), pp. 29–52.
172. Shalaq, *Tajrabatyy*, p. 158.
173. Shalaq, *Tajrabatyy*, pp. 170–1.
174. *al-Safir*, 3 June 1985, p. 7; *al-Safir*, 27 July 1985, p. 5.
175. Shalaq, *Tajrabatyy*, p. 169.
176. The association sent sixty-four students to European and American universities with Hariri Foundation support at the turn of 1984–5: *al-Safir*, 27 December 1984, p. 7; *al-Safir*, 27 February 1985, p. 7. See also Shalaq, *Tajrabatyy*, p. 170.
177. The location of Hariri Foundation offices are from an interview with Mustafa Za'tari, director general of the directorate of education, Hariri Foundation, Beirut, 31 January 2008. A reference to the Biqa' office of the foundation can be found in *al-Safir*, 19 January 1985, p. 7.
178. Hilal Khashan, 'How Grantees Relate to Grantor: A Study on a Lebanese College Scholarship Foundation', *Research in Higher Education*, 33, 2 (1992), p. 269.

179. *al-Safir*, 17 October 1985, p. 7.

180. Khashan, 'How Grantees Relate', p. 269.

181. Khashan, 'How Grantees Relate'.

182. The figures have been rounded up.

183. Khashan, 'How Grantees Relate', p. 266.

184. Salem, *Violence and Diplomacy*, p. 130.

185. The Sa'ib Salam Foundation provided Maqasid scholarships and received LL1 million from Hariri in 1984 and LL1.5 million in 1985: *al-Safir*, 13 July 1984 p. 7; *al-Safir*, 21 June 1985, p. 6.

186. An example is food aid provided by the kingdom in 1988: *al-Nahar*, 6 January 1988, p. 4.

187. *al-Safir*, 8 January 1986, p. 7.

188. Fadl Shalaq publicly praised King Fahd's patronage: *al-Safir*, 18 January 1985, p. 7. A book publicising the Hariri Foundation was dedicated to King Fahd: 'To the Custodian of the Two Holy Mosques, Fahd Ben Abdul Aziz Al-Saud, King of Saudi Arabia, in recognition and gratitude for his limitless generosity' (Hariri Foundation, *Origins*).

189. Blanford, *Killing Mr Lebanon*, p. 14.

190. Interview with Fadl Shalaq, Beirut, 4 April 2008.

191. Hourani, 'Transnational Pathways'.

192. Leenders, *The Spoils of Truce*.

193. Hariri, *Statesmanship in Government*, pp. 16–17.

194. Hourani, 'Transnational Pathways', p. 290.

3. RECONSTRUCTION: 1992–1998

1. World Development Indicators database, available at http://databank.worldbank.org/data/reports.aspx?source=world-development-indicators, accessed 24 February 2015.

2. Wakim, *al-Ayadi al-sud*.

3. Nizameddin, 'Political Economy'.

4. Rent did play a crucial role in the theories of classical economists such as David Ricardo, who used the term to describe the differences in the agricultural productivity of land: David Ricardo, *On the Principles of Political Economy and Taxation*, Kitchener: Batoche Books, 2001, pp. 39–50.

5. Anne Krueger, 'The Political Economy of Rent-Seeking Society', *American Economic Review*, 64, 3 (1974), pp. 291–303.

6. Khan, 'Rents, Efficiency and Growth', p. 24.

7. Mark Neal and Richard Tansey, 'The Dynamics of Effective Corrupt Leadership: Lessons from Rafik Hariri's Political Career in Lebanon', *Leadership Quarterly*, 21, 1 (2010), pp. 33–49; Wakim, *al-Ayadi al-sud*.

8. World Bank, *Helping Countries Combat Corruption*, Washington: World Bank, 1997, p. 8.

9. For an overview of the features of neoliberal urban megaprojects see Erik Swyngedouw, Frank Moulaert and Arantxa Rodriguez, 'Neoliberal Urbanisation in Europe: Large-Scale Urban Development Projects and the New Urban Policy', *Antipode*, 34, 3 (2002), pp. 542–77.

10. Harvey, *Neoliberalism*, p. 160.

11. Rachel Weber, 'Extracting Value from the City: Neoliberalism and Urban Redevelopment', *Antipode*, 34, 3 (2002), pp. 519–40.

12. For a summary of the debate whether a transfer had actually taken place, whether it was voluntary or enforced, see Leenders, *The Spoils of Truce*, pp. 108–13.

13. *Daily Star*, 6 August 2007, p. 4.

14. Solidere, *The Development and Reconstruction of Beirut Central District: Information Booklet 1995*, Beirut: Solidere, 1995, p. 4.

15. *Daily Star*, 6 August 2007, p. 4.

16. For figures see Heiko Schmid, 'Privatized Urbanity or a Politicized Society? Reconstruction in Beirut after the Civil War', *European Planning Studies*, 14, 3 (2006), p. 370; Verdeil, 'Une ville et ses urbanistes', pp. 57, 62.

17. Schmid, 'Privatized Urbanity', p. 370.

18. Solidere, *Development and Reconstruction*, p. 9.

19. Schmid, 'Privatized Urbanity', p. 373.

20. Karim Eid-Sabbagh, 'Reconstruction in Lebanon: Neoliberalism and Spatial Production' Master of Urban Planning thesis, AUB, 2007, p. 138.

21. Solidere, *Development and Reconstruction*, p. 12.

22. Swyngedouw et al., 'Neoliberal Urbanisation', p. 563.

23. Fares el-Dahdah, 'On Solidere's motto: "Beirut: Ancient City of the Future"', in Peter Rowe and Hashim Sarkis (eds.), *Projecting Beirut: Episodes in the Construction and Reconstruction of a Modern City*, Munich: Prestel, 1998, pp. 68–77; Saree Makdisi, 'Laying Claim to Beirut: Urban Narrative and Spatial Identity in the Age of Solidere', *Critical Inquiry*, 23, 3 (1997), pp. 660–705.

24. Economist Intelligence Unit (EIU), *Country Report: Lebanon*, 3rd Quarter, 1994, p. 10; *MEI*, 12 May 1995, p. 15.

25. Leenders, *The Spoils of Truce*, p. 61.

26. Solidere, *Development and Reconstruction*, p. 5.

27. Quoted in *Daily Star*, 6 August 2007, p. 4.

28. Tom Pierre Najem, *Lebanon's Renaissance: The Political Economy of Reconstruction*, Reading: Ithaca, 2000, p. 167.

29. *Lebanon Report*, September 1994, p. 8.

30. According to figures published by the Beirut Stock Exchange (BSE), available at http://www.bse.com.lb/Market/HistoricalData/tabid/90/Default.aspx, accessed 26 January 2010.
31. For evidence of a forced transfer see Leenders' discussion of this issue: Leenders, *The Spoils of Truce*, pp. 108–13.
32. Harvey, *Neoliberalism*, p. 160.
33. Legislative Decree No. 5, Creation of the Council for Development and Reconstruction, 31 January 1977.
34. Sami 'Atallah, 'al-Mu'assasat al-hukumiya wal-tiyat tahdir al-muwazanat', in Lebanese Centre for Policy Studies, *al-Muwazanat wal-tanmiya al-ijtima'iyat fi lubnan*, Beirut: Lebanese Centre for Policy Studies, 2000, pp. 34–6.
35. *ANARAM*, 22 August 1983, p. 4.
36. *ANARAM*, 8 August 1983, pp. 7–8.
37. Iskandar, *Rafiq Hariri*, p. 69.
38. Said Hitti Kemal Shehadi and Rana Houry, *A Framework for Reducing the Lebanese Budget Deficit*, Beirut: Lebanese Centre for Policy Studies, 1998, p. 24; 'Atallah, 'al-Mu'assasat', pp. 34–6.
39. These governance features are enumerated in Swyngedouw et al., 'Neoliberal Urbanisation', which looks at thirteen urban regeneration projects.
40. Swyngedouw et al., 'Neoliberal Urbanisation', p. 572.
41. Swyngedouw et al., 'Neoliberal Urbanisation', p. 574.
42. Solidere, *Development and Reconstruction*, p. 3.
43. Angus Gavin, *Beirut Reborn: The Restoration and Development of the Central District*, London: Academy Editions, 1996, pp. 16–17.
44. Doris Summer, 'Neo-Liberalising the City and the Circulation of City Builders and Urban Images in Beirut and Amman', MA thesis, AUB, 2005.
45. *al-Nahar*, 8 January 1994, pp. 1, 15.
46. Najem, *Lebanon's Renaissance*, p. 167.
47. Najem, *Lebanon's Renaissance*, p. 166.
48. Colin Legum, *Middle East Contemporary Survey*, London: Holmes & Meier, 1992, p. 619; Makassed, *Makassed: Serving Generations, Building Others*, Beirut: Dar el-Kotob, 1998, p. 36.
49. Schmid goes as far as to suggest that Hariri controlled all but one seat on the board of directors: Schmid, 'Privatized Urbanity', p. 371.
50. *Lebanon Report*, October–November 1994, p. 7.
51. Jakob Skovgaard-Petersen, 'The Sunni Religious Scene in Beirut', *Mediterranean Politics*, 3, 1 (1998), p. 77.
52. For instance, the visit of Bahij Tabbara and Fadl Shalaq to Elias 'Audi, the Greek Orthodox Metropolitan of Beirut (*al-Nahar*, 19 December 1990, p. 5).

53. Heiko Schmid, 'Ära Hariri: Wiederaufbau nach dem Bürgerkrieg', *tec21* 5, 33–4 (2005), p. 19.
54. Iskandar, *Rafiq Hariri*, p. 67.
55. Assem Salam, 'The role of government in shaping the built environment', in Rowe and Sarkis (eds.), *Projecting Beirut*.
56. EIU, *Country Report: Lebanon*, 1st Quarter, 1996, p. 10. The government could also use financial pressure against the Beirut municipality, which relied on funds dispersed from the centre. It did so in 1995: EIU, *Country Report: Lebanon*, 4th Quarter, 1995, p. 14.
57. Swyngedouw et al., 'Neoliberal Urbanisation'.
58. Larner, 'Neoliberalism, Mike Moore, and the WTO'.
59. *Financial Times*, 9 July 1993, p. 14.
60. The expression 'new Middle East' refers to a book by then-foreign minister of Israel Shimon Peres, in which he envisioned an integrated economic future for Israel and the Arab states as a basis for peaceful relations: Peres, *The New Middle East*.
61. Interview with Charbel Nahas, Beirut, 2 June 2008.
62. Maha Yahya, 'Let the dead be dead: communal imaginaries and national narratives in the post-civil war reconstruction of Beirut', in Alev Cinar and Thomas Bender (eds.), *Urban Imaginaries: Locating the Modern City*, Minneapolis: University of Minneapolis Press, 2007 pp. 243, 261 FN 18.
63. See for instance the comments by CDR vice-president Butros Labaki, as reported in *Lebanon Report*, March 1994, p. 10.
64. Leenders, *The Spoils of Truce*, p. 67.
65. Aseel Sawalha, '"Healing the wounds of the war": placing the war-displaced in post-war Beirut', in Jane Schneider and Ida Susser (eds.), *Wounded Cities: Destruction and Reconstruction in a Globalised World*, Oxford: Berg, 2003, p. 289, FN 289.
66. EIU, *Country Report: Lebanon*, 3rd Quarter, 1996, p. 20.
67. EIU, *Country Report: Lebanon*, 1st Quarter, 1996, p. 15.
68. EIU, *Country Report: Lebanon*, 1st Quarter, 1998, p. 24; Joumana Ghandour Atallah, 'The northern sector: projects and plans at sea', in Rowe and Sarkis (eds.), *Projecting Beirut*.
69. Harb el-Kak, Mona, 'Post-War Beirut: Resources, Negotiations, and Contestation in the Elyssar Project', *Arab World Geographer*, 3, 4 (2000), pp. 272–88.
70. Marieke Krijnen and Mona Fawaz, 'Exception as the Rule: High-End Developments in Neoliberal Beirut', *Built Environment*, 36, 2 (2010), pp. 245–59.
71. Hourani, 'Aid and Redevelopment'.
72. Marieke Krijnen and Christiaan De Beukelaer, 'Capital, state and con-

flict: the various drivers of diverse gentrification processes in Beirut, Lebanon', in Loretta Lees, Hyun Bang Shin and Ernesto Lopez-Morales (eds.), *Global Gentrifications: Uneven Development and Displacement*, Bristol: Policy Press, 2015, pp. 285–309.

73. Mona Fawaz, 'Neoliberal Urbanity and the Right to the City: A View from Beirut's Periphery', *Development and Change*, 40, 5 (2009), pp. 827–52.

74. Nouriel Roubini and Brad Setser, *Bailouts or Bail-Ins? Responding to Financial Crises in Emerging Economies*, Washington: Institute for International Economics, 2004, p. 39.

75. IMF, *International Finance Statistics*, Washington: IMF, 2007.

76. Data downloaded from the Banque du Liban website, available at http://www.bdl.gov.lb/edata/index.asp, accessed 20 September 2016.

77. *Lebanon Report*, February 1993, p. 9.

78. Data downloaded from the Banque du Liban website, available at http://www.bdl.gov.lb/edata/index.asp, accessed 20 September 2016.

79. IMF, *Lebanon: Selected Issues*, Washington: IMF, 2006, p. 26.

80. Taline Urnéchlian, Sena Eken and Thomas Helbling, 'Dynamics of interest rate movements: an empirical study', in Sena Eken and Thomas Helbling (eds.), *Back to the Future: Postwar Reconstruction and Stabilization in Lebanon*, Occasional Paper 176, Washington: IMF, 1999, p. 37.

81. This account of the movement of treasury bill interest rates follows Makdisi's analysis: Makdisi, *Lessons of Lebanon*, p. 109.

82. Gaspard, *Political Economy*, p. 218.

83. Corm provides a similar calculation: George Corm, 'Overcoming the Debt Trap: Towards an Alternative Development Model in Lebanon', paper presented at the American University Beirut, 21 May 2007, slide 18.

84. Gaspard, *Political Economy*, p. 217.

85. Hariri, *Statesmanship in Government*, p. 51.

86. Data downloaded from the Banque du Liban website, available at http://www.bdl.gov.lb/edata/index.asp, accessed 20 September 2016.

87. Interview with Charbel Nahas, Beirut, 2 June 2008.

88. Robert Wade, 'Wheels within Wheels: Rethinking the Asian Crisis and the Asian Model', *Annual Review of Political Science*, 85, 3 (2000), pp. 85–115.

89. Roubini and Setser, *Bailouts or Bail-Ins?*, p. 39.

90. Roubini and Setser, *Bailouts or Bail-Ins?*, p. 70.

91. These data and the following are from Freddie Baz, *Bilanbanques: Liban*, Beirut: Bankdata Financial Services, various years.

92. Data downloaded from the Banque du Liban website, available at http://www.bdl.gov.lb/edata/index.asp, accessed 20 September 2016.

93. UNDP, *National Human Development Report—Lebanon 2001–2002: Globalisation, towards a Lebanese Agenda*, Beirut: UNDP, 2002, p. 77.
94. *Lebanon Report*, July 1991, p. 6.
95. Data reproduced in Wassim Shahin, 'The Lebanese economy in the twentyfirst century', in Kail Ellis (ed.), *Lebanon's Second Republic: Prospects for the Twenty-first Century*, Gainesville: University Press of Florida, 2002, p. 190.
96. Hariri, *Statesmanship in Government*, pp. 21–4.
97. The interest payments projected in Horizon 2000 are compared with public debt transactions as calculated by the World Bank. Shahin, 'The Lebanese Economy', p. 190; World Bank, *Lebanon: Public Expenditure Reform Priorities for Fiscal Adjustment: Growth and Poverty Alleviation*, Washington: World Bank, 2005, p. 76.
98. Gavin, *Beirut Reborn*, p. 36.
99. *Lebanon Report*, March 1990, p. 2.
100. Bu Habib, *al-Daw'*, p. 178.
101. Makdisi, *Lessons of Lebanon*, pp. 97–8.
102. IMF, *Lebanon: Selected Issues*, p. 26; Urnéechlian et al., 'Dynamics', p. 37.
103. *MEED*, 4 June 1993, p. 27.
104. Siniura had been vice-chairman and managing director at the Mediterranean Investment Group, which owned Banque Mediterranée (1983–92), and chairman and managing director of Banque Mediterranée (1984–92): President of the Council of Ministers, official website, n.d., available at http://www.pcm.gov.lb/Cultures/ar-LB/Menu/%D8%B1%D8%A6%D9%8A%D8%B3+%D9%85%D8%AC%D9%84%D8%B3+%D8%A7%D9%84%D9%88%D8%B2%D8%B1%D8%A7%D8%A1/%D8%AF%D9%88%D9%84%D8%A9+%D8%B1%D8%A6%D9%8A%D8%B3+%D9%85%D8%AC%D9%84%D8%B3++%D8%A7%D9%84%D9%88%D8%B2%D8%B1%D8%A7%D8%A1/, accessed 3 August 2008.
105. Interview with Fu'ad Siniura, London, 30 November 2010.
106. Interview with Fu'ad Siniura, London, 30 November 2010.
107. Dib, *Warlords and Merchants*, p. 223.
108. Interview with Fu'ad Siniura, London, 30 November 2010.
109. Interview with Fu'ad Siniura, London, 30 November 2010; interview with Muhammad Shatah, Beirut, 13 February 2008.
110. Interview with Fu'ad Siniura, London, 30 November 2010. The 'other shocks' may refer to Israeli bombing campaigns that hit Lebanon in 1993 and 1996.
111. Gaspard, *Political Economy*, p. 218.
112. Makdisi, *Lessons of Lebanon*, p. 113.

113. Baz, *Bilanbanques*.
114. Baz, *Bilanbanques*.
115. For instance, Arab Bank and Banque Nationale de Paris Inter-continentale Liban (BNPI) had been the third- and fourth-largest banks by assets in 1991—before the treasury-bill rally—but lost their dominant position in subsequent years.
116. UNDP, *National Human Development*, p. 77.
117. Bassam Fattouh, 'A Political Analysis of Budget Deficits in Lebanon', *SOAS Economic Digest*, June 1997.
118. Axel Schimmelpfennig and Edward Gardner, 'Lebanon—Weathering the Perfect Storms', IMF Working Paper WP/08/17, Washington: IMF, 2008, p. 22.
119. Schimmelpfennig and Gardner, 'Lebanon', p. 20.
120. The case of Capital Investment Services (CIS) and the UK-based Royal Bank of Canada Investment Management is typical. They created a fund of $20 million to invest in high-rate Lebanese government treasury bills. Yet the initiative to invest in these instruments had come from CIS's customers—Lebanese and Arab investors. EIU, *Country Report: Lebanon*, 3rd Quarter, 1996, p. 24. Foreign banks operating in Lebanon such as Germany's Commerzbank tend to engage in trade credit rather than investing in treasury bills.
121. Elizabeth Picard, 'The political economy of civil war in Lebanon', in Steven Heydemann (ed.), *War, Institutions, and Social Change in the Middle East*, Berkeley: University of California Press, 2000, p. 317.
122. The data on public expenditure by functional category are taken from World Bank, *Lebanon: Public Expenditure Reform Priorities*, pp. 75–6.
123. Ramla Khalidi-Beyhum, *Poverty Reduction Policies in Jordan and Lebanon: An Overview*, New York: UN, 1999, p. 61.
124. Walid Ammar, *Health System and Reform in Lebanon*, Beirut: WHO and Ministry of Public Health Lebanon, 2003, p. 56.
125. Nisreen Salti and Jad Chaaban, 'The Role of Sectarianism in the Allocation of Public Expenditure in Post-War Lebanon', *International Journal of Middle East Studies*, 42, 4 (2010), pp. 643, 648.
126. Hitti, and Houry, *A Framework*, p. 24.
127. Sayigh, *Too Many Enemies*, p. 187.
128. Picard, 'Political Economy of Civil War', p. 315.
129. In June 2001, the Council for the South's plan to reconnect southern areas to the national electricity grid had been completed but villages still complained about having no electricity, *MEI*, 1 June 2001, pp. 24–5.
130. Legum, *Middle East Contemporary Survey*, pp. 608–9.
131. For instance *MEI*, 4 September 1998, p. 14.

132. EIU, *Country Report: Lebanon*, 1st Quarter, 1994, p. 13; 'Atallah, 'al-Mu'assasat', p. 25.
133. The number of internally displaced is an estimate of the Ministry of the Displaced from 1996, quoted in Internal Displacement Monitoring Centre, 'Lebanon Overview', Geneva: IDMC, 2010, available at http://www.internal-displacement.org/8025708F004BE3B1/%28httpInfoFiles%29/ADA51C6E3FB628FFC1257809004FD417/$file/Lebanon_Overview_Dec2010.pdf, accessed 15 June 2011. The percentage of internally displaced persons living in poverty is from UNDP, *A Profile of Sustainable Human Development in Lebanon*, Beirut: UNDP, 1997, p. 55.
134. *MEI*, 9 April 1999, p. 11.
135. Aram Nerguizian, *The Lebanese Armed Forces: Challenges and Opportunities in Post-Syria Lebanon*, Washington: CSIS, 2009, p. 78.
136. World Bank, *Lebanon: Public Expenditure Reform Priorities*, pp. 75–6.
137. EIU, *Country Report: Lebanon*, 4th Quarter, 1994, p. 12.
138. The information on Murr is taken from Ziad Abdelnour, 'Dossier: Michel and Elias Murr', *Middle East Intelligence Bulletin*, 5, 6 (June 2003).
139. Blanford, *Killing Mr Lebanon*, p. 49.
140. See for instance Pakradouni, 'Arabising Lebanese Politics'.
141. Harvey, *Neoliberalism*, p. 19.
142. Mirowski, *Never Let a Serious Crisis go to Waste*, p. 40. See also Jessop, 'Liberalism, Neoliberalism, and Urban Governance', p. 454.
143. Stephen Heydemann, 'Upgrading Authoritarianism in the Arab World', Saban Center for Middle East Policy, Brookings Institution, Analysis Paper No. 13, October 2007, available at http://www.brookings.edu/~/media/research/files/papers/2007/10/arabworld/10arabworld.pdf, accessed 20 September 2016.
144. Hanieh, *Capitalism and Class*.
145. Sami Zubaida, 'The nation state in the Middle East', in Zubaida, *Islam, the People and the State*, p. 146.
146. Gill, *Power and Resistance*, p. 154; Leslie Sklair, *The Transnational Capitalist Class*, Malden, MA: Blackwell, 2000, p. 15.
147. Bourdieu, *Language and Symbolic Power*, p. 172.
148. Immanuel Wallerstein, *World Systems Analysis: An Introduction*, Durham: Duke University Press, 2007, p. 40.
149. Even excellent political economies of Lebanon such as those of Gaspard and Makdisi dispense with an analysis of the state. Leenders' book on corruption is a notable exception: Gaspard, *Political Economy*; Makdisi, *Lessons of Lebanon*; Leenders, *The Spoils of Truce*.

4. SOCIAL CRISIS AND HARIRI'S SECTARIAN TURN: 1998–2000

1. Sections of this chapter are based on parts of a chapter in a book published by Karthala. The author would like to thank Karthala for their permission to reproduce parts of the chapter here: Hannes Baumann, 'The ascent of Rafiq Hariri and philanthropic practices in Beirut', in Franck Mermier and Sabrina Mervin (eds.), *Leaders et partisans au Liban*, Paris: Karthala, 2012, pp. 81–106.
2. *Lebanon Report*, December 1993, p. 7.
3. Melani Cammett argued convincingly that 'brick and mortar' clientelism signals commitment to the community where the health centre or school is located: Melani Cammett, *Compassionate Communalism: Welfare and Sectarianism in Lebanon*, Ithaca: Cornell University Press, 2014, p. 90.
4. Makdisi, *Lessons of Lebanon*, p. 185.
5. World Bank, *Private Sector Assessment: Lebanon*, Washington: World Bank, 1995, p. 7.
6. World Bank, *Private Sector Assessment*, p. 9.
7. Roger Nasnas, *Emerging Lebanon*, Beirut: Dar an-Nahar, 2007, pp. 221–42.
8. Banque du Liban, *Quarterly Bulletin*, 4th Quarter, 1998, pp. 67–8: 0.9 percent of beneficiaries accounted for 49.5 percent of credit above LL5 billion.
9. Banque du Liban, *Quarterly Bulletin*, 4th Quarter, 1998, p. 49.
10. World Bank, World Development Indicators database, September 2009, available at Bankhttp://data.worldbank.org/products/wdi#archives, accessed 20 September 2016.
11. UNDP, *Profile of Sustainable Human Development*, pp. 56–7.
12. Gaspard, *Political Economy*, p. 215.
13. Gaspard, *Political Economy*, p. 86.
14. Gaspard, *Political Economy*, p. 96.
15. World Bank, World Development Indicators database, September 2009, available at http://data.worldbank.org/products/wdi#archives, accessed 20 September 2016.
16. Antoine Haddad, *al-Faqr fi Lubnan*, Beirut: ESCWA, 1996, p. 4.
17. EIU, *Country Report: Lebanon*, 1st Quarter, 1997, p. 12; interview with Adib Na'ma, Beirut, 22 February 2008.
18. UNDP, *Mapping of Living Conditions in Lebanon*, Beirut: UNDP, 1998.
19. Khalidi-Beyhum, *Poverty Reduction Policies*, p. 43.
20. Williamson, *Washington Consensus*, pp. 2–3.
21. Abdallah Dah, Ghassan Dibeh and Wassim Shahin, *The Distributional Impact of Taxes in Lebanon: Analysis and Policy Implications*, Beirut: LCPS, 1999, pp. 10–12.

22. World Bank, *Lebanon: Public Expenditure Reform Priorities*, p. 77; Clement Moore Henry and Robert Springborg, *Globalisation and the Politics of Development in the Middle East*, Cambridge: Cambridge University Press, 2001, p. 77.

23. EIU, *Country Report: Lebanon*, 2nd Quarter, 1998, p. 21.

24. Dah et al., *Distributional Impact*, pp. 28–34, 39–42.

25. As was found by surveys of investor choices such as Klaus Meyer, 'Foreign Direct Investment in the Early Years of Economic Transition: A Survey', *Economics of Transition*, 3, 3 (1995), pp. 301–20.

26. EIU, *Country Report: Lebanon*, 4th Quarter, 1994, pp. 16–17.

27. Najem, *Lebanon's Renaissance*, pp. 66–74.

28. Makdisi, *Lessons of Lebanon*, p. 141.

29. While there is a greater number of households with low satisfaction of basic need in urban areas, the level of deprivation is higher among rural households: UNDP, *Mapping of Living Conditions*.

30. Harb el-Kak, 'Post-War Beirut'; Sawalha, '"Healing the wounds of the war"', p. 289, FN 289.

31. Gaspard, *Political Economy*, p. 86.

32. World Bank, *Lebanon: Public Expenditure Reform Priorities*, p. 75.

33. UNDP, *Mapping of Living Conditions*.

34. UNDP, *Mapping of Living Conditions*.

35. Central Administration of Statistics, *Living Conditions of Households: The National Survey of Household Living Conditions 2004*, Beirut: Central Administration of Statistics, 2006, p. 48.

36. UNDP, *Profile of Sustainable Human Development*, p. 63.

37. The only exception is hospitalisation, which is covered by the Ministry of Health for those who have no insurance. Yet hospitals are often reluctant to take in persons of low income because of delays in the disbursement of funds by the ministry and because they fear that they might be unable to pay the 15 per cent of the cost they are required to bear themselves: UNDP, *Profile of Sustainable Human Development*, p. 63.

38. Bradley Chen and Melani Cammett, 'Informal Politics and Inequality of Access to Health Care in Lebanon', *International Journal for Equity in Health*, 23, 11 (2012), p. 6.

39. Sawalha, '"Healing the Wounds of the War"', p. 286.

40. Wakim, *al-Ayadi al-sud*.

41. *MEI*, 11 December 1998, p. 5.

42. *MEI*, 29 January 1999, p. 18.

43. *MEI*, 16 June 2000, pp. 4–5.

44. *MEI*, 11 December 1998, pp. 4–6.

45. *MEI*, 11 December 1998, p. 6; *MEI*, 13 October 2000, p. 16.

46. EIU, *Country Report: Lebanon*, October 2000.

47. *MEI*, 7 May 1999, pp. 16–17; EIU, *Country Report: Lebanon*, July 2002. The moratorium on construction permits was reversed once Hariri was back in office, and from 2001 onwards Solidere once again recorded profits: EIU, *Country Report: Lebanon*, July 2002.

48. EIU, *Country Report: Lebanon*, January 2000.

49. The development of interest rates on two-year Lebanese-pound-denominated T-bills illustrates the highly managed nature of interest rates in Lebanon: they had stood at 16.7 per cent since March 1997, but Corm's arrival led to the managed reduction of the rate to 14.6 per cent.

50. EIU, *Country Report: Lebanon*, October 1999, p. 20.

51. EIU, *Country Report: Lebanon*, July 1999, p. 16; EIU, *Country Report: Lebanon*, January 2000.

52. According to his curriculum vitae, available at http://www.erf.org. eg/CMS/uploads/pdf/1184169330_Nasser_Saidi_CV07.pdf, accessed 1 July 2011.

53. According to an adviser to Salam: interview with Muhammad Mashnuq, Beirut, 6 November 2008.

54. Unless indicated otherwise, the overview of the 1996 election is from *Lebanon Report*, Fall 1996.

55. In Mount Lebanon, electoral districts followed the *qaza*, a small administrative district, favouring Junblat. The *muhafazat* (governorates) of South Lebanon and Nabatiyya were combined into one to favour Birri.

56. EIU, *Country Report: Lebanon*, October 1998, pp. 15–16.

57. Linda Schatkowski, 'The Islamic Maqased of Beirut: A Case Study of Modernisation in Lebanon', MA thesis, AUB, 1969, p. 150.

58. The figure of 17 per cent comes from the current Maqasid president, Amin al-Da'uq. He does not specify whether he is referring to the total number of buildings or built-up area: *al Nahar*, 9 January 2004, p. 13.

59. The current Maqasid president, Amin Da'uq, maintained that Christians used to attend Maqasid schools prior to the civil war: interview with Amin al-Da'uq, Beirut, 30 January 2008. However, the proposed 1968 constitution said explicitly that Maqasid offered education for 'Muslim children': Schatkowski, 'Islamic Maqased', p. 65. Johnson is also under the impression that schools were confined to Muslim children: Michael Johnson, 'Factional Politics in Lebanon: The Case of the "Islamic Society of Benevolent Intentions" (Al-Maqasid) in Beirut', *Middle Eastern Studies*, 14, 1 (1978), pp. 56–75. Shia Muslims constituted only a minority of students and were not represented on the board of directors. Johnson writes that he knows of no non-Sunni or non-Beiruti being elected to the board. See also Kamel Chahine, 'La

Composition de la population scolaire des Makassed', in Nabil Beyhum (ed.), *Reconstruire Beyrouth: les paris sur le possible*, Lyon: Maison de l'Orient, 1991, p. 244.

60. Maqasid started in Beirut and opened its first schools there. Only in Beirut did it maintain secondary schools. While Beirut's Maqasid maintained primary schools in predominantly Sunni rural areas, it stayed out of other Lebanese cities with strong Sunni populations, such as Tripoli or Saida, which were dominated by separate networks of notables. The members of the board of trustees all came from Sunni Beiruti families: Johnson, 'Factional Politics', p. 75, FN 45.

61. Schatkowski, 'Islamic Maqased', pp. 100, 106–7.

62. Johnson, *Class and Client*, p. 111.

63. Johnson, 'Factional Politics'.

64. Schatkowski, 'Islamic Maqased', pp. 84–90, 115, 122.

65. Bourdieu, *Language and Symbolic Power*, p. 204.

66. Johnson, *Class and Client*, p. 199.

67. Chahine, 'La Composition', p. 243.

68. *MEES*, 15 August 1975, p. 12; *MEES*, 10 March 1980, p. II; *al-Nahar*, 9 January 2004, p. 13.

69. *Lebanon Report*, December 1993, p. 7.

70. Al-Ahbash considered such sales to be in contravention of the rules of religious endowments: Skovgaard-Petersen, 'The Sunni Religious Scene', pp. 75–7.

71. According to accounts by both Rougier and Skovgaard-Petersen: Bernard Rougier, *Everyday Jihad: The Rise of Militant Islam among Palestinians in Lebanon*, Cambridge, MA: Harvard University Press, 2007, p. 130–1; Skovgaard-Petersen, 'The Sunni Religious Scene', p. 78–9.

72. For instance, in 1988 Samak discussed the distribution of Saudi aid with Mufti Hassan Khalid: *al-Nahar*, 8 January 1988, p. 4; *Lebanon Report*, April 1994, p. 10.

73. Iskandar, *Rafiq Hariri*, p. 70.

74. Rougier, *Everyday Jihad*, p. 131.

75. Sami Ofeish, 'Lebanon's Second Republic: Secular Talk, Sectarian Application', *Arab Studies Quarterly*, 21, 1 (1999), p. 111. If power struggles within the troika were not involved, Hariri was much less ready to embrace the mufti's pet causes. In 1996 Qabbani was seeking charges against the singer Marcel Khalifa for insulting Islam. Khalifa had used a poem by the Palestinian poet Mahmud Darwish, which contains citations from the Quran. Hariri reportedly suppressed the case by putting pressure on the judiciary and on Qabbani. He was probably afraid for Lebanon's open image. Both Khalifa and Darwish are extremely popular as advocates of the Palestinian cause, and Hariri

would have had very little to gain politically from supporting Qabbani's initiative: *MEI*, 15 October 1999, p. 15.

76. Schatkowski, 'Islamic Maqased', p. 150; Makassed, *Makassed: Serving Generations*, p. 15.
77. Skovgaard-Petersen, 'The Sunni Religious Scene', p. 75.
78. Schmid, 'Ära Hariri', p. 19.
79. *al-Nahar*, 8 January 1994, pp. 1, 15.
80. *al-Nahar*, 9 January 2004, p. 13.
81. *al-Nahar*, 9 January 2004, p. 13; interview with Amin Da'uq, Beirut, 30 January 2008.
82. *al-Nahar*, 8 January 1988, p. 4; *Lebanon Report*, April 1994, p. 10.
83. *al-Safir*, 9 May 1986, p. 10.
84. Ziad Majed and Michael Young, 'The 1996 Elections by Region', *Lebanon Report*, 3 (1996), p. 50.
85. Summer, 'Neo-Liberalising the City', p. 78; LACECO contributed to Oger projects such as a resort in Aqaba and the central district of Jidda, according to the LACECO website, available at http://www.lacecoi.com/kpmasterplan.html and at http://www.lacecoi.com/kpresidential.html, accessed 1 July 2011.
86. Interview with Amin Da'uq, Beirut, 30 January 2008; iInterview with Tammam Salam, Beirut, 23 January 2008.
87. *The Guardian*, 18 June 2007.
88. *al-Nahar*, 9 January 2004, p. 13.
89. Website of the Directorate of Health and Social Services of the Hariri Foundation, available at http://www.Haririmed.org/ourMedicalCenters.aspx, accessed 21 January 2008.
90. Ras Beirut, Ras al-Naba', Dharif, Bashura and 'Aramun–Bshamun.
91. For instance, the health centres in Tariq al-Jadida and Tripoli received financial support from Saudi businessman Prince Walid bin Talal, while the health centre in 'Akkar was supported by the Kuwait Fund: *al-Nahar*, 31 December 1999, p. 4; *al-Nahar*, 10 May 2002, p. 2002; *al-Nahar*, 7 October 2002, p. 20.
92. *al-Nahar*, 22 July 2000, p. 16.
93. Website of the Beirut Association for Social Development, available at http://www.beirutassociation.org/, accessed 1 December 2009.
94. Social centres are located in Dharif, Nahr, Watta Musaitba, Tariq al-Jadida, 'Aramun and Ras al-Naba'.
95. *al-Nahar*, 31 October 1995, p. 3.
96. In December 1996, for instance, a delegation of the Hariri Foundation alumni association headed by its president Bilal Hammad visited Nabih Birri: *al-Nahar*, 21 December 1996, p. 20.
97. *al-Nahar*, 9 January 2004, p. 13.

98. *al-Nahar*, 9 January 2004, p. 13; *al-Nahar*, 10 January 2004, p. 10.

99. Huss put his campaign expenses at $273,940 while Hariri said he spent $2 million on himself and his seventeen allies. *MEI* writes that the figure was even higher and Hariri spent $50 million in Beirut and the districts of his allies. That support included paying for a student's university or technical education or $200 in food vouchers for anyone pledging support for a candidate: *MEI*, 15 September 2000, pp. 4–6.

100. Interview with Tammam Salam, Beirut, 23 January 2008.

101. *al-Nahar*, 18 February 2003, p. 15. Newcomers considered close to Hariri included Walid Kibbi, Amin 'Itani and Khalid Qabbani.

102. *al-Nahar*, 9 January 2004, p. 13.

103. Maqasid is associated with the Sa'ib Salam Foundation, which gives university scholarships, and runs the Salim Salam dispensary: Maqasid, *al-Maqasid wal-'ata' mustammir*, Beirut: Maqasid, 2003, p. 10.

104. As observed by the author during visits to a Hariri Foundation health centre and an office of the foundation, 22 January 2008 and 29 January 2008.

105. According to several Hariri Foundation representatives: Nur al-Din al-Kush, general manager, directorate of health and social services, Hariri Foundation, presentation at the AUB, 6 February 2008; interview with Suha al-'Akkar, Beirut, 29 January 2008.

106. Information about the centres is available on the website of the directorate of health and social services of the Hariri Foundation, available at http://www.haririmed.org/ourMedicalCenters.aspx, accessed 21 January 2008. See also *al-Nahar*, 28 July 2001, p. 19.

107. In their study on welfare and clientelism in Lebanon, Cammett and Issar take the spatial location of clinics, hospitals and schools as a reflection of the target communities of providers: 'The locations of sectarian party welfare institutions provide an appropriate measure of targeting strategies, or the communities that parties seek to serve. There are few if any legal or practical restrictions on the locations of private institutions, providers acknowledge that they purposively target specific communities with welfare programs, and beneficiaries interpret the locations of party-based welfare agencies as evidence for territorial and communal favouritism of sectarian organizations', Melani Cammett and Sukriti Issar, 'Bricks and Mortar Clientelism: Sectarianism and the Logics of Welfare Allocation in Lebanon', *World Politics*, 63, 2 (2010), pp. 388–9.

108. Cammett, *Compassionate Communalism*, pp. 148–9.

109. Cammett and Issar, 'Bricks and Mortar Clientelism'.

110. Interview with Rania Za'tari al-Kush, Beirut, 22 January 2008.

111. Interview with Suha al-'Akkar, Beirut, 29 January 2008.

112. Suha 'Akkar related the story of an attack by March 8 partisans on a Hariri Foundation health centre in Bashura at the start of a sit-in in December 2006: interview with Suha al-'Akkar, Beirut, 29 January 2008.

113. Ward Vloeberghs, 'The Genesis of a Mosque: Negotiating Sacred Space in Downtown Beirut', EIU Working Papers, Florence: European University Institute, 2008, p. 13.

114. Unless indicated otherwise, the information contained in the following two paragraphs is from two interviews with Hariri Foundation representatives: interview with Suha al-'Akkar, Beirut, 29 January 2008; interview with Rania Za'tari al-Kush, Beirut, 22 January 2008.

115. The figure was quoted by Nur al-Din al-Kush, general manager, directorate of health and social services, Hariri Foundation, at a presentation at the American University Beirut on 6 February 2008.

116. For information on the importers' cartel see Consumer Lebanon, *Consumers*.

117. Helena Cobban, *The Making of Modern Lebanon*, London: Hutchinson, 1985.

118. Ussama Makdisi, *The Culture of Sectarianism: Community, History and Violence in Nineteenth-Century Lebanon*, Berkeley: University of California Press, 2000.

119. Samih Farsoun, '*E pluribus plura* or *e pluribus unum*? Cultural pluralism and social class in Lebanon', in Halim Barakat (ed.), *Toward a Viable Lebanon*, London: Croom Helm, 1988, pp. 99–132.

120. See for instance Michael Billig, *Banal Nationalism*, London: Sage, 1995; Rogers Brubaker, 'Ethnicity without Groups', *European Journal of Sociology*, 40, 2 (2002), pp. 163–89.

121. Billig, *Banal Nationalism*.

122. Cammett, *Compassionate Communalism*, p. 90.

123. Benedict Anderson, *Imagined Communities*; London: Verso, 2006.

124. Wallerstein, *World Systems Analysis*, p. 40.

125. Wallerstein had written that the 'cadres' of capitalist management are recruited according to universal principles to ensure a smooth running of the economy, while particularist populism fragments class-based resistance: Wallerstein, *World Systems Analysis*, pp. 40–1.

5. RETURN TO POLITICAL CRISIS AND ASSASSINATION: 2000–2005

1. Halliday, *Second Cold War*.

2. International Crisis Group, *Syria under Bashar (I): Foreign Policy Challenges*, Brussels: ICG, 2004, p. 9.

3. Despite Syria's fundamental opposition to the invasion, it still tried to appear conciliatory by giving the USA occasional support at the UN. In November 2002 Syria voted in favour of UN Security Council Resolution 1441, which called on Iraq to allow weapons inspectors back in.

4. The two Ba'thist regimes had been regional rivals, but from 1997 there was a rapprochement based on mutual economic benefit: From November 2000 onwards Syrian pipelines were carrying 150,000–200,000 barrels of Iraqi crude oil daily. While Iraq could thus side-step UN 'oil-for-food' sanctions, Syria pocketed an estimated $1 billion annually: ICG, *Syria under Bashar (I)*, p. 16.

5. ICG, *Syria under Bashar (I)*, p. 4.

6. John Mearsheimer and Stephen Walt, *The Israel Lobby and US Foreign Policy*, New York: Farrar, Strauss & Giroux, 2006, p. 274.

7. Madawi Al-Rasheed, 'Saudi Arabia: the challenge of the US invasion of Iraq', in Rick Fawn and Raymond Hinnebusch (eds.), *The Iraq War: Causes and Consequences*, Boulder: Lynne Rienner, 2006, p. 153.

8. Neil Quilliam, 'Jordan: appeasing the hegemon', in Rick Fawn and Raymond Hinnebusch (eds.), *The Iraq War: Causes and Consequences*, Boulder: Lynne Rienner, 2006, p. 143.

9. ICG, *Syria under Bashar (I)*, p. 17.

10. Daniel Pipes and Ziad Abdelnour, *Ending Syria's Occupation of Lebanon: The US Role*, Washington: Middle East Forum, 2000; Flynt Leverett, *Inheriting Syria: Bashar's Trial by Fire*, Washington: Brookings Institution Press, 2005, p. 144.

11. ICG, *Syria under Bashar (I)*, p. 14.

12. *MEI*, 13 October 2000, p. 15; *MEI*, 20 April 2001, p. 13; *MEI*, 14 September 2001, p. 15.

13. The gathering included Amin Gemayel, deputies such as Nassib Lahoud, and the editor of the newspaper *al-Nahar*, Jibran Tuwayni.

14. *MEI*, 15 June 2001, pp. 10–12.

15. EIU, *Country Report: Lebanon*, January 2001; EIU, *Country Report: Lebanon*, April 2001.

16. EIU, *Country Report: Lebanon*, July 2002.

17. EIU, *Country Report: Lebanon*, April 2001.

18. *MEI*, 30 June 2000, p. 9.

19. *MEI*, 22 December 2000, p. 12; *MEI*, 23 March 2001, p. 13; EIU, *Country Report: Lebanon*, October 2001; *MEI*, 7 December 2001, p. 20.

20. EIU, *Country Report: Lebanon*, October 2001.

21. EIU, *Country Report: Lebanon*, October 2002.

22. *MEI*, 23 March 2001, p. 13.

23. *MEI*, 22 December 2000, p. 11; *MEI*, 29 June 2001, p. 21; Leverett, *Inheriting Syria*, p. 108.

24. EIU, *Country Report: Lebanon*, January 2001. *MEI*, 15 June 2001, pp. 10–12.

25. *Le Monde*, 12 February 2001.

26. Rafiq Hariri, interview with Kyodo news agency, 31 January 2001, available at http://www.rhariri.com/news.aspx?ID=68&Category= Interviews, accessed 20 September 2016.

27. In February 1996 the General Confederation of Workers in Lebanon (GCWL) called for strikes and a day of demonstrations linking issues of social justice with calls to respect democratic rights on a 'national day in defence of liberties, democracy and daily bread': *MEI*, 15 March 1996. The Hariri government reacted with repression: on 27 February 1996 it declared a 'semi-state of emergency', which formally transferred responsibility for security to the army for three months and allowed for trials by military courts under martial law: *al-Nahar*, 28 February 1996; EIU, *Country Report: Lebanon*, 2nd Quarter, 1996. Hariri in effect mobilised the army against the trade unions.

28. This is particularly ironic considering that this issue became a rallying cry for the anti-Syrian movement led by Sa'd Hariri after his father's death: Human Rights Watch, *Syria/Lebanon: An Alliance beyond the Law*, Washington: HRW, 1997, available at http://www.hrw.org/en/ node/24483/section/2, accessed 20 September 2016.

29. *MEI*, 22 December 2000, p. 12.

30. *MEI*, 31 August 2001, p. 11–14.

31. Quoted in EIU, *Country Report: Lebanon*, October 2001.

32. EIU, *Country Report: Lebanon*, October 2002.

33. Rafiq Hariri, interview with Radio France International, 9 September 2002, available at http://www.rhariri.com/news.aspx?ID=726&Cate gory=Interviews, accessed 20 September 2016.

34. EIU, *Country Report: Lebanon*, July 2003.

35. *Financial Times*, 18 May 2001, p. 9.

36. EIU, *Country Report: Lebanon*, January 2002. Rafiq Hariri, interview with *al-Sharq al-Awsat*, 14 October 2001, available at http://www. rhariri.com/news.aspx?ID=469&Category=Interviews, accessed 20 September 2016.

37. For instance in an interview with *al-Nahar*, 3 January 2002, available at http://www.rhariri.com/news.aspx?ID=294&Category=Interviews, accessed 20 September 2016.

38. Interview with *Le Monde*, 12 February 2001, available at http://www. rhariri.com/news.aspx?ID=65&Category=Interviews, accessed 20 September 2016.

39. Interview with *al-Sharq al-Awsat*, 14 October 2001, available at http:// www.rhariri.com/news.aspx?ID=469&Category=Interviews, accessed 20 September 2016.

40. EIU, *Country Report: Lebanon*, January 2002.
41. *MEI*, 23 November 2001, p. 17.
42. *MEI*, 9 March 2001, p. 19.
43. *MEI*, 9 March 2001, p. 19.
44. Quoted in *MEI*, 4 May 2001, pp. 10–12.
45. EIU, *Country Report: Lebanon*, July 2001.
46. *MEI*, 6 April 2001, p. 16.
47. *MEIB*, July 2001.
48. Interview published in *al-Sharq al-Awsat*, 8 February 2001, available in the official Syrian translation at http://www.al-bab.com/arab/countries/syria/bashar0102b.htm, accessed 21 June 2010.
49. EIU, *Country Report: Lebanon*, July 2003.
50. EIU, *Country Report: Lebanon*, July 2003.
51. Leverett, *Inheriting Syria*, p. 62.
52. *MEI*, 16 June 2000, p. 7.
53. EIU, *Country Report: Lebanon*, January 2003.
54. The title of this section is borrowed from Brynen's study of international aid to the Palestinians: Rex Brynen, *A Very Political Economy: Peacebuilding and Foreign Aid in the West Bank and Gaza*, Washington: USIP, 2000.
55. Gaspard, *Political Economy*, p. 217.
56. Data downloaded from the Banque du Liban website, available at http://www.bdl.gov.lb/edata/index.asp, accessed 20 September 2016.
57. Data downloaded from the Banque du Liban website, available at http://www.bdl.gov.lb/edata/index.asp, accessed 20 September 2016.
58. Data downloaded from the Banque du Liban website, available at http://www.bdl.gov.lb/edata/index.asp, accessed 20 September 2016.
59. *Financial Times*, 30 July 2001, p. 6.
60. Baz, *Bilanbanques*.
61. EIU, *Country Report: Lebanon*, July 2002.
62. *Financial Times*, 30 July 2001, p. 6.
63. For instance, Andre Crockett, 'Strengthening the international financial architecture', in Dilip Das (ed.), *An International Finance Reader*, London: Routledge, 2003, pp. 87–103.
64. Duménil and Lévy, *Capital Resurgent*; Peter Gowan, *The Global Gamble: Washington's Faustian Bid for World Dominance*, London: Verso, 1999; Harvey, *Neoliberalism*; Wade, 'Wheels within Wheels'.
65. These four relationships are derived from a survey of the literature on financial crisis, including Andrew Cooper and Bessma Momani, 'Negotiating out of Argentina's Financial Crisis: Segmenting the International Creditors', *New Political Economy*, 10, 3 (2005), pp. 305–20; Ngaire Woods, 'Understanding Pathways to Financial Crises and the

Impact of the IMF: An Introduction', *Global Governance*, 12, 4 (2006), pp. 373–93; Harvey, *Neoliberalism*; Joseph Stiglitz, *Globalisation and its Discontents*, London: Penguin, 2002; Wade, 'Wheels within Wheels'.

66. For instance, Japan's suggestion of an Asian Monetary Fund to tackle the regional crisis in 1997–8 were opposed by the USA and the IMF: Stiglitz, *Globalisation*, p. 112.

67. Rafiq Hariri, interview with LBC, 1 September 2001, available at http://www.rhariri.com/news.aspx?ID=145&Category=Interviews, accessed 27 January 2010.

68. EIU, *Country Report: Lebanon*, April 2001.

69. *Financial Times*, 28 February 2001, p. 11.

70. EIU, *Country Report: Lebanon*, July 2002.

71. Woods, 'Pathways to Financial Crises'.

72. Hanna described himself as part of the team that was negotiating with the IMF, led by minister of economy and trade Bassil Fulayhan: interview with Mazin Hanna, Beirut, 3 March 2008.

73. According to IMF resident representative in Lebanon, Edward Gardner. He became the head of the IMF mission in Beirut after Paris II but was familiar with IMF thinking at the time of Paris II: interview with Edward Gardner, Beirut, 28 May 2008.

74. IMF, 'IMF Concludes Article IV Consultation with Lebanon', Public Information Notice 01/109, 2001.

75. On devaluation, the IMF document suggested differences in opinion among directors: 'some Directors also recommended keeping open the option of an exchange rate adjustment, in conjunction with appropriate fiscal and monetary policies and ambitious structural reforms. While acknowledging the need for strong macroeconomic and structural policies, other Directors, pointing to Lebanon's circumstances, and the risks involved, saw however, little merit in pursuing the option of exchange rate action': IMF, 'IMF Concludes Article IV Consultation'.

76. Hariri, *Statesmanship in Government*.

77. EIU, *Country Report: Lebanon*, January 2001.

78. Interview with Mazin Hanna, Beirut, 3 March 2008.

79. Lebanese Republic, *Lebanon: Paris II Meeting—Beyond Reconstruction and Recovery, towards Sustainable Growth*, Beirut: Lebanese Republic, 2002, pp. 1–2, Annex II.

80. Interview with Mazin Hanna, Beirut, 3 March 2008.

81. Interview with Mazin Hanna, Beirut, 3 March 2008.

82. EIU, *Country Report: Lebanon*, July 2002.

83. Interview with Mazin Hanna, Beirut, 3 March 2008.

84. Stiglitz, *Globalisation*, p. 202.

85. EIU, *Country Report: Lebanon*, January 2003.

86. *MEI*, 20 December 1996, p. 15.
87. Rafiq Hariri, interview with *Le Figaro*, 2 July 2002, available at http://www.rhariri.com/news.aspx?ID=613&Category=Interviews, accessed 20 September 2016.
88. EIU, *Country Report: Lebanon*, October 2002.
89. Gill, *Power and Resistance*, p. 154.
90. Susanne Soederbergh, *The Politics of the New International Financial Architecture: Reimposing Neoliberal Domination in the Global South*, London: Zed Books, 2004; Stiglitz, *Globalisation*; Wade, 'Wheels within Wheels'.
91. Unless otherwise indicated, the following data about Paris II are derived from EIU, *Country Report: Lebanon*, January 2002.
92. EIU, *Country Report: Lebanon*, January 2003.
93. This account of Hariri's early activities in France is based on Naba, *Rafic Hariri*, pp. 20–1.
94. Naba, *Rafic Hariri*, pp. 20–1.
95. *MEI*, 12 April 1996, pp. 7–9.
96. *Lebanon Report*, Spring 1996; *Lebanon Report*, Summer 1996, pp. 14–15.
97. Iskandar, *Rafiq Hariri*, p. 79.
98. Elizabeth Picard, 'Great Expectations, Limited Means: France and the 2006 Israeli–Lebanese War', *MIT Electronic Journal of Middle East Studies*, 6 (Summer 2006), p. 146.
99. Schimmelpfennig and Gardner, 'Lebanon'.
100. Schimmelpfennig and Gardner, 'Lebanon', p. 19.
101. One of the authors also mentions Saudi and Kuwaiti aid during the 2006 war when interviewed by the BBC, showing that Saudi Arabia was the main source of the 'implicit guarantee': BBC News Online, 5 December 2008.
102. The loan was reported to originate from the Saudi monetary authorities. The interest rate stood at 5 per cent for three years: EIU, *Country Report: Lebanon*, 1st Quarter, 1999, p. 12.
103. Other buyers were Malaysia, other Gulf states and local investors: *MEES*, 8 July 2002, pp. B3–4; EIU, *Country Report: Lebanon*, July 2002.
104. Data downloaded from the Banque du Liban website, available at http://www.bdl.gov.lb/edata/index.asp, accessed 20 September 2016.
105. Beblawi, 'The Rentier State', p. 97.
106. Data downloaded from the Banque du Liban website, available at http://www.bdl.gov.lb/edata/index.asp, accessed 20 September 2016.
107. Data downloaded from the Banque du Liban website, available at http://www.bdl.gov.lb/edata/index.asp, accessed 20 September 2016.

108. As measured in commercial bank claims on the public and private sector. Data downloaded from the Banque du Liban website, available at http://www.bdl.gov.lb/edata/index.asp, accessed 20 September 2016.

109. Data downloaded from the Banque du Liban website, available at http://www.bdl.gov.lb/edata/index.asp, accessed 20 September 2016.

110. One such financial operation illustrates how the burden of financing government debt was shifted from the government to the central bank: in April 2004 the EIU reported that the central bank had provided treasury bills worth $430 million to the government at an interest rate of only 4 per cent and at a maturity of four years. The operation was financed through the sale of CDs to commercial banks at a rate of 11 per cent. The cost differential was to be borne by the central bank, while official government statistics would show a reduction in debt servicing cost: EIU, *Country Report: Lebanon*, April 2004.

111. Baz, *Bilanbanques*.

112. *MEI*, 11 December 1998, p. 6; *MEI*, 13 October 2000, p. 16.

113. EIU, *Country Report: Lebanon*, October 2000.

114. *MEI*, 7 May 1999, pp. 16–17; EIU, *Country Report: Lebanon*, July 2002.

115. EIU, *Country Report: Lebanon*, January 2002.

116. EIU, *Country Report: Lebanon*, April 2002.

117. EIU, *Country Report: Lebanon*, January 2004

118. EIU, *Country Report: Lebanon*, April 2001.

119. Rafiq Hariri, interview with the Saudi newspaper *al-Jazira*, 20 April 2001, available at http://www.rhariri.com/news.aspx?ID=63&Category=Interviews, accessed 27 January 2010.

120. EIU, *Country Report: Lebanon*, April 2001.

121. EIU, *Country Report: Lebanon*, January 2002.

122. EIU, *Country Report: Lebanon*, July 2002; *MEIB*, January 2003.

123. *Forbes*, 10 March 2010; *MEED*, 21 November 2008, p. 74; *ANARAM*, 19 December 1983, p. 8; James Exelby, 'The Post-War Reconstruction of the Telecommunications Sector in Lebanon', *Japanese Institute of Middle Eastern Economies Review*, 41 (1998), p. 27.

124. *EIU*, July 2002.

125. Majed and Young, 'The 1996 Elections', p. 53.

126. *EIU, Country Report: Lebanon*, July 2002; John Sfakianakis, 'Gray Money, Corruption and the Post-September 11 Middle East', *Middle East Report*, 222 (Spring 2002), p. 34.

127. EIU, *Country Report: Lebanon*, 4th Quarter, 1995, p. 14; EIU, *Country Report: Lebanon*, 1st Quarter, 1996, p. 14; EIU, *Country Report: Lebanon*, October 2000.

128. EIU, *Country Report: Lebanon*, July 2001.
129. EIU, *Country Report: Lebanon*, April 2002.
130. EIU, *Country Report: Lebanon*, July 2002.
131. International Telecommunications Union, *Arab States Telecommunications Indicators 1992–2001*, Geneva: ITU, 2002.
132. World Bank, *Lebanon: Public Expenditure Reform Priorities*, p. 77.
133. EIU, *Country Report: Lebanon*, July 2002.
134. EIU, *Country Report: Lebanon*, January 2003; EIU, *Country Report: Lebanon*, April 2003.
135. EIU, *Country Report: Lebanon*, October 2003.
136. World Bank, *Public Expenditure Reform Priorities*, p. 77.
137. Irene Gendzier, *Notes from the Minefield: United States Intervention in Lebanon and the Middle East, 1945–1958*, New York: Columbia University Press, 1999, pp. 101–5.
138. *ANARAM*, 10 December 1984, p. 4; *MEED*, 11 January 1986, p. 16.
139. *Lebanon Report*, Summer 1996.
140. *Lebanon Report*, Summer 1996.
141. *Business Middle East (BME)*, 5 January 1997, p. 7.
142. Possible reasons why Birri agreed to the takeover include Hariri's threat to buy up the shares of Kuwaiti and Qatari investors in Intra, which amounted to a combined 35 per cent of the holding: *Lebanon Report*, Summer 1996.
143. *BME*, 1 January 1998, p. 5.
144. *al-Akhbar*, 31 January 2010.
145. EIU, *Country Report: Lebanon*, July 2001.
146. *BME*, 5 January 1997, p. 7.
147. When MEA was preparing for job cuts in 1996 it reportedly drew up three lists of possible redundancies: those who could be released for medical reasons; those nearing retirement age; and those who were hired during the war under pressure from political figures: *Lebanon Report*, Summer 1996. The preponderance of Shia employees at MEA was not just due to Birri doling out jobs: during the war it was easier and safer for inhabitants of the predominantly Shia neighbourhoods around the airport to reach it than people from other areas of the city, while the technical college in the predominantly Shia area of Harat Hurayk was training future airport employees: *MEI*, 13 July 2001, pp 16–17.
148. *MEI*, 6 April 2001, p. 17.
149. EIU, *Country Report: Lebanon*, April 2001.
150. EIU, *Country Report: Lebanon*, July 2001.
151. *BME*; 16 June 2001, p. 4.
152. EIU, *Country Report: Lebanon*, January 2002.

153. *MEED*, 5 December 2003, p. 33.

154. Oxford Business Group, *Emerging Lebanon*, London: Oxford Business Group, 2005, p. 89.

155. EIU, *Country Report: Lebanon*, April 2001.

156. Oxford Business Group, *Emerging Lebanon*, pp. 90–1.

157. EIU, *Country Report: Lebanon*, 2nd Quarter, 2000.

158. EIU, *Country Report: Lebanon*, October 2003.

159. EIU, *Country Report: Lebanon*, 3rd Quarter, 1999, p. 17; EIU, *Country Report: Lebanon*, April 2002.

160. EIU, *Country Report: Lebanon*, April 2002.

161. World Bank, *Public Expenditure Reform Priorities*, p. 77.

162. Data downloaded from the Banque du Liban website, available at http://www.bdl.gov.lb/edata/index.asp, accessed 20 September 2016.

163. Data downloaded from the Banque du Liban website, available at http://www.bdl.gov.lb/edata/index.asp, accessed 20 September 2016.

164. Banque du Liban, *Quarterly Bulletin*, various issues.

165. Data downloaded from the Banque du Liban website, available at http://www.bdl.gov.lb/edata/index.asp, accessed 20 September 2016.

166. Nasnas, *Emerging Lebanon*, pp. 221–42.

167. Ministry of Social Affairs, *Development of Mapping of Living Conditions in Lebanon 1995–2004*, Beirut: MOSA, 2007, p. 19.

168. MOSA, *Development of Mapping of Living Conditions*, p. 25.

169. MOSA, *Development of Mapping of Living Conditions*, p. 25, FN 14.

170. MOSA, *Development of Mapping of Living Conditions*, p. 26.

171. Heba Laithy, Khalid Abu-Ismail and Kamal Hamdan, *Poverty, Growth, and Income Distribution in Lebanon*, Brasilia: International Poverty Centre, 2008, pp. 1, 4.

172. EIU, *Country Report: Lebanon*, 1st Quarter, 1994, p. 12.

173. World Bank, *Public Expenditure Reform Priorities*, pp. 29, FN 44.

174. Interview with Muhammad Shatah, Beirut, 13 February 2008.

175. Interview with Fu'ad Siniura, London, 30 November 2010.

176. The biographical information on Nadim Munla is derived from his CV, published on websites advertising his speaking engagements: website of Shafik Gabr, available at http://www.gabr.com/layout1/speeches/speeches_97_1.html, accessed 14 July 2011; MIT Arab Alumni Association website, available at http://www.mitpanarabconf.org/wp-content/uploads/2009/08/2002_Conference.pdf, accessed 14 July 2011.

177. According to Bassil Fulayhan's CV, published on the website of the

Bassil Fuleihan Foundation, available at http://www.basilfuleihan-foundation.org/cv.htm, accessed 14 May 2010.

178. Interview with Mazin Hanna, Beirut, 3 March 2008.
179. Interview with Mazin Hanna, Beirut, 3 March 2008.
180. Interview with Mazin Hanna, Beirut, 3 March 2008.
181. Interview with Mazin Hanna, Beirut, 3 March 2008.
182. Interview with Asma Fulayhan, *Executive Magazine*, May 2006.
183. Interview with Mazin Hanna, Beirut, 3 March 2008.
184. Interview with Mazin Hanna, Beirut, 3 March 2008.
185. Dani Rodrik, 'What is Wrong (and Right) in Economics?', Dani Rodrik's personal blog, 7 May 2013, available at http://rodrik.type-pad.com/dani_rodriks_weblog/2013/05/what-is-wrong-and-right-in-economics.html, accessed 4 November 2013.
186. Hariri, *Statesmanship in Government*, p. 67.
187. Interview with Mazin Hanna, Beirut, 3 March 2008; EIU, *Country Report: Lebanon*, April 2002; See also the website of the Bassil Fulayhan Foundation, available at http://www.basilfuleihanfoundation.org/cv.htm, accessed 14 May 2010.
188. According to the website of the Bassil Fulayhan Foundation, available at http://www.basilfuleihanfoundation.org/cv.htm, accessed 14 May 2010.
189. *Lebanon Opportunities*, March 2005, p. 9.
190. See for instance Nikolaos van Dam, *The Struggle for Power in Syria: Politics and Society under Asad and the Ba'th Party*, London: I.B. Tauris, 1996.
191. Blanford, *Killing Mr Lebanon*, pp. 54–5; Leverett, *Inheriting Syria*, p. 29.
192. EIU, *Country Report: Lebanon*, October 2004.
193. EIU, *Country Report: Lebanon*, July 2004.
194. Blanford, *Killing Mr Lebanon*, p. 100; Detlev Mehlis, *Report of the Independent International Investigation Commission Established Pursuant to Security Council Resolution 1595 (2005)*, Beirut: UNIIIC, 2005.
195. EIU, *Country Report: Lebanon*, October 2004.
196. United Nations Security Council, Resolution 1559, 2 September 2004, available at http://www.un.org/News/Press/docs/2004/sc8181.doc.htm, accessed 20 September 2016.
197. Mearsheimer and Walt, *The Israel Lobby*, p. 277.
198. International Crisis Group, *Syria after Lebanon, Lebanon after Syria*. Brussels: ICG, 2005, p. 9.
199. Blanford, *Killing Mr Lebanon*, p. 104.
200. ICG, *Syria after Lebanon*, p. 9.
201. Blanford, *Killing Mr Lebanon*, p. 104.

202. Rafiq Hariri, interview with *al-'Arabiyya* TV, 15 December 2004, available at http://www.rhariri.com/news.aspx?ID=2985&Category =Interviews, accessed 20 September 2016.

203. Rafiq Hariri, interview with *al-'Arabiyya* TV, 15 December 2004, available at http://www.rhariri.com/news.aspx?ID=2985&Category =Interviews, accessed 20 September 2016.

204. Blanford, *Killing Mr Lebanon*, pp. 104, 109.

205. Blanford, *Killing Mr Lebanon*, p. 104. 'Abd al-Halim Khaddam would later claim that Assad's suspicions against Hariri stemmed from a disinformation campaign by the security establishment around Lahoud, masterminded by Jamil Sayyid: 'Abd al-Halim Khaddam, interview with *al-'Arabiyya* TV, 8 January 2006, available in translation at http://yalibnan.com/site/archives/2006/01/full_text_of_kh.php, accessed 2 August 2010.

206. EIU, *Country Report: Lebanon*, October 2004; ICG, *Syria after Lebanon*, p. 26.

207. EIU, *Country Report: Lebanon*, July 2004.

208. Blanford, *Killing Mr Lebanon*, p. 97.

209. EIU, *Country Report: Lebanon*, January 2005.

210. EIU, *Country Report: Lebanon*, July 2004.

211. EIU, *Country Report: Lebanon*, January 2005.

212. ICG, *Syria after Lebanon*, p. 13, FN 97.

213. Blanford, *Killing Mr Lebanon*, p. 4.

214. ICG, *Syria after Lebanon*, p. 13.

215. Elias Muhanna, 'Hizballah and Rational Choice', 30 May 2013, available at http://qifanabki.com/2013/05/30/hizbullah-and-rational-choice/Muhanna 2013, accessed 23 December 2013.

216. Mehlis, *Report*.

217. Daniel Bellemare, *Tenth Report of the International Independent Investigation Commission Established Pursuant to Security Council Resolutions 1595 (2005), 1636 (2005), 1644 (2005), 1686 (2006) and 1748 (2007)*, Beirut: UNIIIC, 2008.

218. *Der Spiegel*, 23 May 2009.

219. BBC News Online, 3 July 2011.

6. CONCLUSIONS

1. Harvey, *Neoliberalism*.

2. Cited in Ralph Miliband, *The State in Capitalist Society*, London: Weidenfeld & Nicolson, 1969, p. 55.

3. Pierre Bourdieu and Loic Wacquant, *An Invitation to Reflexive Sociology*, Cambridge: Polity Press, 1992.

4. Najib Hourani, 'Lebanon: Hybrid Sovereignties and US Foreign Policy', *Middle East Policy*, 20, 1 (2013), p. 43.
5. In the words of economist Dani Rodrik, who was speaking about economists' tendency to turn a blind eye to anti-market policies pushed by corporate interests: Rodrik, 'What is Wrong (and Right) in Economics?'.
6. Mirowski, *Never Let a Serious Crisis go to Waste*, p. 43.
7. Prior to the Paris II conference in 2002 Hariri and his technocrats failed to persuade key IMF directors of the need to defend the currency peg, including managing director Horst Köhler, the director of the Middle East department Paul Chabrier, and deputy managing director Eduardo Aninat, who was responsible for the Lebanon file: interview with Mazin Hanna, Beirut, 3 March 2008.
8. Leenders, *The Spoils of Truce*.
9. Swyngedouw et al., 'Neoliberal Urbanisation'.
10. Gaspard, *Political Economy*, p. 217.
11. Mirowski, *Never Let a Serious Crisis go to Waste*, p. 40. See also Jessop, 'Liberalism, Neoliberalism, and Urban Governance', p. 454.
12. Bourdieu, *Acts of Resistance*, p 2.
13. Hourani, 'Aid and redevelopment', p. 205.
14. Hariri Foundation, *A Promising Future*, p. 12.
15. Khashan, 'How Grantees Relate'.
16. Wallerstein, *World Systems Analysis*, p. 40.
17. Hanieh, *Capitalism and Class*.
18. A UN Security Council resolution (1757) was required because Nabih Birri refused to convene parliament to ratify the establishment of the tribunal.
19. Shehadi and Wilmshurst, *Special Tribunal*.
20. International Crisis Group, *Trial by Fire: The Politics of the Special Tribunal for Lebanon*, Brussels: ICG, 2010; Are Knudsen, 'Special Tribunal for Lebanon: homage to Hariri?', in Michael Kerr and Are Knudsen (eds.), *Lebanon after the Cedar Revolution*, London: Hurst, 2012, pp. 219–234.
21. Shehadi and Wilmshurst, *Special Tribunal*, p. 8.
22. Mehlis, *Report*.
23. Bellemare, *Tenth Report*.
24. EIU, *Country Report: Lebanon*, October 2009, p. 11.
25. BBC News Online, 6 September 2010.
26. *New York Times*, 22 April 2009, p. A1.
27. According to the website of the Hariri Foundation Directorate for Health and Social Services, available at http://www.haririmed.org/ourMedicalCenters.aspx, accessed 21 January 2008; http://www.haririmed.org/pages/frmCenters.aspx?pageid=1, accessed 15 January 2014.

28. Cammett and Issar, 'Bricks and Mortar Clientelism', p. 395.

29. International Crisis Group, *Lebanon's Politics: The Sunni Community and Hariri's Future Current*, Middle East Report, Brussels: ICG, 2010, p. 12.

30. *Los Angeles Times*, 12 May 2008.

31. ICG, *Sunni Community*, p. 13.

32. The government had also accused Hizballah of monitoring air traffic at Beirut airport, allegedly in preparation for a terrorist attack.

33. ICG, *Sunni Community*, p. 22.

34. *al-Akhbar*, 3 September 2011.

35. International Crisis Group, *A Precarious Balancing Act: Lebanon and the Syrian Conflict*, Brussels: ICG, 2012, p. 4

36. The following analysis is from Marwa Boukarim and Marwan Kaabour, 'Tariq al Jdide: Alternative Model of Political Propaganda', 2012, available at http://www.signsofconflict.com/Publications/essay_details?id=19, accessed January 16, 2014.

37. EIU, *Country Report: Lebanon*, July 2009, p. 12.

38. EIU, *Country Report: Lebanon*, September 2010, p. 13.

39. Central bank figures on international cash transfers in the first six months of 2009 show that the Gulf is the main source of remittances: the UAE accounted for 25.8 per cent, Saudi Arabia for 15.5 per cent and Qatar for 9.3 per cent, with 7.4 per cent from other Gulf Arab states (EIU, *Country Report: Lebanon*, April 2010, p. 14). In the same year the value of remittances reached 21.8 per cent of GDP: World Bank, World Development Indicators database, December 2013, available at http://databank.worldbank.org/data/databases.aspx, accessed 20 September 2016.

40. EIU, *Country Report: Lebanon*, February 2011, p. 8.

41. EIU, *Country Report: Lebanon*, June 2011, p. 8.

42. EIU, *Country Report: Lebanon*, February 2011, p. 8.

43. Passenger statistics from Beirut airport contain tourists' origins. In the first nine months of 2010 18 per cent of arrivals came from the UAE, 12 per cent from Saudi Arabia, 9.8 per cent from France—mainly Lebanese expatriates—and 7.3 per cent from Kuwait: EIU, *Country Report: Lebanon*, November 2011, p. 13.

44. Cited in Suzanne Maloney, 'The Gulf's Renewed Oil Wealth: Getting it Right this Time', *Survival* 50, 6 (2008), p. 129.

45. These figures are cited by Eid and Momani, relying on data by the Institute for International Finance, investment firm Samba and the Inter-Arab Investment Guarantee Corporation (IAIGC): Florence Eid, 'The new face of Arab investment', in John Nugee and Paola Subacchi (eds.), *The Gulf Region: A New Hub of Global Financial Power*, London: Chatham House, 2008, pp. 71–2; Bessma Momani, 'Shifting Gulf Arab

investments in the Mashreq: underlying political economy rationales?',
in B. Momani and M. Legrenzi (eds.), *Shifting Geo-Economic Power of
the Gulf: Oil, Finance and Institutions*, Farnham: Ashgate, 2011, p. 169.

46. In January 2008 reports indicated that five companies had expressed
    an interest in buying Lebanon's mobile phone networks: Etisalat of
    the UAE, Qatar Telecom, Zain of Kuwait, and Batelco of Bahrain, with
    Orascom Telecom of Egypt being the only non-Gulf bidder (EIU,
    Country Report: Lebanon, January 2008, p. 12).

47. The value of total deposits in Lebanese commercial banks increased
    from $57 billion in February 2005, at the time of Rafiq Hariri's death,
    to $141 billion in November 2013: data downloaded from the Banque
    du Liban website, available at http://www.bdl.gov.lb/edata/index.asp,
    accessed 20 September 2016. Over the same period, the value of non-
    resident deposits almost tripled from $9.3 billion to $27.1 billion.
    This measure is only indicative. Much Gulf capital is invested by the
    Lebanese diaspora, who are also counted as resident in Lebanon if
    they have a local address.

48. The share of credits to individuals rose from 17.4 per cent of total
    credit extended by the Lebanese financial sector in 2005 to 26.4
    per cent in 2012 (Association of Lebanese Banks, various years). The
    value of foreign assets owned by Lebanese banks rose from $12.8 bil-
    lion at Hariri's death in February 2005 to $24.6 billion in November
    2013: data downloaded from the Banque du Liban website, available
    at http://www.bdl.gov.lb/edata/index.asp, accessed 20 September
    2016.

49. Data downloaded from the Banque du Liban website, available at
    http://www.bdl.gov.lb/edata/index.asp, accessed 20 September 2016.

50. EIU, *Country Report: Lebanon*, October 2006, pp. 23–4.

51. EIU, *Country Report: Lebanon*, March 2008, p. 11.

52. EIU, *Country Report: Lebanon*, July 2009, p. 16.

53. EIU, *Country Report: Lebanon*, October 2008, p. 11.

54. al-Arabiya News, 19 May 2011; Naharnet, 2 July 2011.

55. EIU, *Country Report: Lebanon*, February 2011, p. 8; EIU, *Country Report:
    Lebanon*, February 2012, p. 14.

56. Nahas appears to have found this alliance frustrating, eventually fall-
    ing out with his political sponsor, Michel Aoun: EIU, *Country Report:
    Lebanon*, March 2012, p. 11.

57. I am indebted to Jamil Mouawad for alerting me to this point.

58. *The Guardian*, 10 October 2012.

59. *New York Times*, 26 October 2013, p. A1.

60. *Daily Star*, 4 January 2014.

61. The weakening of Sa'd Hariri's grip on the Sunni community has been
    regularly noted, for instance by ICG, *Sunni Community*.

BIBLIOGRAPHY

Archives consulted

American University of Beirut, Library Archives.

Periodicals consulted

Business Middle East (BME).
Daily Star.
Economist Intelligence Unit, *Country Report: Lebanon.*
Lebanon Report.
Middle East Economic Digest (MEED).
Middle East Economic Survey (MEES).
Middle East Intelligence Bulletin (MEIB).
Middle East International (MEI).
al-Nahar.
an-Nahar Arab Report and Memo (ANARAM).
al-Safir.

Databases and data collections consulted

Baz, Freddie, *Bilanbanques: Liban*, Beirut: Bankdata Financial Services, various years.
Banque du Liban website.
Banque du Liban, *Quarterly Bulletin.*
IMF, *International Finance Statistics*, Washington: IMF, 2007.
World Bank, World Development Indicators, various editions.

Bibliography

Abdelnour, Ziad, 'Dossier: Michel and Elias Murr', *Middle East Intelligence Bulletin*, 5, 6 (June 2003), available at https://www.meforum.org/meib/articles/0306_ld.htm, accessed 20 September 2016.

BIBLIOGRAPHY

Abu Khalil, As'ad, 'Determinants and characteristics of the Saudi role in Lebanon: the post-civil war years', in Madawi Al-Rasheed (ed.), *Kingdom without Borders: Saudi Political, Religious and Media Frontiers*, London: Hurst, 2008.

Altan-Olcay, Özlem, 'Defining "America" from a Distance: Local Strategies of the Global in the Middle East', *Middle Eastern Studies*, 44, 1 (2008), pp. 29–52.

Ammar, Walid, *Health System and Reform in Lebanon*, Beirut: WHO and Ministry of Public Health Lebanon, 2003.

Anderson, Benedict, *Imagined Communities*; London: Verso, 2006.

'Atallah, Sami, 'al-Mu'assasat al-hukumiya wal-tiyat tahdir al-muwazanat', in Lebanese Centre for Policy Studies, *al-Muwazanat wal-tanmiya al-ijtima'iyat fi Lubnan*, Beirut: Lebanese Centre for Policy Studies, 2000.

Ayubi, Nazih, *Over-Stating the Arab State: Politics and Society in the Middle East*, London: I.B. Tauris, 2001.

Baumann, Hannes, 'The ascent of Rafiq Hariri and philanthropic practices in Beirut', in Franck Mermier and Sabrina Mervin (eds.), *Leaders et partisans au Liban*, Paris: Karthala, 2012.

———— 'The "new contractor bourgeoisie" in Lebanese politics: Hariri, Miqati and Faris', in Are Knudsen and Michael Kerr (eds.), *Lebanon: After the Cedar Revolution*, New York: Oxford University Press, 2014/London: Hurst, 2012.

Beblawi, Hazem, 'The Rentier State in the Arab World', in Giacomo Luciani (ed.), *The Arab State*, London: Routledge, 1990.

Bellemare, Daniel, *Tenth Report of the International Independent Investigation Commission Established Pursuant to Security Council Resolutions 1595 (2005), 1636 (2005), 1644 (2005), 1686 (2006) and 1748 (2007)*, Beirut: UNIIIC, 2008.

Billig, Michael, *Banal Nationalism*, London: Sage, 1995.

Blanford, Nicholas, *Killing Mr Lebanon: The Assassination of Rafik Hariri and its Impact on the Middle East*, London: I.B. Tauris, 2006.

Boas, Taylor and Jordan Gans-Morse, 'Neoliberalism: From New Liberal Philosophy to Anti-Liberal Slogan', *Studies in Comparative International Development*, 44, 2 (2009), pp. 137–61.

Bogaerts, Koenraad, *Paradigms Lost in Morocco: How Neoliberal Urban Projects Challenge our Understanding of Politics in the Arab Region*, Minneapolis: University of Minnesota Press, forthcoming.

Bonne, Emmanuel, *Vie publique. Patronage et clientèle: Rafic Hariri à Saida*. Beirut: CERMOC, 1995.

Bourdieu, Pierre, *Acts of Resistance: Against the Tyranny of the Market*, New York: New Press, 1998.

———— *Language and Symbolic Power*, Cambridge: Polity, 1991.

BIBLIOGRAPHY

Bourdieu, Pierre and Loic Wacquant, *An Invitation to Reflexive Sociology*, Cambridge: Polity Press, 1992.

Brenner, Neil, 'Urban Governance and the Production of New State Spaces in Western Europe, 1960–2000', *Review of International Political Economy*, 11, 3 (2004), pp. 447–88.

Bronson, Rachel, 'Understanding US–Saudi Relations', in Paul Aarts and Gerd Nonneman (eds.), *Saudi Arabia in the Balance: Political Economy, Society, Foreign Affairs*, London: Hurst, 2005.

Brynen, Rex, *A Very Political Economy: Peacebuilding and Foreign Aid in the West Bank and Gaza*, Washington: USIP, 2000.

Brubaker, Rogers, 'Ethnicity without Groups', *European Journal of Sociology*, 40, 2 (2002), pp. 163–89.

Bu Habib, 'Abdallah, *al-Daw' al-asfar: al-siyyasat al-Amirkiyya tijah Lubnan*, Beirut: Sharikat al-Matbu'at lil-Tawazi' wal-Nashar, 2007.

Cammett, Melani, *Compassionate Communalism: Welfare and Sectarianism in Lebanon*, Ithaca: Cornell University Press, 2014.

Cammett, Melani and Sukriti Issar, 'Bricks and Mortar Clientelism: Sectarianism and the Logics of Welfare Allocation in Lebanon', *World Politics*, 63, 2 (2010), pp. 381–421.

Central Administration of Statistics, *Living Conditions of Households: The National Survey of Living Household Living Conditions 2004*, Beirut: Central Administration of Statistics, 2006.

Chahine, Kamel, 'La Composition de la population scolaire des Makassed', in Nabil Beyhum (ed.), *Reconstruire Beyrouth: les paris sur le possible*, Lyon: Maison de l'Orient, 1991.

Chen, Bradley and Melani Cammett, 'Informal Politics and Inequality of Access to Health Care in Lebanon', *International Journal for Equity in Health*, 23, 11 (2012), pp. 1–8.

Chubin, Shahram and Charles Tripp, *Iran–Saudi Arabia Relations and Regional Order: Iran and Saudi-Arabia in the Balance of Power in the Gulf*, Oxford: Oxford University Press, 1996.

Cobban, Helena, *The Making of Modern Lebanon*, London: Hutchinson, 1985.

Consumer Lebanon, *The Consumers and the Exclusive Agencies in Lebanon*, Beirut: Consumer Lebanon, 2005.

Cooper, Andrew and Bessma Momani, 'Negotiating out of Argentina's Financial Crisis: Segmenting the International Creditors', *New Political Economy*, 10, 3 (2005), pp. 305–20.

Corm, George, *Le Liban contemporain: histoire et société*, Paris: Découverte, 2005.

——— 'Overcoming the Debt Trap: Towards an Alternative Development Model in Lebanon', paper presented at the American University Beirut, 21 May 2007.

BIBLIOGRAPHY

————— 'The war system: militia hegemony and reestablishment of the state', in Deirdre Colling (ed.), *Peace for Lebanon? From War to Reconstruction*, Boulder: Lynne Rienner, 1994.

Crockett, Andre, 'Strengthening the international financial architecture', in Dilip Das (ed.), *An International Finance Reader*, London: Routledge, 2003.

Dah, Abdallah, Ghassan Dibeh and Wassim Shahin, *The Distributional Impact of Taxes in Lebanon: Analysis and Policy Implications*. Beirut: LCPS, 1999.

el-Dahdah, Fares, 'On Solidere's motto: "Beirut: Ancient City of the Future"', in Peter Rowe and Hashim Sarkis (eds.), *Projecting Beirut: Episodes in the Construction and Reconstruction of a Modern City*, Munich: Prestel, 1998.

Deeb, Marius, 'Saudi Arabian policy toward Lebanon since 1975', in Halim Barakat (ed.), *Toward a Viable Lebanon*, London: Croom Helm, 1988.

Dekmejian, Hrair, *Patterns of Political Leadership: Egypt, Israel, Lebanon*, New York: State University of New York Press, 1975.

Denoeux, Guilain and Robert Springborg, 'Hariri's Lebanon: Singapore of the Middle East or Sanaa of the Levant?' *Middle East Policy* 6, 2 (1998), pp. 158–73.

Dib, Kamal, *Warlords and Merchants: The Lebanese Business and Political Establishment*, Reading: Ithaca, 2004.

Dubar, Claude and Salim Nasr, *Les Classes sociales au Liban*, Paris: Presses de la Fondation Nationale des Sciences Politiques, 1976.

Duménil, Gérard and Dominique Lévy, *Capital Resurgent: Roots of the Neoliberal Revolution*, Cambridge, MA: Harvard University Press, 2004.

Eid, Florence, 'The new face of Arab investment', in John Nugee and Paola Subacchi (eds.), *The Gulf Region: A New Hub of Global Financial Power*, London: Chatham House, 2008.

Eid-Sabbagh, Karim, 'Reconstruction in Lebanon: Neoliberalism and Spatial Production', Master of Urban Planning thesis, AUB, 2007.

El Khazen, Farid, *The Breakdown of the State in Lebanon*, London: I.B. Tauris, 2000.

Exelby, James, 'The Post-War Reconstruction of the Telecommunications Sector in Lebanon', *Japanese Institute of Middle Eastern Economies Review*, 41 (1998), pp. 18–34.

Farsoun, Samih, '*E pluribus plura* or *e pluribus unum*? Cultural pluralism and social class in Lebanon', in Halim Barakat (ed.), *Toward a Viable Lebanon*, London: Croom Helm, 1988.

Fattouh, Bassam, 'A Political Analysis of Budget Deficits in Lebanon', *SOAS Economic Digest*, June 1997.

Fawaz, Mona, 'Neoliberal Urbanity and the Right to the City: A View from Beirut's Periphery', *Development and Change*, 40, 5 (2009), pp. 827–52.

Gaspard, Toufic, *A Political Economy of Lebanon 1948–2002: The Limits of Laissez-Faire*, Leiden: Brill, 2004.

BIBLIOGRAPHY

Gates, Carolyn, *The Merchant Republic of Lebanon: Rise of an Open Economy*. London: I.B. Tauris, 1998.

Gavin, Angus, *Beirut Reborn: The Restoration and Development of the Central District*, London: Academy Editions, 1996.

Gendzier, Irene, *Notes from the Minefield: United States Intervention in Lebanon and the Middle East, 1945–1958*, New York: Columbia University Press, 1999.

George, Alan, *Syria: Neither Bread Nor Freedom*, London: Zed Books, 2003.

Gerges, Fawaz, 'Lebanon', in Yezid Sayigh and Avi Shlaim (eds.), *The Cold War and the Middle East*, Oxford: Oxford University Press, 1997.

Ghandour Atallah, Joumana, 'The northern sector: projects and plans at sea', in Peter Rowe and Hashim Sarkis (eds.), *Projecting Beirut: Episodes in the Construction and Reconstruction of a Modern City*, Munich: Prestel, 1998.

Gill, Stephen, *Power and Resistance in the New World Order*, Basingstoke: Palgrave Macmillan, 2003.

Glyn, Andrew, *Capitalism Unleashed: Finance, Globalization, and Welfare*, Oxford: Oxford University Press, 2006.

Gowan, Peter, *The Global Gamble: Washington's Faustian Bid for World Dominance*, London: Verso, 1999.

Haddad, Antoine, *al-Faqr fi Lubnan*, Beirut: ESCWA, 1996.

Hakim, Sam and Saad Andary, 'The Lebanese Central Bank and the Treasury Bills Market', *Middle East Journal*, 51, 2 (1997), pp. 230–41.

Halliday, Fred, *The Making of the Second Cold War*, London: Verso, 1986.

Hanf, Theodor, *Coexistence in Wartime Lebanon: Decline of a State and Death of a Nation*, London: I.B. Tauris, 1993.

Harb el-Kak, Mona, 'Post-War Beirut: Resources, Negotiations, and Contestation in the Elyssar Project', *Arab World Geographer*, 3, 4 (2000), pp. 272–88.

Hanieh, Adam, *Capitalism and Class in the Gulf Arab States*, London: Palgrave Macmillan, 2011.

Hariri, Rafiq, *Statesmanship in Government: Emerging from War and Entering the Future*, Beirut: Arab United Press, 1999.

Hariri Foundation, *Hariri Foundation: The Origins and Prospects*, Beirut: Hariri Foundation, 1992.

———— *A Promising Future*, Beirut: Hariri Foundation, 2004.

Harvey, David, *A Brief History of Neoliberalism*, Oxford: Oxford University Press, 2005.

Henry, Clement Moore, 'Prisoners' Financial Dilemma: A Consociational Future for Lebanon?', *American Political Science Review*, 81, 1 (1987), pp. 201–18.

Henry, Clement Moore and Robert Springborg, *Globalisation and the Politics of Development in the Middle East*, Cambridge: Cambridge University Press, 2001.

BIBLIOGRAPHY

Hertog, Steffen, 'The Sociology of the Gulf Rentier Systems: Societies of Intermediaries', *Comparative Studies in Society and History*, 52, 2 (2010), pp. 282–318.

Heydemann, Stephen, 'Upgrading Authoritarianism in the Arab World', Saban Center for Middle East Policy, Brookings Institution, Analysis Paper No. 13, October 2007, available at http://www.brookings.edu/~/media/research/files/papers/2007/10/arabworld/10arabworld.pdf, accessed 20 September 2016.

Hitti, Said, Kemal Shehadi and Rana Houry, *A Framework for Reducing the Lebanese Budget Deficit*, Beirut: Lebanese Centre for Policy Studies, 1998.

Hourani, Najib, 'Aid and redevelopment: international finance and the reconstruction of Beirut', in Daniel Bertrand Monk and Jacob Mundy (eds.), *The Post-Conflict Environment: Investigation and Critique*, Ann Arbor: University of Michigan Press, 2014.

———— 'Lebanon: Hybrid Sovereignties and US Foreign Policy', *Middle East Policy*, 20, 1 (2013), pp. 39–55.

———— 'Transnational Pathways and Politico-Economic Power: Globalisation and the Lebanese Civil War', *Geopolitics*, 15, 2 (2010), pp. 290–311.

Human Rights Watch, *Syria/Lebanon: An Alliance beyond the Law*, Washington: HRW, 1997, available at http://www.hrw.org/en/node/24483/section/2.

IMF, 'IMF Concludes Article IV Consultation with Lebanon', *Public Information Notice 01/109*, 2001.

———— *International Finance Statistics*, Washington: IMF, 2007.

———— *Lebanon: Selected Issues*, Washington: IMF, 2006.

Internal Displacement Monitoring Centre, 'Lebanon Overview', Geneva: IDMC, 2010, available at http://www.internal-displacement.org/assets/library/Middle-East/Lebanon/pdf/Lebanon-December-2010.pdf, accessed 20 September 2016.

International Crisis Group, *Lebanon's Politics: The Sunni Community and Hariri's Future Current*, Middle East Report, Brussels: ICG, 2010.

———— *A Precarious Balancing Act: Lebanon and the Syrian Conflict*, Brussels: ICG, 2012.

———— *Syria under Bashar (I): Foreign Policy Challenges*, Brussels: ICG, 2004.

———— *Syria after Lebanon, Lebanon after Syria*, Brussels: ICG, 2005.

———— *Trial by Fire: The Politics of the Special Tribunal for Lebanon*, Brussels: ICG, 2010.

International Telecommunications Union, *Arab States Telecommunications Indicators 1992–2001*, Geneva: ITU, 2002.

Iskandar, Marwan, *Rafiq Hariri and the Fate of Lebanon*, London: Saqi, 2006.

Jessop, Bob, 'Liberalism, Neoliberalism, and Urban Governance: A State-Theoretical Perspective', *Antipode*, 34, 3 (2002), pp. 452–72.

Johnson, Chalmers, 'The developmental state: odyssey of a concept', in

BIBLIOGRAPHY

Meredith Woo-Cumings (ed.), *The Developmental State*, Ithaca: Cornell University Press, 1999.

Johnson, Michael, *Class and Client in Beirut:The Sunni Muslim Community and the Lebanese State 1840–1985*, London: Ithaca Press, 1986.

———— 'Factional Politics in Lebanon: The Case of the "Islamic Society of Benevolent Intentions" (Al-Maqasid) in Beirut', *Middle Eastern Studies*, 14, 1 (1978), pp. 56–75.

Kerr, Michael, *Imposing Power-Sharing: Conflict and Coexistence in Northern Ireland and Lebanon*, Dublin: Irish Academic Press, 2005.

Khalidi-Beyhum, Ramla, *Poverty Reduction Policies in Jordan and Lebanon: An Overview*, NewYork: UN, 1999.

Khan, Mushtaq, 'Rents, efficiency and growth', in Mushtaq Khan and Jomo Kwame Sundaram (eds.), *Rent, Rent-Seeking and Economic Development*, Cambridge: Cambridge University Press, 2000.

Khan, Mushtaq and Jomo Kwame Sundaram, 'Introduction', in Mushtaq Khan and Jomo Kwame Sundaram (eds.), *Rent, Rent-Seeking and Economic Development*, Cambridge: Cambridge University Press, 2000.

Khashan, Hilal, 'How Grantees Relate to Grantor: A Study on a Lebanese College Scholarship Foundation', *Research in Higher Education*, 33, 2 (1992), pp. 263–73.

Knudsen, Are, 'SpecialTribunal for Lebanon: homage to Hariri?', in Michael Kerr and Are Knudsen (eds.), *Lebanon after the Cedar Revolution*, London: Hurst, 2012.

Krijnen, Marieke and Christiaan De Beukelaer, 'Capital, state and conflict: The various drivers of diverse gentrification processes in Beirut, Lebanon', in Loretta Lees, Hyun Bang Shin and Ernesto Lopez-Morales (eds.), *Global Gentrifications: Uneven Development and Displacement*, Bristol: Policy Press, 2015.

Krijnen, Marieke and Mona Fawaz, 'Exception as the Rule: High-End Developments in Neoliberal Beirut', *Built Environment*, 36, 2 (2010), pp. 245–59.

Krueger, Anne, 'The Political Economy of Rent-Seeking Society', *American Economic Review*, 64, 3 (1974), pp. 291–303.

al-Kush, Nur al-Din, presentation at the American University Beirut, 6 February 2008.

Laithy, Heba, Khalid Abu-Ismail and Kamal Hamdan, *Poverty, Growth, and Income Distribution in Lebanon*, Brasilia: International Poverty Centre, 2008.

Larner, Wendy, 'Neoliberalism, Mike Moore, and the WTO', *Environment and Planning*, 41, 7 (2009), pp. 1576–93.

———— 'Neo-Liberalism, Policy, Ideology, Governmentality', *Studies in Political Economy*, 63 (2000), pp. 5–25.

Lebanese Republic, *Lebanon: Paris II Meeting—Beyond Reconstruction and Recovery,Towards Sustainable Growth*, Beirut: Lebanese Republic, 2002.

BIBLIOGRAPHY

Leenders, Reinoud, *The Spoils of Truce: Corruption and State-Building in Post-War Lebanon*, Ithaca: Cornell University Press, 2012.

Legum, Colin, *Middle East Contemporary Survey*, London: Holmes & Meier, 1992.

Leverett, Flynt, *Inheriting Syria: Bashar's Trial by Fire*, Washington: Brookings Institution Press, 2005.

Majed, Ziad and Michael Young, 'The 1996 Elections by Region', *Lebanon Report*, 3 (1996).

Makassed, *Makassed: Serving Generations, Building Others*, Beirut: Dar el-Kotob, 1998.

Makdisi, Samir, *Lessons of Lebanon: The Economics of War and Development*, London: I.B. Tauris, 2004.

Makdisi, Saree, 'Laying Claim to Beirut: Urban Narrative and Spatial Identity in the Age of Solidere', *Critical Inquiry*, 23, 3 (1997), pp. 660–705.

Makdisi, Ussama, *The Culture of Sectarianism: Community, History and Violence in Nineteenth-Century Lebanon*, Berkeley: University of California Press, 2000.

Maloney, Suzanne, 'The Gulf's Renewed Oil Wealth: Getting it Right This Time', *Survival* 50, 6 (2008), pp. 129–50.

Maqasid, *al-Maqasid wal-'ata' mustammir*, Beirut: Maqasid, 2003.

Mearsheimer, John and Stephen Walt, *The Israel Lobby and US Foreign Policy*, New York: Farrar, Strauss & Giroux, 2006.

Mehlis, Detlev, *Report of the Independent International Investigation Commission Established Pursuant to Security Council Resolution 1595 (2005)*, Beirut: UNIIIC, 2005.

Meyer, Klaus, 'Foreign Direct Investment in the Early Years of Economic Transition: A Survey', *Economics of Transition*, 3, 3 (1995), pp. 301–320.

Miliband, Ralph, *The State in Capitalist Society*, London: Weidenfeld & Nicolson, 1969.

Mills, C. Wright, *The Power Elite*, New York: Oxford University Press, 1959.

———— *The Sociological Imagination*, Oxford: Oxford University Press, 2000.

Ministry of Social Affairs, *Development of Mapping of Living Conditions in Lebanon 1995–2004*, Beirut: MOSA, 2007.

Mirowski, Philip, *Never Let a Serious Crisis go to Waste*, London: Verso, 2013.

Mitchell, Timothy, 'No Factories, No Problems: The Logic of Neoliberalism in Egypt', *Review of African Political Economy*, 26, 82 (1999), pp. 455–86.

Momani, Bessma, 'Shifting Gulf Arab investments in the Mashreq: underlying political economy rationales?', in B. Momani and M. Legrenzi (eds.), *Shifting Geo-Economic Power of the Gulf: Oil, Finance And Institutions*, Farnham: Ashgate, 2011.

Naba, René. *Rafic Hariri: un homme d'affaires premier ministre*, Paris: Harmattan, 1999.

Najem, Tom Pierre, *Lebanon's Renaissance: The Political Economy of Reconstruction*, Reading: Ithaca, 2000.

BIBLIOGRAPHY

Nasnas, Roger, *Emerging Lebanon*, Beirut: Dar an-Nahar, 2007.

Nasr, Salim, 'Backdrop to Civil War: The Crisis of Lebanese Capitalism', *MERIP Reports*, 73 (1978).

——— 'The political economy of the Lebanese conflict', in Nadim Shehadi and Bridget Harney (eds.), *Politics and the Economy in Lebanon*, Oxford: Centre for Lebanese Studies, 1989.

Neal, Mark and Richard Tansey, 'The Dynamics of Effective Corrupt Leadership: Lessons from Rafik Hariri's Political Career in Lebanon', *Leadership Quarterly*, 21, 1 (2010), pp. 33–49.

Nerguizian, Aram, *The Lebanese Armed Forces: Challenges and Opportunities in Post-Syria Lebanon*, Washington: CSIS, 2009.

Nizameddin, Talal, 'The Political Economy of Lebanon under Rafiq Hariri: An Interpretation', *Middle East Journal*, 60, 1 (2006), pp. 95–114.

Ofeish, Sami, 'Lebanon's Second Republic: Secular Talk, Sectarian Application', *Arab Studies Quarterly*, 21, 1 (1999), pp. 97–116.

Ohlin Wright, Erik, 'Understanding Class', *New Left Review*, 60 (2009), pp. 101–16.

Ong, Aihwa, and Stephen J. Collier, 'Global assemblages and anthropological problems', in Aihwa Ong and Stephen J. Collier (eds.), *Global Assemblages: Technology, Politics, and Ethics as Anthropological Problems*, Oxford: Wiley-Blackwell, 2008.

Oxford Business Group, *Emerging Lebanon*, London: Oxford Business Group, 2005.

Owen, Roger, *Imperialism, Globalization and Internationalism: Some Reflections on their Twin Impacts on the Arab Middle East in the Beginning of the Twentieth and Twenty-First Centuries*, Washington: Center for Contemporary Arab Studies, 2004.

——— *Lord Cromer: Victorian Imperialist, Edwardian Proconsul*, Oxford: Oxford University Press, 2004.

Pakradouni, Karim, 'Arabising Lebanese Politics', *Middle East International*, 16 May 1997, pp. 21–2.

Panitch, Leo and Sam Gindin, 'Global capitalism and American empire', in Leo Panitch and Colin Leys (eds.), *The New Imperial Challenge*, London: Merlin Press, 2003.

Peck, Jamie and Adam Tickell, 'Neoliberalising Space', *Antipode* 34, 3 (2002), pp. 380–404.

Peres, Shimon, *The New Middle East*, New York: Henry Holt, 1993.

Picard, Elizabeth, 'Great Expectations, Limited Means: France and the 2006 Israeli–Lebanese War', *MIT Electronic Journal of Middle East Studies*, 6 (Summer 2006), pp. 141–51.

——— 'The political economy of civil war in Lebanon', in Steven Heydemann (ed.), *War, Institutions, and Social Change in the Middle East*, Berkeley: University of California Press, 2000.

BIBLIOGRAPHY

Pollock, David, 'Saudi Arabia's King Khaled and King Fahd', in Barbara Kellerman and Jeffrey Rubin (eds.), *Leadership and Negotiation in the Middle East*, New York: Praeger, 1988.

President of the Council of Ministers, official website, n.d., available at http://www.pcm.gov.lb/Cultures/ar-LB/Menu/%D8%B1%D8%A6% D9%8A%D8%B3+%D9%85%D8%AC%D9%84%D8%B3+%D8%A7% D9%84%D9%88%D8%B2%D8%B1%D8%A1/%D8%AF%D 9%88%D9%84%D8%A9+%D8%B1%D8%A6%D9%8A%D8%B3+%D 9%85%D8%AC%D9%84%D8%B3++%D8%A7%D9%84%D9%88%D 8%B2%D8%B1%D8%A7%D8%A1/, accessed 20 September 2016.

Qassem, Naim, *Hizbullah: The Story from Within*, Beirut: Saqi, 2007.

Quilliam, Neil, 'Jordan: appeasing the hegemon', in Rick Fawn and Raymond Hinnebusch (eds.), *The Iraq War: Causes and Consequences*, Boulder: Lynne Rienner, 2006.

Pipes, Daniel and Ziad Abdelnour, *Ending Syria's Occupation of Lebanon: The US Role*, Washington: Middle East Forum, 2000.

Al-Rasheed, Madawi, 'Saudi Arabia: the challenge of the US invasion of Iraq', in Rick Fawn and Raymond Hinnebusch (eds.), *The Iraq War: Causes and Consequences*, Boulder: Lynne Rienner, 2006.

Rettig, Marco, 'The Role of the Banking Sector in the Economic Process of Lebanon before and after the Civil War', M.Sc. thesis, SOAS, 2004.

Ricardo, David, *On the Principles of Political Economy and Taxation*, Kitchener: Batoche Books, 2001.

Rodrik, Dani, 'What is Wrong (and Right) in Economics?', Dani Rodrik's personal blog, 7 May 2013, available at http://rodrik.typepad.com/ dani_rodriks_weblog/2013/05/what-is-wrong-and-right-in-economics. html.

Roubini, Nouriel and Brad Setser, *Bailouts or Bail-Ins? Responding to Financial Crises in Emerging Economies*, Washington: Institute for International Economics, 2004.

Rougier, Bernard, *Everyday Jihad: The Rise of Militant Islam among Palestinians in Lebanon*, Cambridge, MA: Harvard University Press, 2007.

Ruggie, John Gerard, 'International Regimes, Transactions, and Change: Embedded Liberalism in the Postwar Economic Order', *International Organisation*, 36, 2 (1982), pp. 379–415.

Salam, Assem, 'The role of government in shaping the built environment', in Peter G. Rowe and Hashim Sarkis (eds.), *Projecting Beirut: Episodes in the Construction and Reconstruction of a Modern City*, Munich: Prestel, 1998.

Salem, Elie, *Violence and Diplomacy in Lebanon: The Troubled Years, 1982–1988*, London: I.B. Tauris, 1995.

Salti, Nisreen and Jad Chaaban, 'The Role of Sectarianism in the Allocation of Public Expenditure in Post-War Lebanon', *International Journal of Middle East Studies*, 42, 4 (2010), pp. 637–55.

BIBLIOGRAPHY

Sawalha, Aseel, "'Healing the wounds of the war'": placing the war-displaced in post-war Beirut', in Jane Schneider and Ida Susser (eds.), *Wounded Cities: Destruction and Reconstruction in a GlobalisedWorld*, Oxford: Berg, 2003.

———— 'Post-War Beirut: Place Attachment and Interest Groups in Ayn al-Mreisi', *ArabWorld Geographer* 3, 4 (2000), pp. 289–302.

Sayigh, Rosemary, *Too Many Enemies: The Palestinian Experience in Lebanon*, London: Zed Books, 1994.

Schatkowski, Linda, 'The Islamic Maqased of Beirut: A Case Study of Modernisation in Lebanon', MA thesis, AUB, 1969.

Schimmelpfennig, Axel and Edward Gardner, 'Lebanon—Weathering the Perfect Storms', IMF Working Paper WP/08/17, Washington: IMF, 2008.

Schmid, Heiko, 'Ära Hariri: Wiederaufbau nach dem Bürgerkrieg', *tec21* 5, 33–4 (2005), pp. 16–20.

———— 'Privatized Urbanity or a Politicized Society? Reconstruction in Beirut after the Civil War', *European Planning Studies*, 14, 3 (2006), pp. 365–381.

Sfakianakis, John, 'Gray Money, Corruption and the Post-September 11 Middle East', *Middle East Report*, 222 (Spring 2002), pp. 32–9.

Shahin, Wassim, 'The Lebanese economy in the twentyfirst century', in Kail Ellis (ed.), *Lebanon's Second Republic: Prospects for the Twenty-first Century*, Gainesville: University Press of Florida, 2002.

Shalaq, Fadl, *Tajrabatyy ma'a al-Hariri*, Beirut: Arab Scientific Publishers, 2006.

Shehadi, Nadim, *The Idea of Lebanon: Economy and the State in the Cénacle Libanais 1946–54*, Oxford: Centre for Lebanese Studies, 1987.

Shehadi, Nadim and Elizabeth Wilmshurst, *The Special Tribunal for Lebanon: The UN on Trial?* London: Chatham House, 2007.

Shils, Edward, 'The prospects for Lebanese civility', in Leonard Binder (ed.), *Politics in Lebanon*, NewYork: Wiley, 1966.

Simpson, William, *The Prince: The Secret Story of theWorld's Most Intriguing Royal, Prince Bandar al-Sultan*. NewYork: Regan, 2006.

Sklair, Leslie, *The Transnational Capitalist Class*, Malden, MA: Blackwell, 2000.

Skovgaard-Petersen, Jakob, 'The Sunni Religious Scene in Beirut', *Mediterranean Politics*, 3 1 (1998), pp. 69–80.

Soederbergh, Susanne, *The Politics of the New International Financial Architecture: Reimposing Neoliberal Domination in the Global South*, London: Zed Books, 2004.

Solidere, *The Development and Reconstruction of Beirut Central District: Information Booklet 1995*, Beirut: Solidere, 1995.

Spiro, David, *The Hidden Hand of American Hegemony: Petrodollar Recycling and International Markets*, Ithaca: Cornell University Press, 1999.

Stiglitz, Joseph, *Globalisation and its Discontents*, London: Penguin, 2002.

BIBLIOGRAPHY

Stork, Joe, 'Report from Lebanon', *MERIP Reports*, 118 (1983), pp. 3–13, 22.

Summer, Doris, 'Neo-liberalising the City and the Circulation of City Builders and Urban Images in Beirut and Amman', MA thesis, AUB, 2005.

Sunayama, Sonoko, *Syria and Saudi Arabia: Collaboration and Conflicts in the Oil Era*, London: I.B. Tauris, 2007.

Swyngedouw, Erik, Frank Moulaert and Arantxa Rodriguez, 'Neoliberal Urbanisation in Europe: Large-Scale Urban Development Projects and the New Urban Policy', *Antipode*, 34, 3 (2002), pp. 542–77.

Towe, Christopher, *Exchange Rate 'Fundamentals' versus Speculation: The Case of Lebanon*, Washington: IMF, 1988.

Traboulsi, Fawwaz, *A History of Modern Lebanon*, London: Pluto, 2007.

————— *Social Classes and Political Power in Lebanon*, Beirut: Heinrich Böll Stiftung, 2014.

Tripp, Charles, 'States, elites, and the "management of change"', in Hassan Hakimian and Ziba Moshaver (eds.), *The State and Global Change: The Political Economy of Transition in the Middle East and North Africa*, Richmond: Curzon, 2001.

UNDP, *Mapping of Living Conditions in Lebanon*, Beirut: UNDP, 1998.

————— *National Human Development Report—Lebanon 2001–2002: Globalisation, towards a Lebanese Agenda*, Beirut: UNDP, 2002.

————— *A Profile of Sustainable Human Development in Lebanon*, Beirut: UNDP, 1997.

Urnéchlian, Taline, Sena Eken and Thomas Helbling, 'Dynamics of interest rate movements: an empirical study', in Sena Eken and Thomas Helbling (eds.), *Back to the Future: Postwar Reconstruction and Stabilization in Lebanon*, Occasional Paper 176, Washington: IMF, 1999.

van Dam, Nikolaos, *The Struggle for Power in Syria: Politics and Society under Asad and the Ba'th Party*, London: I.B. Tauris, 1996.

Verdeil, Eric, 'Reconstructions manquées à Beyrouth', *Les Annales de la recherche urbaine*, 91 (2001), pp. 65–73.

————— 'Une ville et ses urbanistes: Beyrouth en reconstruction', Ph.D. thesis, Université de Paris I Sorbonne, 2002.

Vitalis, Robert, *America's Kingdom: Mythmaking on the Saudi Oil Frontier*. London: Verso, 2009.

————— 'The Democratization Industry and the Limits of the New Interventionism', *Middle East Report*, 187/8 (1994), pp. 45–60.

Vloeberghs, Ward, 'The Genesis of a Mosque: Negotiating Sacred Space in Downtown Beirut', EIU Working Papers, Florence: European University Institute, 2008.

Wade, Robert, 'Wheels within Wheels: Rethinking the Asian Crisis and the Asian Model', *Annual Review of Political Science*, 85, 3 (2000), pp. 85–115.

Wakim, Najah, *al-Ayadi al-sud*, Beirut: Sharika al-Matbu'at lil-Tawzir wal-Nashar, 2006.

BIBLIOGRAPHY

Wallerstein, Immanuel, *World Systems Analysis: An Introduction*, Durham: Duke University Press, 2007.

Weber, Rachel, 'Extracting Value from the City: Neoliberalism and Urban Redevelopment', *Antipode*, 34, 3 (2002), pp. 519–40.

Williamson, John, *A Short History of the Washington Consensus*, Barcelona: Fundación CIDOB, 2004.

Woodward, Bob, *Veil: The Secret Wars of the CIA 1981–1987*, New York: Simon & Schuster, 2005.

Woods, Ngaire, 'Understanding Pathways to Financial Crises and the Impact of the IMF: An Introduction', *Global Governance*, 12, 4 (2006), pp. 373–93.

World Bank, *Private Sector Assessment: Lebanon*, Washington: World Bank, 1995.

———— *Helping Countries Combat Corruption*, Washington: World Bank, 1997.

———— *Lebanon: Public Expenditure Reform Priorities for Fiscal Adjustment: Growth and Poverty Alleviation*, Washington: World Bank, 2005.

Yahya, Maha, 'Let the dead be dead: communal imaginaries and national narratives in the post-civil war reconstruction of Beirut', in Alev Cinar and Thomas Bender (eds.), *Urban Imaginaries: Locating the Modern City*, Minneapolis: University of Minneapolis Press, 2007.

Young, Michael, 'Two Faces of Janus: Post-War Lebanon and its Reconstruction', *Middle East Report*, 209 (1998), pp. 4–7, 44.

Zubaida, Sami, *Islam, the People and the State: Political Ideas and Movements in the Middle East*, London: I.B. Tauris: London, 1993.

———— 'The nation state in the Middle East', in Sami Zubaida, *Islam, the People and the State: Political Ideas and Movements in the Middle East*, London: I.B. Tauris, 1993.

INDEX

INDEX

INDEX